Death, Memory and
Material Culture

MATERIALIZING CULTURE
. . . .

Series editors: Paul Gilroy, Michael Herzfeld and Danny Miller

Barbara Bender, *Stonehenge: Making Space*

Gen Doy, *Materializing Art History*

Laura Rival (ed.), *The Social Life of Trees: Anthropological Perspectives on Tree Symbolism*

Victor Buchli, *An Archaeology of Socialism*

Marius Kwint, Christopher Breward and Jeremy Aynsley (eds), *Material Memories: Design and Evocation*

Penny van Esterik, *Materializing Thailand*

Michael Bull, *Sounding Out the City: Personal Stereos and the Management of Everyday Life*

Anne Massey, *Hollywood Beyond the Screen: Design and Material Culture*

Judy Attfield, *Wild Things*

Daniel Miller (ed.), *Car Cultures*

Elizabeth Edwards, *Raw Histories: Photographs, Anthropology and Museums*

David E. Sutton, *Remembrance of Repasts: An Anthropology of Food and Memory*

Eleana Yalouri, *The Acropolis: Global Fame, Local Claim*

Death, Memory and Material Culture

Elizabeth Hallam and Jenny Hockey

Oxford • New York

First published in 2001 by
Berg
Editorial offices:
150 Cowley Road, Oxford, OX4 1JJ, UK
838 Broadway, Third Floor, New York, NY 10003-4812, USA

Berg is the imprint of Oxford International Publishers Ltd.

Library of Congress Cataloging-in-Publication Data

A catalogue record for this book is available from the Library of
Congress.

British Library Cataloguing-in-Publication Data

A catalogue record for this book is available from the British Library.

ISBN 1 85973 374 3 (Cloth)
      1 85973 379 4 (Paper)

Typeset by JS Typesetting, Wellingborough, Northants.
Printed in the United Kingdom by Antony Rowe Ltd, Chippenham,
Wiltshire.

For Josie Hallam
7 February 1942–3 July 2000

Contents

Acknowledgements

This book has been researched and written with the generous support of many people. The British Academy and the Faculty of Arts and Divinity at the University of Aberdeen granted research funds in the early stages of the research. Many thanks go to staff at the Science Museum, London, especially Georgina Hooper, Alice Nicholls and Mark Abbott. Staff at Marischal Museum, University of Aberdeen are always very helpful and Neil Curtis has been very generous with his time and in guiding me through the ethnographic collection. Peter Johnston's support has made it possible for me to conduct research in the Anatomy Museum at the University of Aberdeen. Ann Louise Luthi's advice and the access she has granted to collections has been extremely welcome and rewarding. Archivists at Canterbury Cathedral Archive and Library have kindly assisted my search for materials and Andrew Butcher has continued to provide ideas, years after my doctoral studies. Thanks are also extended to members of the Aberdeen University Anthropology Seminar and the Manchester University History and Anthropology Seminar for their comments and suggestions. The staff in Cultural History at Aberdeen have been very supportive and encouraging – many thanks to Ben Marsden and Phil Withington for their help.

For reasons known to my family and friends, the completion of this book has been both very difficult and personally significant. I wish to thank my family – especially Jackie, Frank and Myra for their kindness. Ian Maclachlan, well beyond his invaluable intellectual insight, has made it all bearable. My mother, who died in July 2000, has been a constant source of inspiration. It seems to me that she was always keenly aware of her own past, as well as the pleasures and difficulties of living with her memories. This book has been written both with and without my mother and it is to her that it belongs – Josie Hallam – mother, sister and friend.

Elizabeth Hallam

Jenny Hockey would like to thank friends and colleagues for their helpful comments on a paper entitled 'Motionless Memories: death, material culture and social space' presented at the Death, Dying and Disposal Conference, Glasgow Caledonian University, September 1998; and Katherine Earle at Berg for the initial inspiration and continued support she has provided for this study. Jenny also warmly acknowledges her debt to Elizabeth Hallam who brings a unique historical and aesthetic perspective to anthropology and whose enthusiasm for this project has profoundly enriched her thinking.

Jenny Hockey

List of Figures

Introduction: Remembering as Cultural Process

This book is about relationships between death, memory and material culture. Death is a life crisis, a conjuncture of changes and transformations of the physical body, social relations and cultural configurations. Death is a phase of transition involving loss and adjustment and throughout this study we examine the ways in which memory comes into play as an important aspect of the process of dying, mourning and grief. Facing death, either of the self or of others, has come to entail ritualized social practices that mobilize domains of material objects, visual images and written texts. Focusing upon Western experiences, we attend to a diverse range of materials, associated with death in historical and contemporary contexts. In doing so we examine issues of metaphor, temporality, and social space, all of which impinge upon and shape memory as a cultural process and a social experience. By process we mean sets of interconnected practices that unfold over time, involving material and embodied dimensions. Developing anthropological and historical perspectives we find memories at work in visual images of death, in textual forms and in rituals which we trace as interconnected fields, related in their focus on the body – its structures, capacities and limits. We explore memory through the material objects that acquire meanings and resonances through embodied practice – such as the wearing of mourning attire, or the ritualized writing of wills, together with the material objects that come to represent or form extensions of the body – from funeral effigies to photographs. This takes us into personalized interior spaces and domestic settings as emotional realms of dying, mourning and remembrance. Thus we analyse the 'everyday' contexts of memory making that have received comparatively less attention when we note the sociological and historical work devoted to large scale, public forms of memorial and commemoration

1

(Morley 1971; J. Davies 1993; Winter 1995; A. King 1998; Rowlands 1999). The relationships between material objects and subjectivity, materiality and imaginative processes are explored throughout this study, which seeks to account for the cultural ramifications of death as a salient figure in the making of memories.

Material culture mediates our relationship with death and the dead; objects, images and practices, as well as places and spaces, call to mind or are made to remind us of the deaths of others and of our own mortality. Whether in the form of personal memento or public memorial, material objects and embodied social practices associated with the dead have been viewed from a variety of perspectives, which might be personal, social or political. We highlight a diversity of social values and cultural meanings that are attributed to mementoes and memorials, and examine the ways in which these are perceived to recall or represent death and the dead. These processes often entail value judgements, for instance in the cultural politics that render certain persons or social groups memorable or publicly visible in dedicated monuments. While the deaths of royalty or political leaders are marked, others might be marginalized or forgotten. Here we analyse 'ordinary', 'mundane' deaths as well as material objects associated death and memory that have been overlooked. In examining these themes we explore the ways in which material objects evoke the dead and this leads us to consider methodological and analytical issues faced by anthropologists and cultural historians. Emphasizing the centrality of material cultures and embodied social practices in producing and sustaining memories, we draw upon original research, focusing on England. Throughout our study historical and cross-cultural comparisons serve to highlight and expose the institutions and social practices that constitute Western perceptions of memory and their relation to death.

Memory Making

Central to this project is the shifting and often elusive field of memory and the way in which memory practices provide perspectives on the past as well as inflecting views of the future, situating us in time as well as social space. Important starting points are 'everyday' or naturalized conceptions of memory that have become axiomatic or regarded as 'common-sense' orientations towards the social world. As we bring this set of precedents into critical focus, we explore culturally constituted conceptions of 'internal' states, where memory intersects with emotional or imaginative experience. To understand the ways in which internal processes and external material objects are linked in the production of subjectivity and identity requires an analysis of material culture as well as the discourses and practices that define and situate objects in relation to the self. Our work identifies memory through its distinctive vocabularies, metaphors and images that structure and shape remembering, whilst feeding into the formation of social identities and relationships.

'Memory' is commonly envisaged as both the facility to remember and as the mental representation or trace of that which is remembered, both of which are crucially mediated by a variety of cultural forms. In contemporary Western societies, 'memories' are often conceived as possessions: we 'keep' and 'preserve' our memories almost as though they are objects in a personal museum. We choose when to disclose or display our memories to others, either in the form of personal narratives or photographs. They are, therefore, associated with individual agency in the sense that we imagine ourselves to be responsible for, or 'in control' of, our memories. While they are attributed something approximating an object status, memories are also routinely regarded as 'static', as imprints retained and fixed such that the dimensions of creativity or imaginative reconstruction that remembering entails often remains as a latent, only dimly perceived and sometimes troubling awareness.

Alongside this orientation toward fixity is the notion that a memory and the experience it arises out of are identical – this may be explained in terms of the influence of scientific disciplines on the conception of memories as 'real' or 'true' (Lambek and Antze 1996: xiv). Yet these concepts require further analysis in relation to death and its attendant trauma, loss, and emotional difficulty. They also require contextual and comparative analysis, which reveals their historical and cultural specificity as well as the ways in which memory and death are caught up in processes of personal transformation and social change. Memory practices and experiences shift over time as perceptions of the past are reworked in the context of the present and in anticipation of the future. Here we trace connections between the crises of death and the formation of memory, the relationships between loss and recovery, how memories operate to render present that which is absent and here we find concepts of death and memory intimately bound together. Indeed, we witness death acting as a deep incentive to remember and the process of dying can give licence to intense phases of memory making with all of its attendant material complexity – from the disposal of the corpse to the repeated act of returning to the graveside with flowers.

The material presented in this book reveals the social and cultural dimensions of memory and memory making in a diversity of locations that might be interior or exterior to the body, stimulated and anchored in private or public domains. It is in relation to death, as event, idea and experience, that we situate this exploration of memory. It is at the time of death that embodied persons disappear from view; that their relationships with others come under threat; that the unfolding of their affairs and their influence may cease. Emotionally, socially and politically, therefore, much is at stake at the time of death; memories and memory making in this context can be highly charged and heavily loaded. Indeed, in contemporary contexts, the threat of death is very much bound up with the possibility of oblivion. Not only may individuals or groups believe that there is no independent existence after death; they also face the possibility of *social* erasure and the annihilation of identities that they have lived out. Memories of the dead, as we will show, are as much a bulwark against the terror of the forgettable self as an inescapable aftermath of lives which have come to an end.

Materialities and Social Practices

Mementoes, memorials, words and artefacts can be understood as external cultural forms functioning to sustain thoughts and images that are conceived of as part of the internal states of living persons. These relations between internal and external domains are subject to change over time as well as to cross-cultural variation. Perceptions of memorializing practices and their emotional resonance are often acutely sensitive and receptive to changes in broader social orientations and attitudes. For example, a Western tendency to wear jewellery made from enduring parts of the corpse such as hair was not uncommon in the nineteenth century yet came to be seen as unsavoury during the twentieth. The carrying of a deceased husband's skull in a basket was expected of New Caledonian widows, yet to do so in contemporary Western society might invite a clinical diagnosis (Taylor 1983). Western practices that have developed around the prenatal deaths of infants, such as photographing and measuring the body, giving it a name, a death certificate and a grave, are recent cultural innovations. Prior to the 1970s foetal remains were disposed of with no religious or institutional attempt to provide them with a social body and therefore a memorable identity. Similarly the practice of memorial photography has taken place within quite specific cultural boundaries. Ruby (1995) shows how carefully composed photographic portraits of relatives, taken after death, were common in nineteenth-century American homes, appearing in frames on parlour walls. However during the twentieth century, especially since World War Two, post-mortem photographs in both Europe and America have been subject to restricted viewing as they are kept in guarded family photograph collections or in the institutionalized filing systems of professionals (such as the police) who deal with death.

Whilst highlighting patterns of change in the material dimensions of memory our study also explores the striking tenacity of certain memory-making practices in which many generations have invested. In their appeal to continuity, memory acts such as the demarcation of spaces dedicated to the dead and the use of visual images to invoke persons deceased, carry the historical weight of hundreds of years. As we shall see, the resilience of flowers as expressive materials of memory may be explained, paradoxically, in terms of their fragility. Camporesi observes that '[t]ime ... dominates floral symbolism because of the ephemeral nature of flowers, their rapid discoloration and premature putrefaction, which relate them to human life' (1994: 34). The interplay of longevity and transience inhabits many of the material and cultural dynamics that we trace in our study. We are reminded not to disregard the most fragile, paper-thin fragments of material cultures in our search for the most tenacious of memories associated with death.

Our analysis of material objects requires a nuanced focus on the embodied experience of socially structured space, as it unfolds over time. The cultural meanings ascribed to spaces of the dead and dying are invoked through social practices and it is this nexus of social space and practice that reproduces potent death-related memories. We therefore analyse a diversity of spaces – sacred, public and domestic – which serve as sites of memory making: museums, memorials and cemeteries, attics, nurseries and gardens. Spaces of death, and their significance in memory making, have been transformed across historical time in both their material form and their metaphorical potential. Our discussion moves from medieval conceptions of memory, in which valued images were recalled through their location in real and imaginary places, to the way in which death-related objects and practices have emerged and have been transformed in contemporary society. We question the predominant argument that the dead are sequestered and instead chart the ways in which lost generations and dead friends and lovers remain manifest – through well-worn garments, memorial prizes, photographs, street names, residual drops of perfume, war memorials. The deceased can always be provided with a powerful presence within the here and now, something which is increasingly evident in the appropriation of public space for private grief at times of collective disaster or traumatic loss. Drawing on these materials, we examine a concept of 'memory' as a labyrinth of mutually interacting materialized cultural forms and images which emerge over time and in relation to the spatial location of the dead and dying.

Practices associated with death, together with the experiences of memory and emotion that they invoke, can be observed across a spectrum that ranges from an individual visit to a grave to the collective participation in state funerals. While these practices vary in scale, duration and intensity, they may share a common ground in prevailing cultural codes and values. There are, however, divergent perceptions of death rituals that emerge along, for instance, lines of gender, ethnicity, age and social group. Contested views of highly visible public funerals, for instance, mark different levels of social involvement and personal identification that affect emotional experiences and memory. We might cite the example of the funeral of Diana, Princess of Wales in 1997, which gave rise to media debates regarding the significance of collective mourning and grief. How could a multiplicity of individuals, each of whom stood in a different relationship to this member of the Royal Family, nonetheless find commonality in their grief? Large-scale mourning was clearly a newsworthy phenomenon that had erupted in response to a quite extraordinary death. In practice, however, the representation of collectivity and shared emotionality was rapidly called into question. Criticized for whipping up 'false' emotion, the media were said to have fostered the events and indeed the emotions in which many participated (Merrin 1999). Clearly the reporting of a collective emotional response angered many people and on the first anniversary of her death newspapers were filled with letters and articles that challenged an assumed universality of grief. These letter writers refused to have their particular individual emotions subsumed within corporate statements and insisted upon a diversity of personal responses – including an absence of any interest whatsoever in her death.

Taking account of their effects upon self perception and identity, this book explores processes of grief, mourning and remembrance, as culturally constituted and socially shared. At the same time the meanings of these practices are diverse, often socially negotiated and politically contested. Rather than focusing on psychological explanations, we provide cultural and historical accounts of how the dead and the living find proximity via material objects and places.

Memory Materials in Cultural and Historical Perspectives

In the absence suggested by death we find potent cultural materials and strategies, including objects, visual images and texts that constitute systems of recall for persons and social groups that have been threatened or traumatized by loss. Throughout the book we analyse the materiality of things at the edge of social life – the ways in which social disappearance has been perceived and counteracted. In many instances, death is provided with a visibility through material cultures and we analyse the cultural politics and social repercussions of this visibility. Cultural preservation, of persons or objects, requires investments and these might be economic, political and emotional so that the cultural practices involved in memory making exist at macro as well as micro levels of societies. Memory, in relation to death, can be seen at work in public spaces, sacred sites, Church institutions, state bureaucracies, national museums as well as in locations devoted to personal collections, including domestic interiors. Thus we explore the spaces of death and memory, observing their internal organization and symbolism together with their external connections and references to wider social and cultural formations – these are spaces of immense as well as intimate proportions. Responses to death and the evocation of memories during processes of dying, grief and mourning have been rendered in the form of the large-scale monument and the miniature memento – here we attend to the implications of scale and substance. In tracing the formation and practice of memory we explore its temporal dimensions. How is the material culture of death instrumental in the maintenance of particular memory configurations? Why do certain memories persist as others are seen to fade into a distant past? Why are certain aspects of society and culture afforded a permanence that others are denied? How do social, cultural and political factors impinge on the resonances and associations that material objects amass and shed as they circulate, come to rest or are actively resurrected?

These are key questions that we address through a study of materials that have a place in contemporary and historical contexts associated with dying and death. Whilst material objects retain a certain historical specificity, rooted in their production within a particular historical moment, we witness their varied uses at later stages in their social lives. Moving (being transported, translated) from one cultural or temporal zone to another, objects are re-contextualized and made to mean in different ways – for example, having once operated as a focus of personal remembrance and emotional connection, objects such as mourning jewellery may be displayed in museums as evidence of past mourning rituals. Thus materials once inhabiting a domain of subjectivity, and used predominantly for the fashioning of personal memory, may be later assigned object status, for viewing in public domains as an aspect of national cultural heritage. Conversely, objects seen to possess a social relevance or value at one time may be redefined as worthless or even dangerous or disturbing at others. Objects once central to public forms of remembrance – village war memorials or public statues – may become virtually 'invisible' as a result of habitual viewing, and therefore marginal in longer term processes of memory maintenance. Objects themselves may suffer a social death, being discarded or passing into storage in archives or attics – although, while they may lie dormant, they are still potentially available for reactivation. Thus our enquiry leads us to consider why it is that certain objects are infused with the capacity to endure time, persisting and rejuvenated *in* memory, whereas others are constrained in their temporal reach as ephemera, as *only* memories, barely present as fading traces that may be cut adrift by the passing away of certain generations or individuals.

Throughout the book we analyse a range of death related objects, images and texts including tombs, relics, wills, mourning jewellery and costume, commemorative flowers, sculpture and painting, memorial photographs, printed and painted images. The range of materials available for analysis in the study of memory and death is staggering and this is testimony to the cultural investment in memory at times of personal, social and political crisis invoked by the cessation of life. These materials have been woven into the fabric of daily life, establishing their significance within routine social interactions, but some of them have been marked out as spectacular, staged in their arresting impact and elevated through ritual practices. We move between objects highly charged in their devastating relation to traumatic death and objects that mobilize only a tangential connection to distant sorrows. In exploring the cultural significance of death in relation to memory we seek out the meanings and symbolic associations of material objects – objects rendered in stone, wood, bone, wax, metal, cloth and paper as well as objects incorporating once living forms such as flowers, hair and flesh itself.

These materials have connotations of transience as well as permanence which feed into the metaphors used to describe and account for the capabilities of memory. There is often a cultural politics of memory which reaches across public and private spaces and which designates what is worth preserving in the face of loss. While memory is sustained through the social circulation of material objects – for example, family photographs and albums, the visibility of certain material forms is also implicated in what is forgotten. To make such objects socially visible – through, for example, strategies of framing or displaying are exercises in selective emphasis where certain meanings are foregrounded at the expense of others. Here we trace material cultures of death, exploring those aspects that have been provided with visibility as well as those that have remained secluded. The rituals of death involve material objects that are meant for preservation, to be kept in view for the living, and others that are deliberately allowed to decay, having only a temporary role in the visual order of this rite of passage. For example, the clothing of the corpse and the coffin remain in view during the brief but highly emotive ritual of the funeral and are then released into invisibility and decay. The interplay between what is made visible and what is buried, that which is retained and that which is lost in the material cultures of death, has an impact in terms of the possibilities of memory and forgetting.

From contemporary perspectives, death-related objects surviving from earlier times offer the opportunity to reconstruct aspects of memory practices as they were perceived in the past as well as a means of tracing the play of historical reference and allusion in contemporary material cultures of death. Objects serving the practice of memory in the past are, in the context of the present, a resource for the reinterpretation of history. Contemporary social spaces, both public and private, retain a multiplicity of death-related objects that have accrued over time and are now enmeshed in the spatio-temporal conjuncture of the present; for example, the furniture, ornaments and crockery of previous generations can, through inheritance, remain in use in the households of surviving relatives. Some of these objects are distanced as temporally 'other' in their unfamiliar iconography or displaced symbolism, which would once have had powerful mnemonic effects. For example, the figure of death personified as a decaying corpse was once a commonly accepted memento mori – an object or image intended to remind viewers of their inevitable physical end. Now bereft of their association with memory processes, largely due to their dislocation from a framework of Christian spiritual belief, sculpted figures of Death tend to stand as 'historical rarities'. This is exemplified in the current (1999) display of such items at the Victoria and Albert Museum in London, where Death in the guise of 'animated' skeletons can be found on shelves of a case labelled 'Cabinets of Curiosities' (Sculpture and Architecture Gallery).

Further objects, although tied in terms of their production, materials, forms and structural compositions to historically specific settings, possess attributes that are more closely aligned with familiar understandings of death; for example, flowers, trees and other organic forms have provided a language to express responses to death and the effort of memory over at least the last five centuries. These continue to be active in the reproduction of memory. Tracing continuities and discontinuities, we note that death-related objects from the past may be used, over time, as a creative resource in the present, constituting relations of distance and proximity with the past. We therefore analyse different historical contexts of cultural production and reception, acknowledging the significance of systems of collection, reproduction and simulation which keep death in memory from medieval to modern times.

The materials that we analyse throughout this study are the products of different, historically emergent technologies including writing, print and photography, which provide diverse means of recording, storing and retrieving experiences of death. Le Goff refers to 'mnemotechnologies' as the various 'systems of training memory' that differ according to historical context (1992: 51–2). We approach cultural materials, produced through various technologies, from perspectives within anthropology and cultural history, and attend to the relationships between texts, visual images and material objects. Our methods combine ethnographic fieldwork with archival and museum research in England to explore aspects of death, memory and material culture that have yet to receive scholarly attention. Our aim, while acknowledging the cultural significance of established public memorial forms, has been to recover marginalized memory practices associated with death and dying. For instance, we draw upon rich archival and museum collections that have been underexploited in terms of their capacity to enhance our understanding of death and memory. Whereas social historians have concentrated on collections of texts and objects that refer to public memory practices (for example funerary rituals and public memorials), we have tended to shift attention from these towards other practices, for example, those located in domestic spheres such as deathbed rituals and the preservation of personal mementoes. Equally, our fieldwork in contemporary settings (together with our uses of other anthropological studies) brings into the analytic frame the more mundane memory practices of the household or the hospital, the less spectacular rituals observed within the home or at the graveside. This enables us to re-evaluate established or culturally dominant modes of remembrance in relation to marginalized domains of material culture, memory and death. Yet many of the materials that we analyse through-out this study owe their existence and historical survival to the develop-ment of archives and museums – powerful institutions devoted to the storage and preservation of cultural products. The study we present here has entailed the recovery of historical materials from these spaces, their re-interpretation and re-contextualization placing them in relation to contemporary ethnographic descriptions.

Bodies in Time/Materials in memory

The significance of the body has been explored in recent anthropo-logical studies which highlight the importance of embodied experience, including the senses, in the making of memories. These highlight the importance of 'everyday', mundane practices involving 'ordinary' material objects. Seremetakis, for instance, outlines a 'reception theory' of material culture that deploys concepts of embodiment, performance and memory in the context of contemporary European societies (1994). The theoretical perspectives which Seremetakis develops are relevant to the cross-cultural analysis of death and memory in the social contexts pursued throughout our study. Seremetakis suggests that there are connections between the senses, agency, memory and history which are established through embodied emotional and aesthetic experiences and are informed by patterns of social and cultural power. She maintains that '[m]emory cannot be confined to a purely mentalist or subjective sphere. It is a culturally mediated material practice that is activated by embodied acts and semantically dense objects' (1994: 9). The field of sensory experience is not clearly bounded as an aspect of the inner self as there is an exchange which is established between internal states and the 'social-material' domain external to the body (1994: 5–6). While this exchange is socially and materially grounded in embodied perform-ance, the interaction of senses and material objects builds up over time and is retained as an accumulated 'emotional and historical sedimenta-tion' within objects (1994: 7). This sedimentation is capable of trigger-ing further embodied actions, which, in turn, transform the significance of material objects as the process unfolds. Embodied performances establish connections with objects to form creative acts that draw upon previous experience, constituting 'a mutation of meaning and memory that refracts the mutual insertion of the perceiver and the perceived in historical experience' (1994: 7). However, these connections are not overconstrained by established cultural codes, since social acts of mean-ing and memory making may diverge from the officially sanctioned or publicly endorsed memory and economies that designate the dominant values of material objects. Thus embodied performances can involve cultural transformation as much as repetition and this can work to reconstitute the meanings assigned to objects that may have been previously disregarded.

The recovery of discarded objects and the reinterpretation of those things that are overlooked, devalued or remain 'invisible' from domi-nant social, economic or political perspectives, has been an important strategy in artistic discourses of the twentieth century. For example, Cardinal points to the projects of the German artist Kurt Schwitters (1887–1948) who accounted for his work as 'a campaign to combat chaos by salvaging the broken pieces left after the Great War' (1994: 72). Producing collages made of materials that he found in the streets (transport tickets, used stamps, playing cards, bits of newspaper, cigarette packets), Schwitters stated that 'One can still cry out by way of bits of rubbish, and that is what I did by glueing or nailing them together . . . Nothing was left intact anyway, and the thing was to build something new out of the broken pieces' (quoted in Cardinal 1994: 72). This orientation towards used material fragments still resonates when translated into the personal worlds of those facing loss through the death of loved ones: the entire contents of a house shaken by a recent death, from old shopping lists to worn shoes, may speak to years of accumulated memories. Hence it can be that memories flood forward through marginal materials or objects so ordinary that they once com-manded no special attention. It is with an eye to this immense field of mundane objects that the significance of dedicated memorials can be re-evaluated.

In academic debate we find a concern with spheres of cultural production that emerge through the interaction of the powerful and the marginalized. In an anthropological discussion of cultural change in modernity, Seremetakis comments upon the 'discourse on loss' as an aspect of public culture and official ideology that operates through the repression of memory and the redefinition of the past that becomes 'defamiliarized' for those on the cultural periphery (1994: 8–9). Here she is referring to the loss of sensory memory, which has consequences in the fragmentation of social identities and the relocation of socially shared experience to the space of the personal and the privatized. Seremetakis points out that the recovery of sensory memory, and the material forms through which it operates, has been the concern of social theorists and artists such as the surrealists. Via their work she finds that 'the cosmos of economically discarded cultural artefacts constitutes a vast social unconscious of sensory-emotive experience that potentially offers up hidden and now inadmissible counter-narratives of once valued lifeworlds' (1994: 10). There is a multiplicity of marginalized perceptions and values that might be acknowledged by attending to objects that have been cast aside in peripheral spaces. In these it is possible to appreciate the 'cultural procreation in the lost, negated, de-commodified attics and basements of everyday life', and to discover in these sites social memory that may run counter to dominant discourses (1994: 10).

While we describe and account for the layering of meanings and memories within the material cultures of death, we emphasize the significance of embodied social practices, engaging with issues of power and perception, sensation and emotion. Connerton argues that 'memory is sedimented or amassed in the body' through social action, which he defines as 'incorporating' or 'inscribing' practices (1989: 72). Incorporating practices include the range of bodily actions, gestures or movements all of which 're-enact[s] the past in our present conduct', whereas inscribing practice is that which involves a cultural means of storing information, such as print and photographs (1989: 72–3). Throughout this study we explore the interaction between these two forms of practice, focusing on the constitution of memory in the relationships between embodied action and material objects. The ways in which material forms are fashioned into memory objects – objects that retain and hold traces of previous experiences – and become enmeshed in subjective processes, require detailed contextual analysis. Emotion and identity are also bound into memory as articulated through the interplay of embodied action and material objects; for example the wearing of memorial or inherited jewellery enacts a series of connections and identifications between the body of the mourner and that of the deceased relative. A diverse range of sensations and impressions from the powerfully felt to the diffuse and barely perceived are associated with and reproduced through domains of material objects and social practices. Memory feeds into processes involving the construction of identity and notions of the self, just as emotional experiences impinge upon and help to create memories. Thus we are interested in objects associated with death, objects which acquire a density of meaning and significance, objects engaged in grief, fear, anxiety, love, disgust, anger, sorrow, fascination and curiosity.

Material objects are circulated at different stages of the dying process, acquiring significance for the self and others, namely during preparations for death and after the event of a death. For example, last gestures of gift giving may create treasured memories of physical contact during the final phase of a life, while the distribution of property via a will may infuse objects with other familial connotations. The temporal and spatial positioning of objects during phases of dying, death and mourning often inflects their meanings together with the relationship they bear to the living or the dead body. Appadurai's perspective on rites of passage, including death, is illuminating here. He states that '[w]hat affects social salience is the nature, timing, scale and social visibility of the material transactions that constitute the ritual processes of the rites' (1996: 69). We might note then, that it is these features of ritualized 'material transactions' (their nature, timing, scale and social visibility) that are formative in terms of their potential in the sphere of memory.

Understood as central aspects of memory processes we explore the embodied practices of the living and the cultural treatment of the dying and dead body, focusing on their material dimensions. Within the social contexts that we analyse, what 'remains' of the deceased in either material or symbolic form is central to the cultural operations of memory. We examine the continuities of subject and object where material forms are made to represent and sometimes to incorporate the once living body. The point at which the body of the deceased ends and the material object (for example the memorial, the tomb, the casket of ashes) begins is often a porous boundary and this linkage with the body often reinforces the object's mnemonic capacity. With reference to the later twentieth century, the corpse has been defined as 'a presence that manifests an absence' (quoted in Vincent 1991: 265). The ways in which this absence is dealt with through material objects owes much to the cultural apparatus devoted to memory. Memory sites are often, although not exclusively, those associated with the body of the deceased, as Vincent asks:

> What lies beneath the durable marble headstone that loved ones like to visit and decorate with flowers? A body . . . Attention has been shifted, in a kind of metonymy from the contents to the vessel. How can the memory of the deceased be preserved while the state of the decomposing body is forgotten? With photographs, films and tapes – the modern ways of preserving information. (1991: 267)

Forty makes a similar point with regard to the function of separation at death as performed by material objects such as tombs which contain and are substituted for the decaying physical body (1999). Again, material objects are relied upon to provide concrete renderings of what is deemed culturally acceptable to remember. As we show, however, attitudes to bodily processes in death are culturally and historically specific and these inflect the nature of memory objects as well as their ritual contexts. Experiences of bodily decline, decay and preservation shift over time and are displayed, masked or made visible in a variety of ways which shape memories of death.

In the following chapters we aim to develop theoretical work on memory with specific reference to the dying and dead body as it is imaged and transformed in the material cultures of death, and in the relationships that have been sustained between the bodies of the deceased and those of the living. Links between the human body, memory and death have deep historical roots. In the thirteenth century Thomas Aquinas provided four mnemonic rules that extended their influences upon theories of memory, theology, education and art into the seventeenth century. According to these rules, memory was aided by its associations with the body or 'corporeal similitudes' as well as order, repetition, attention and intention (Le Goff 1992). With regard to memory and death, Le Goff traces the oscillation of memory processes in relation to the dead over the last millennium. From the eighth century, popular Christian memory focused on the dead as the tombs of martyrs (memoria) were located at the centre of churches and saints were commemorated on the days associated with their deaths. Prayers for the dead became customary in the early Christian Church when *Libri memoriales* (known from the seventeenth century as necrologies or obituaries) registered the names of the dead to be collectively remembered. An annual celebration, to be held in memory of the faithful dead on November the second (All Souls Day) was introduced in the eleventh century, and from the twelfth century, masses and prayers preserving memories of the departed were necessary in reducing the time spent by souls of the departed in Purgatory (Le Goff 1992: 71–3). Christian belief and ritual practice, therefore, ensured that 'memory enters into the definition of the mourned dead, they are "of good" or of "splendid memory"' (1992: 73).

Following Aries and Vovelle, Le Goff asserts that during the seventeenth and the eighteenth centuries the links between memory and death were less pronounced as evidenced, for example, in the simplification of tomb designs and the lack of cemetery maintenance. This he attributes to the effects Protestantism and Enlightenment, together with the development of an 'increasingly rich technical, scientific memory' influenced by print (1992: 85). The relationship between death and memory was, however, reasserted from the later eighteenth century with renewed investment in the material culture associated with the deceased: '[t]he great period of cemeteries begins, with new kinds of monuments, funeral inscriptions, and the rite to visit the cemetery. The tomb outside the Church has become once again the centre of remembrance. Romanticism accentuates the attraction of the cemetery linked to memory' (Le Goff 1992: 85–6).

We can note that during the late eighteenth century memory was not only linked to spheres of cultural creativity such as the imagination and poetry but also to politics. The national commemoration of mass deaths, for example, after the French Revolution and, later, the American Civil War, highlighted the memory of death as a large-scale political issue. Collective memories of past generations were further shaped by the foundation of centralized archives, museums and libraries that were open to the public. During the nineteenth century national commemoration in the form of coins and medals as well as inscriptions on street signs and plaques extended the range of materials and public spaces dedicated to collective memories of the dead. Finally, Le Goff notes two further developments of the nineteenth and twentieth centuries in the relationship between death and collective memory: war memorials and photography. While monuments to the dead such as the 'Tomb of the Unknown Soldier', erected after the First World War, expanded public funerary commemoration via a 'nameless body', photography, especially in family albums, provided a means by which the visual memory of particular individuals was preserved (Le Goff 1992: 89).

The social experiences of dying and death, together with memory processes that are activated in relation to them, are therefore enmeshed in wider political, religious and intellectual factors. These influence or sustain (or, conversely, work to erode) solitary as well as collective remembering so that we need to attend to the individual body and its relation to the social body in the act of making memories. The conditions and meanings of either individual or mass deaths also inflect memory processes: while preparation for the 'good death' often makes way for the production of memories, violent or voluntary death (for example in the cases of accidents or suicides) creates different memory contexts. Mass deaths resulting from epidemic disease or war, again resonate in different ways within social memory. Rowlands (1999) for example, notes the profound difficulties associated with memorials for Holocaust victims, deaths that, in his view, cannot be transformed into worthwhile sacrifices. In circumstances such as these the representation of personal and social loss, through a density of enmeshed words, texts, images and material objects, collective rituals and institutional sites, is often made to convey the weight of power just as it is forced to bear the tension of cultural conflict.

Material Memories: Contemporary Concerns

Throughout this study we move between different sites and senses of memory, finding that the significance of material objects, in mediating relationships between the living and the dead, is negotiated and contested. Authoritative discourses and the professionalized spheres of knowledge relating to death and memory, alongside complex economic factors in the twentieth century, influence the perceived significance of material domains. While this study takes its theoretical perspectives from anthropology and cultural history, we acknowledge the historical emergence of these disciplines as an aspect of the (specialized) cultural production of memory. As Le Goff points out, the emergence and development of the social sciences has had a significant effect upon the ways in which memory, especially collective memory, has been conceptualized. He suggests that there is a mutually reinforcing relationship between academic interest in memory and wider social perceptions of memory as an important dimension of lived experience:

> This pursuit, rescue, and celebration of collective memory, no longer in single events but over a long period, this quest for collective memory, less in texts than in the spoken word, images, gestures, rituals and festivals, constitutes a major change in historical vision. It amounts to a conversion that is shared by the public at large, which is obsessed by the fear of losing its memory in a kind of collective amnesia – a fear that is awkwardly expressed in the taste for the fashions of earlier times, and shamelessly exploited by nostalgia-merchants; memory has thus become a best-seller in a consumer society. (1992: 95)

While recognizing the broad trends that Le Goff identifies, we address a more specific field of memory making in relation to death and material culture: a field that is fraught with difficulty and tension. How have material objects relating to death been defined in dominant discourses and wider economic relations which have a bearing upon memory in the twentieth century? As different social groups make competing claims to shape the value of objects in memory processes relating to death, divergent definitions of the material world and its 'objects' emerge through the discourses of medicine and psychiatry. From the later nineteenth century to the present day, what have been identified as the 'sciences of memory' emerge with professionalization and the development of expert knowledge (Antze and Lambek 1996: 65). At the same time, processes of commercialization and commodification in the twentieth century affect notions of value, patterns of consumption, what is retained and what becomes disposable – all of which act as formative influences upon the material cultures of death and memory.

Relevant here is Appadurai's argument that one of the effects of mass merchandising in the later twentieth century has been to 'underline the inherent ephemerality of the present' (1996: 78). This not only invents sentiments of loss but fuels patterns of consumption:

> The valorization of ephemerality expresses itself at a variety of social and cultural levels. The short shelf life of products and lifestyles; the speed of fashion change; the velocity of expenditure; the polyrhythms of credit, acquisition, and gift; the transience of television product images; the aura of periodization that hangs over both products and lifestyles in the imagery of the mass media. The much-vaunted feature of modern consumption – namely, the search for novelty – is only the symptom of a deeper discipline of consumption in which desire is organised around the aesthetic of ephemerality. (Appadurai 1996: 84)

If these factors, together with the emphasis on transience, set up a 'radically new relationship among wanting, remembering, being and buying' (Appadurai 1996: 84), how are we to understand their impact upon the material cultures of death? Arguably, death (and the images used to represent it) instances the ephemerality of the material world in the most powerful of ways, producing desires for permanence as a counteractive force. In the chapters that follow we explore perceptions of the ephemeral in different historical periods to document a wide range of cultural responses to actual and imagined sensations of loss.

The capacity of material objects to bind the living and the dead, to hold a fragile connection across temporal distance and to preserve a material presence in the face of an embodied absence, may be appreciated, questioned or problematized from different personal or professional perspectives. As Lupton notes, objects that have become part of the 'territory of the self' lose their exchange value as commodities and become unattractive to other consumers (1998: 144). Juliet Ash, in an exploration of the sensations of absence, writes powerfully of the way clothing can evoke the deceased (1996). Yet she also feels constrained to ask: 'Does it trivialise a person to feel close to and/or image even a part of them through an item of clothing?' (1996: 220). This book concentrates therefore on sites of ambiguity and uncertainty, the varying and unstable relationships between individuals and objects providing distinctive foci of enquiry.

In the contemporary context, to wear the personal possessions of deceased relatives such as their watches, or to enshrine their clothing and cherish their photographs and letters, provides a means of coping with personal loss. Emotive media images of weeping widows pictured stifling their sobs in their dead husbands' handkerchiefs, or wistfully smiling adults holding lockets and framed photographs of their deceased parents, provide collective reference points for a shared understanding of the object's role in personal grieving. Objects and images are infused with a bittersweet quality evoking that which they cannot replace and providing touchstones for inchoate feelings of grief. They may also be avoided as sources of pain as when well-meaning relatives notoriously dispose of clothing that might upset someone newly bereaved. Yet these objects, although providing an important resource for personal meaning making, might be trivialized as merely 'sentimental'. For instance, they may be coded as disparate fragments residing in a 'female' domain of excessive emotion and irrational, possessive impulses.

These objects have also been pathologized. Profound attachment to an object may be perceived as an overvaluation of a material item, which exceeds 'acceptable' limits through its estimation over and above the lost person with whom it is associated. Furthermore, such a subjective involvement with material objects may be interpreted as a symptom of mental disturbance. In the discourse of psychiatry, relationships with powerful objects can be pathologized if their importance for the individual becomes overwhelming and a 'dependency' is suspected. Cast in this light, objects become a resource through which professional practitioners intervene in clients' emotional responses to a death, in cases where their responses are diagnosed as 'unhealthy'. Parkes, for example, argues that the use of objects to 'mitigate' the pain of loss is acceptable only as a temporary defence mechanism that allows bereaved people to gradually adjust to 'reality' – that the dead person is lost to them (1972: 77). Worden (1991), a therapist who regards letting go of the deceased as necessary to the client's wellbeing, distinguishes between keepsakes, which act merely as 'mementoes' or 'tokens of remembrance', and 'linking objects' (Volkan 1972). The latter represent the symbolic merger of two individuals' psychic boundaries and can 'hinder the satisfactory completion of the grieving process' (1991: 84). Though one person is dead, the other uses the object 'to handle separation anxiety and . . . provide a "token of triumph" over the loss. [They] mark a blurring of psychic boundaries between the patient and the one mourned, as if representations of the two persons or parts of them merge externally through their use' (Volkan, cited in Worden 1991: 84–87). Similarly the meaning attributed to objects is another focus for professional intervention. In Volkan's view objects embody the dead selectively and can represent positive memories to the exclusion of more negative ones. Again, aspects of bereavement are not acknowledged but become obstacles to 'balanced' personal well-being. As psychiatrists and psychologists, Parkes, Volkan and Worden construct the mediating object as a hindrance to the mental health of the individual, legitimating their knowledge claims through the authority vested in medical science.

Miller argues that within some areas of social science the significance of material objects in social processes is not fully realised as a result of dominant notions 'that the relation of persons to objects is in some way vicarious, fetishistic or wrong; that primary concerns should lie with direct social relations and "real" people' (Miller, cited in Lupton 1998: 137). When addressed by therapeutically oriented theorists, this area can provoke the reservations exemplified in Volkan's notion of the 'linking object' (Volkan, cited in Worden 1991: 85). His view is premised upon a model of the self that privileges psychic differentiation as necessary to the mental health of individuals conceived of as independent, discrete and bounded selves. Such conceptions, as Lakoff and Johnson (1980) point out, rely upon a prevalent cultural metaphor of the self as a 'container' that is embedded in Western, masculine ideologies (Battersby 1993; Lawton 1998).

Throughout this book we examine the materials that have constituted memories in anticipation of and in the aftermath of death. Our central arguments reside in the assertion that material dimensions of memory making are significant not just in the marking of deaths, but also in the social and cultural processes through which lives are remembered and futures are imagined. Death can initiate deeply felt desires to remember, just as it might generate the need to forget and in the following chapters we trace the ramifications of this life crisis in the field of memory.

In the following chapter we explore the metaphors through which memory, as a capacity, has been conceptualized in Western societies – focusing on the ways in which salient metaphors have assigned material qualities to memory. This leads to a consideration of relationships posited between persons and their material environments – between bodies and material forms and, ultimately, between human subjects and material objects. We will discover that where material objects are designated as aspects or extensions of persons, they can become potent resources of memories. Chapter 3 moves on to consider dimensions of time in the production of memory and in the imagery used to represent temporality and death. It traces the distinctive imagery of time and its passage deployed in material objects which have been made to remind the living both of their own mortality and of others now deceased. The spatial dimensions of death and memory lie at the heart of Chapter 4, where we analyse a range of ways in which material spaces have formed sites for the dead to reside and for the departed to be remembered. Here we highlight the inter-connections between spaces, embodied actions and material objects in the formation of highly personalized, yet socially recognizable, memories. Memories have often been materialized in order to stabilize and preserve them, but in Chapter 5 we note the disturbing and sometimes threatening qualities of memories associated with death. Attempts to map and control the materials of memories, which seem possessed of their own intrusive agency, then become crucial in the personal and collective management of recall.

The significance of visual images and written texts in the shaping of memories is examined in Chapters 6 and 7, focusing upon relationships that obtain between these cultural forms and the bodies of both the living and the dead. Here we argue that images and texts have important material dimensions and/or bear connections with embodied persons which inflect their potential as memory 'objects'. Finally, Chapter 8 explores the ritualized practices through which persons and 'everyday' material environments become vehicles of death related memories. Throughout the book we analyse the often complex relationships between death, memory and material culture that have persisted and transformed over time. And throughout our examination of these processes in Western contexts we are also concerned with 'otherness', variously perceived as an aspect of the non-Western, the deep historical past or a condition that the self passes into at the end of life.

Figuring Memory: Metaphors, Bodies and Material Objects

This chapter examines the apprehension of memory or the cultural devices through which it has been imagined both in lay and learned terms. In dealing with personal and social memories that are perceived as distinctively 'intangible', recourse to metaphor has provided a means by which they are made accessible. Indeed, recent studies have stated that the use of metaphor is essential if memories are to be grasped (Antze and Lambek 1996). Similarly death, as a field of experience that cannot be 'known' in a direct sense, has been elaborated extensively through metaphors and cultural representations. Here we can note that '[m]etaphor is, at its simplest, a way of proceeding from the known to the unknown' (Nisbet 1969, quoted in Turner 1974: 25). If the capacity of memory and the act of remembering are couched in distinctive vocabularies, discourses and images we need to understand how these inform and inflect memories. Furthermore, within the scope of this study, the relationship between conceptions of memory and the materiality of social domains requires elucidation.

Cross-cultural and historical studies of memory highlight not only the multiplicity of socio-cultural means by which memories are conceived, but also the changing nature of these formulations and experiences. So, for instance, a late twentieth-century growing 'fascination, even obsession with historical memory' occurs at a time of renewed concerns with guilt associated with war and Holocaust (Davis and Starn 1989: 1). In addition to concepts of memory as historically defined and delineated within culturally specific settings we find an emphasis on memory as *process* that involves complex negotiations such that what is recalled is always amenable to revision: 'that one's memory of any given situation is multiform and that its many forms are situated in place and time from the perspective of the present' (Davis

23

and Starn 1989: 2). From current anthropological and historical per-spectives, memory may be analysed as a shifting construct that is highly dependent on context, but these perspectives are themselves historically emergent. As Davis and Starn suggest, memory, formulated within academic discourse as a construct, is very different from conceptions of memory as knowledge or truth (Davis and Starn 1989: 2). Whether the past can be 'recovered' or only 'reinvented', together with questions regarding the significance of lived experience in relation to the making of memories, are key questions that impinge upon the epistemological status of memory. The tensions between what is regarded as historical actuality and its subsequent representation in collective memories are politically fraught, especially when these memories involve death – a seemingly indisputable fact. The politics of denial and manipulation that unfold around mass death, and indeed, the multi-faceted dimen-sions of personal loss, which, as we argue throughout this book, often involve a recovery of the dead as social (if not physically present) agents, open memories of death and the dead to retrospective reconstruction. Given these complexities, memories cannot be conflated with actuality:

> If memory is an index of loss, and notoriously malleable besides, how can we remember truly? The obstacles are formidable – sheer forgetful-ness, suggestibility, censorship, hindsight, conflicting recollections, the force of interests that frame whatever we remember ... if memory is shaped by mythologies, ideologies, and narrative strategies why should we even try to remember what actually happened in the past? And yet if we give up trying, where does this leave history except as a special category of fiction? (Davis and Starn 1989: 4)

Thus we are presented with a set of unresolved dilemmas that carry implications for the ways in which the relationships between memory, politics, society, culture and, indeed, identity are construed. It is cert-ainly the case that memory remains a contested terrain in which claims to truth and fiction are variously made with reference to historical 'evidence', personal testimony and experience. This contestation may be manifest at national, local or individual levels and what might crystallize as dominant memory forms is open to dispute through 'counter-memory' or instances of memory that provide alternatives to 'official' versions (Davis and Starn 1989: 2). We therefore need to attend to memory as generated and maintained by marginalized or subordin-ated social groups as well as to memories that, by virtue of their form or content, are regarded as problematic, disturbing or dangerous from dominant viewpoints.

Davis and Starn point out that 'people do worry about the fit between what actually happened and received narratives about the past' (1989: 5). Such anxieties are fuelled by the cultural positioning of memories as sources of identity and self-understanding: 'personal identity is constituted by memory. Any type of amnesia results in something being stolen from oneself; how much worse if it is replaced by false memories, a nonself' (Hacking 1994: 458). If memories, which are afforded a genuine truth value or a certain authenticity, are so crucial in the maintenance of self and identity, we have to address the ways in which perceived connections between the 'real' and the 'remembered' are sustained. Which particular qualities and attributes make certain memories resonate or 'ring true' for persons or social groups who invest in them? Taking these questions forward from an anthropological perspective entails a rejection of 'objective' history in favour of approaches which acknowledge that 'what happened is inseparable from the conventions of meaning and power that shape the horizon of happening. In such a view, our sense of "truth" is always provisional, our evidence contextual' (Comaroff 1994: 465). Where memories and the contexts to which they refer are always mediated by 'conventions of meaning and power' we explore the significance of material forms in efforts to secure in memory what is potentially dissolved through death.

In the later twentieth century it is claimed that: '[m]emory is of course a substitute, surrogate, or consolation for something that is missing' (Davis and Starn 1989: 3). The ways in which absence is addressed have come to involve various material forms such as written texts, visual images and material objects all of which are brought into play as a means to recall persons, relationships and events that are no longer immediately present. If death is regarded as loss, departure or journey – displacements that create distance, either spatial or temporal – memories stand as mediators that connect accessible with what threaten to become inaccessible domains. As Bronfen argues, 'death emphasises the impermanence of social experience and elicits attempts to preserve some aspects of it in permanent form' (1992: 77). This impulse to preserve in the face of death is enacted through the use of material forms that provide tangible substance as mnemonic resource. Thus, Bronfen refers to eighteenth-century literary works that, in terms of their narratives of death, situate texts (such as letters) as materials that nourish memories: recollecting the death of a loved one in writing serves to 'assure a tangible possession of the otherwise receding deceased' (1992, 79). Material objects also acquire capacities in sustaining memory relations between survivors and the departed. As Parkin demonstrates, objects gathered by refugees prior to forced displacement provide materials through which attempts to secure continuity of personal and cultural identity are articulated. Parkin refers to situations in later twentieth-century Africa that reveal that, under extreme pressure to depart from their homes, people would gather items required for basic survival as well as 'reminders of who they are and where they came from' (Parkin 1999: 13). Objects such as photographs, letters, beads, keys form accessible 'non-commodity, gift-like objects' that are 'inscribed with narrative and sentiment' (Parkin 1999: 13). In contexts where people have lost the majority of their possessions, these mementoes are made to 'encapsulate' personhood to the extent that to take away these few remaining markers of identity could lead to social death for their owners. Furthermore, these objects provide materials through which those who lose their lives may be commemorated (Parkin 1999: 13–14).

We also note that the body, either living or dead, can be regarded as material that sustains memory. In this respect, Roach argues that '[i]nto the cavities created by loss through death or other forms of departure . . . survivors attempt to fit satisfactory alternates' (1996: 2). He defines this as a process of surrogation where, for instance, in ritual performances such as funerals, effigies (copies of absent originals or models fashioned in the likeness of the *once* living) as well the bodies of the *now* living, become mediators of memory.

Where the material dimensions of texts, images, objects and bodies enter into the sustenance of memories at points of social and personal crisis such as death, we need to examine the ways in which memory has been conceptualized in relation to materiality. Antze and Lambek suggest that memory can be grasped only via the metaphors through which it is represented and communicated: 'it is virtually impossible to imagine memory – what it is, how it works, where it lies – without recourse to metaphor' (1996: xi). Highlighting the centrality of metaphors used to convey ideas about memory, they ask '[i]s memory a storehouse, a computer, a filing system, an encyclopaedia, or a landscape, a cathedral, a city?' (1996, xi). Thus, a range of metaphors convey different facets of memory, as a container, or architectural structure, or as an unstable process like the weather (Antze and Lambek 1996: xi, xxviii). Memory can therefore take on substance via metaphor. The immaterial aspect of an inner world, like thoughts, emotions, dreams and imaginings that are unavailable to any direct gaze, is fused metaphorically with material objects which possess distinct structures and boundaries (for example rooms and shelves).

Metaphors of memory often highlight the notion of containment and so the ability to remember is frequently represented as the act of storing something in a vessel or structure. On the other hand, the ephemeral or fleeting nature of memories is acknowledged with the recognition that memories 'fade' or threaten to wither or die and consequently need to be 'kept alive'. That memories recede only to be enlivened later can be conveyed through metaphorical chains of association with visible aspects of the elements. The elements are brought into play, for instance, through images of memories 'rekindled': memory is figured as a flame and this finds its concrete rendering in the lighting of candles at shrines or other foci of remembrance. Such repetitive commemorative actions, while suggesting a certain vulnerability, allude to a continuity of light and this principle is expressed more directly in the maintenance of eternal flames of remembrance. In these instances, the destruction of matter by fire produces a more lasting (and in religious contexts, spiritual) manifestation in the form of the flame. As such, metaphors of memory, which connect the intangible with the material, either convey notions of fixity and stability or they highlight process and transformation. At either end of this spectrum, however, metaphors of memory always allude at some level to continuity.

Furthermore, metaphors not only provide a means to represent memory: they impact upon memory as lived experience. As Skultans points out '[m]etaphor reaches into the fractured and irreconciled corners of people's lives. Its centripetal force brings life to similarities and patterns which would otherwise not be perceived' (1998: 31). Here Skultans highlights metaphor as a cultural device, operative within narratives, which produces meaning and in particular draws together disparate aspects of past and present experience. This is especially the case, as her study of memory in Latvia demonstrates, in social contexts disrupted and fragmented by war and exile. For instance, Skultans cites the example of the farmstead, which has become, after the dislocation of communities from their homes, an important metaphor for well-being in shared stories of the past: '[t]he farmstead comes to be seen as an embodiment of happiness and virtue, a pastoral metaphor for the good life. Thus the geography and physical attributes of the farmstead are infused with moral and emotive attributes' (Skultans 1998: 31). In addition, Lakoff and Johnson have challenged the notions that metaphor is a marginal, poetic flourish and demonstrated its centrality not only to societies' conceptual systems but also their practices (1980). Drawing upon Ricoeur's work, they show how our apparently unmediated grasp of fundamental aspects of life – eating, arguing, organizing our time – is shaped metaphorically in terms of other sets of ideas and experiences. 'I'm running out of time' appears to describe our experience directly; but nonetheless draws upon a specifically Western capitalist metaphor of time as a commodity that is in short supply. Intangible aspects of life such as time or emotion are often a particular focus for metaphorical elaboration; and in this respect both memory and death attract a proliferation of metaphorical representation.

This chapter moves on to examine a range of metaphors through which memory has been conceptualized and experienced; but death itself is similarly understood in terms of other tangible figures, objects or experiences. It has been represented as a mirror that reminds viewers of their fleshly fragility, an unavoidable presence who dances amongst the living, a withered skeleton, as friend or seductress (Guthke 1999). With the prospect of death, individuals living in different times and places have anticipated peace, sleep, judgement, bliss, reunification with loved ones, damnation, oblivion, a journey, rebirth. In forms borrowed from other domains, therefore, death is made tangible or at least 'thinkable'. Each image, whether a personification, an entity or an experience, carries what Lakoff and Johnson describe as a system of entailments: 'metaphoric entailments can characterise a coherent system of metaphorical concepts and a corresponding coherent system of metaphorical expressions for those concepts' (1980: 9). The primary or root metaphors through which we understand both memory and death, therefore, have consequences. For example, 'sleep' is the domain that many Westerners draw upon, metaphorically, to think about and manage death. In this context, material cultures of death include churchyards full of the stone 'beds' in which the dead lie in their white nightdress shrouds, stretched out on their backs in familial proximity to those they shared a bed with in life. The coherence of this system of metaphoric entailments is extended in the behaviour of living visitors who keep their voices down and take care not to step onto the graves' flowery coverlets. The following sections of this chapter examine, firstly, the ways in which memory has been connected with materiality and secondly, the social practices and cultural associations that link persons or subjects with material objects. Thus we move from a consideration of metaphors of memory, which reveal the deep-seated association of memory with material domains in Western discourse, to an exploration of relationships between material objects and persons. This circuit of association, we will argue, is crucial if material objects are to function as memory resources.

Metaphors and the Materiality of Memory

Certain contemporary Western conceptions, which designate memory as highly individualized and interior to the individual, are underscored when memory is seen as an innate biological capacity. The links between biology and memory extend back to the eighteenth century as evidenced in research on the biological passage of inter-generational traits and, through the nineteenth century, in work on heredity (Le Goff 1992: 92). Le Goff notes the '"metaphorical" effect' of these developments, which established analogies between biological and mechanical memory as, for instance, in the statement that ' "heredity functions like the memory of a calculating machine" ' (Jacob, cited in Le Goff 1992: 92). Thus expressed, we can recognize metaphors of memory as having been generated within historically emergent structures of knowledge together with their supporting technologies.

The uses of metaphor to describe memory processes, however, have deeper historical roots in Western cultures. For instance, Carruthers identifies two key sets of related metaphors that shaped medieval memory. During this period, memory was regarded as an aspect of knowledge either as 'waxed tablets upon which material is inscribed', or as a 'storehouse or inventory. These models are complementary; they are also archetypal Western commonplaces' (Carruthers 1990: 14). Memory was thus figured as a written surface and as part of a process involving the inscription or marking of the body:

> A memory is a mental picture (phantasm; Latin *simulacrum* or *imago*) . . . which is inscribed in a physical way upon that part of the body which constitutes memory. This phantasm is the final product of the entire process of sense perception, whether its origin be visual or auditory, tactile or olfactory. Every sort of sense perception ends up in the form of a phantasm in memory. (Carruthers 1990: 16–17)

The metaphor of memory as a wax tablet established connections between the body, sensory experience and material objects. The inscription of sensory perception upon the body and hence memory was likened to the imprint of wax seals achieved through the application of signet rings (see Chapter 7). While these metaphors convey notions of memory as material matter, the body was also seen as necessary in the generation of memories. The somatic nature of memory was conveyed through ideas about the heart, which received impressions, and the brain which stored these messages. Furthermore, 'heart' was used metaphorically to refer to 'memory'. The health of the body was seen to improve the activity of recollection but after death, in the absence of a body, the soul existed in the past being unable to generate new memories. A further feature of embodied, sensory memory was that it involved emotion – memory was made more effective through emotional associations (Carruthers 1990: 46–60).

Another metaphor prevalent in medieval educated memory was that of the thesaurus or storage room. This conveys notions about the contents and internal structure of memory and highlights collecting, sorting, ordering and containing impressions, which are thus made available for recall: 'places of memory, appropriate to rhetoric, dialectic, poetry and jurisprudence – this structure gathers into one place (the trained memory) everything human knowledge has gained of the world' (Carruthers, 1990, 33). This conception of the memory process is one that emphasized deliberate effort – memory was actively built and learned as opposed to innate or passively acquired. Memory was located in a particular 'place' and required sorting and organizing in order to function properly. As Carruthers demonstrates, the metaphor of the storage room and also the strongbox provided connections between memory, systematised spaces and orderly sets of objects. The metaphor provided a means to visualise these connections and to establish a 'network' or a '"texture" of associations', which were crucial in memory techniques (Carruthers 1990: 36). Carruthers stresses that medieval memory images themselves were partially material in that they consisted of 'matter' and occupied a physical location in the brain (1990: 27) and she provides examples of the complex metaphorical linkage of memory and material aspects of the lived environment. Memory was visualized in the form of spaces and objects including the strong room containing treasures, the library, cells or compartments for books, the hives of bees, book-boxes for the storage of ecclesiastical records and relics, caves and inner chambers, shrines and also books decorated in the manner of shrines with jewels and ivory (1990: 35–42). These metaphors deployed images of structures and vessels to store and contain memories in the form of gathered flowers, fruits, precious stones and coins. The untrained memory was represented, on the other hand, as a forest without clear routes and pathways (Carruthers 1990: 33).

Metaphors of memory were primarily spatial and the importance of the visual sense in securing memory was emphasized. Perceptions (phantasmata) were stored in the mind as 'representations' or ('copies') but these were most effectively recalled through a process that was like seeing. Material received through other sensory modes was provided with visual associations in order to place it in memory (Carruthers 1990: 95). However, as re-presentations, memory images were 'of the past'. As Carruthers states, '[t]heir temporal nature also means that memory's re-presentation is less importantly mimetic, or objectively reiterative of the original perception, than it is temporal, because it makes the past perception present' (1990: 60). Thus, in medieval memory processes, representations did not claim to imitate, rather, they recalled past experiences in ways that entailed the mobilization of emotion and imagination. Memory images, which set up spatial and visual associations produced the 'immense hall of memory' – a rich and imaginative architecture (Le Goff 1992: 70). The internal visualization of spaces with depths and different regions is apparent in St Augustine's writings, which figure memory as 'spacious palaces' so that memories are retrieved from an 'inner receptacle'. The notion of the spatiality of memory is illustrated in the perception that when memories rush forward they might be swept away 'with the hand of my heart from the face of my remembrance; until what I wish for be unveiled, and appear in sight out of its secret place' (quoted in Le Goff 1992: 70). The imaginative dimensions of memory were acknowledged in thirteenth century claims that 'fable, the marvellous, and the emotions that lead to metaphor are an aid to memory' (Le Goff 1992: 78).

Fifteenth- and sixteenth-century ideas about memory continued to emphasize spatial and visual dimensions. Yates has described the complex spatial structures that were generated as part of the art of memory. Memory was imagined, described and drawn in treatises as, for instance, an abbey together with objects such as books, flowers, beads, ecclesiastical garments, furniture and sacred paraphernalia to be mentally placed and remembered in the different areas of this structure (Yates, 1992: 116). Imaginary places, such as the spheres of the universe, containing zones for the elements, planets and stars provided maps for memorizing as did actual places. With regard to the latter, one treatise from 1491 advised that the best spaces in which to place and fix memories were those that were quiet, for instance an empty church that one could walk around whilst attaching memories to particular features within its interior (Yates, 1992: 120). A further treatise from 1533, defining several systems of placement for memories, pointed to the cosmos, the zodiac and real buildings. Alongside these spatial arrangements, the role of the visual was again foregrounded in alphabets used to aid memory where letters were represented by images. For example by imagining birds and animals, letters were recalled (Ass = A) providing an effective means of 'making inscriptions on memory' (Yates 1992: 125). Yates shows how images held internally by learned persons were constructed as a method to memorize vast fields of knowledge from the sciences to the arts. Yet as treatises that provided instructions in this 'mnemotechnic' became increasingly detailed, they were criticised for fuelling 'wild imaginative indulgence', or 'strange fantasia', crowded with 'mysterious inscriptions' and puzzles (Yates, 1992: 130). However, as Yates goes on to argue, the art of memory with its characteristic spaces and visual appeal continued to inform conceptions of memory theatres. This is not to deny that during the sixteenth century, the role of images as stimulating and emotive within memory received criticism – the Protestant rejection of material images as false and spiritually corrupting placed emphasis on the word as a purer form.

Fentress and Wickham point to a shift in models of memory that occurred in relation to scientific and philosophical work conducted during the seventeenth century. Conceptions of memory as a 'source of knowledge' were gradually eroded so that memory came to designate the zone of the personal and the private. They argue that theatres of memory came to be regarded as overly complex and prone to the confusion of fact and fiction. Instead the 'textual paradigm of knowledge' was prioritized (1992: 8). One of the effects of this epistemological shift, combined with the increasing use of print technology, was to define textual forms of memory as 'objective' and 'rational' in contrast with memories or those impressions derived from the senses which came to be designated as 'subjective' and 'non-rational' (Fentress and Wickham 1992: 16). Further important factors in these developments were literacies that facilitated the articulation of knowledge in textual form. However, as Watt points out, the textual and the visual were never entirely separate, rather, they were mutually interacting as, for instance, in cheap printed pamphlets that were widely circulated during the seventeenth century (Watt 1994). In Chapter 7 we trace relationships between words and images as deployed in material cultures that sustain memories of the dead. Here we must be careful not to overstate the impact of textual forms on the perceived efficacy of visual images in memory making as the social practices and cultural processes we examine throughout this study are often testimony to the sustained interaction of the visual and the textual.

Pierre Nora has provided an account of memory that emphasizes the transformation or metamorphosis of memory in modern times (see Chapters 5 and 8). This metamorphosis entails a radical shift from what he calls 'true' memory to a form of memory that is 'not memory but already history' and, in this latter state, memory is 'voluntary and deliberate, experienced as duty, no longer spontaneous; psychological, individual, and subjective; but never social, collective or all encompassing' (1989: 13). Nora outlines the contours of a 'lost memory', which is 'life', 'a perpetually actual phenomenon', 'affective and magical', as 'multiple and yet specific', as something that 'takes root in the concrete, in spaces, gestures, images and objects' and as a form that 'has taken refuge in gestures and habits, in skills passed down by unspoken traditions, in the body's inherent self-knowledge, in unstudied reflexes' (1989: 8–13). In Nora's analysis, the break which effects the transformation of this 'immediate' memory into modern ('indirect') memory comes about through changes which eroded 'peasant culture', institutions (such as the church and family) and ideologies which had upheld collective values. Global mass culture and media also fragment 'collective heritage' and focus instead upon the contemporary in their obsession with 'current events' (1989: 7–8).

Modern memory emerges with certain predominant features: for example, 'archive-memory' and 'duty-memory' (Nora 1989: 13, 16). The former refers to an externally materialized memory form whereas the latter designates an internalized compulsion to engage in specific acts of remembering. The archive-memory is one that relies upon the recording and amassing of documentation to preserve the past. It is dependent upon 'the materiality of the trace' and 'the visibility of the image' and forms a 'gigantic and breathtaking storehouse of a material stock of what it would be impossible for us to remember, an unlimited repertoire of what might need to be recalled' (1989: 13). Institutions dedicated to preservation and record making, such as public archives, museums and libraries have expanded enormously and these provide, in Nora's view, 'exterior scaffolding' for memories: external structures for the maintenance of memory become increasingly important when memory as an 'interior' experience declines (1989: 13). A further consequence of the archive-memory (especially in contemporary societies where the present is unstable and the future seems radically unpredictable) is the impulse to collect and retain everything as a potential reminder of the past. Nora states that there is a 'disinclination to destroy anything' such that almost any material form, including 'remains, testimonies, documents, images, speeches, any visible sign of what has been' becomes potentially significant as a memory object (1989: 13). The responsibility to remember has been, in Nora's view, transferred to the individuals who feel the duty to remember and record their pasts as an obligation tied to the maintenance of their identities. Furthermore, this 'duty memory' is reinforced through the 'psychologisation of contemporary memory' (1989: 15).

Of particular relevance to our study are the 'sites of memory' which, Nora suggests, are in existence due to the loss of 'real environments of memory' (1989: 7). He identifies memory sites as simultaneously material, symbolic and functional. For example a historical generation is material in that it is constituted by persons, functional in that it passes on memories and symbolic in that it represents experiences common to a particular group (1989: 19). Sites of memory are extensive and various (ranging from archives to calendars) and they are

> mixed, hybrid, mutant, bound intimately with life and death, with time and eternity; enveloped in a Mobius strip of the collective and the individual, the sacred and the profane, the immutable and the mobile. For if we accept that the most fundamental purpose of the *lieu de memoire* is to stop time, to block the work of forgetting, to establish the state of things, to immortalize death, to materialize the immaterial . . . it is also clear that *lieu de memoire* only exist because of their capacity for metamorphosis. (1989: 19)

Thus Nora defines memory as a vast field of sites which concentrate and locate memory in a multiplicity of materials which stand in an external relation to individuals. These sites are 'immutable' in that they allude to a degree of fixity which prevents forgetting, but they are also mutable and open to change – to an 'endless recycling of their meaning' (Nora 1989: 19). It is notable that one of the main categories of modern sites of memory, as outlined by Nora, is defined by those associated with the dead. In the chapters that follow we trace the material objects which have come into play as powerful reminders of the deceased. However, the case studies and examples that we explore suggest that the radical transformation of memory described by Nora overemphasizes the discontinuity of pre-modern and modern memory forms and practices. For instance, there was an emphasis on the materiality of memory prior to the modern period as in the metaphors used to conceptualise it, such as the 'theatre'. Indeed a physical model of the memory theatre as conceived by Giulio Camillo was built during the 1530s as a wooden structure 'large enough to be entered by at least two people at once' (Yates 1992). And during the modern period memories can be generated and sustained through certain embodied actions and gestures – a feature of the 'true' memory that Nora considers to have been lost. In many ways, Nora's emphasis on sites as a means to grasp modern memory reiterates the importance of the spatial and the visual – but rather than residing in the mind, the 'scaffolding' of memory he refers to is built outside of the body. It is to the relations between 'interior' memories and 'external' material forms that our study returns, focusing upon these relations as configured through experiences of death.

Metaphors used to conceptualise memory in the twentieth century continue to deploy spatial and visual images. Despite Hutton's claim that in the nineteenth century '[t]he image of memory as a brightly lit theatre of the world was replaced by one better attuned to the kind of inquiry with which the art of memory was henceforth to be allied – that of memory as a mirror of the dark abyss of the mind' (Hutton 1987: 380), we can note that the metaphor of shady depths remains primarily spatial. So too are notions in Freud's work such as 'screen memories' that 'displace deeper, hidden memories' often of a traumatic or painful nature which reside in the unconscious mind (Hutton 1987: 388). Likewise the idea that memory fragments might 'surface' in dreams is dependent upon a spatial conception of interior mental zones – albeit ones that are difficult to map or interpret. Rather than the clearly structured and stable theatres of memory, the conception of internal mental space as ever expanding throughout the life span of individuals is characteristic of certain psychological models of memory: the 'long term' memory is described by Wilkinson and Campbell as 'a relatively permanent storehouse of information and contains everything we know about the world . . . [it] seems to have an almost limitless storage capacity' (1997). While distinctions are made here between long- and short-term memory, where the latter is seen as less enduring, long term memory is also vulnerable to losses which emerge over time. Thus, Legg asks 'do we lose bits of information at random so that our memories develop holes, like an old pair of curtains that is being eaten by moths . . . ?' (1998: 85). While deploying notions of an internal space, which exhibits features of permanence and mutation, psychological models also allude to processes unfolding in time. For instance, memory is characterized as 'an active information processing system that as well as storing information, also receives it, organises it, alters it and recovers it' (Wilkinson and Campbell 1997: 61). Here, memory is animated through allusions to mechanized communication and information systems such as radio transmissions and bureaucratic filing.

In psychological discourses, memories are assigned materiality through metaphors, but the human body acts as a source of such images. This is especially the case with emotionally charged memories, which in lay perceptions might constitute those that are most cherished or most burdensome. The early psychologist William James posited that '[a]n experience may be so exciting emotionally as to almost leave a scar on the cerebral tissues' (cited in Rosenzweig et al 1999). The image of painful memory as a form of physical damage – a scar or wound – comes into play with regard to memories of responses to death. Writing about bereavement as physical damage, Elizabeth Jenning's poem *Words about Grief* (1967) expresses the physicality of memory:

> Time does not heal,
> It makes a half stitched scar
> That can be broken and you feel
> Grief as total as in its first hour.[1]

In these images we find memories residing on the vulnerable surface of the body as wounds that cannot be soothed – the force of memories of death are likened here to breaches in the skin which defy the supposed healing power of time. In later chapters we trace relationships between embodiment and memories of the deceased (see Chapter 6), but here we can note the powerful materiality of memories as conveyed through images of bodily sensations. These are memories that seem possessed of their own agency – they are difficult to live with even as they occupy the physical self.

Bodies and Material Objects

Our discussion so far has concentrated on the significance of metaphors that establish cultural connections between memory and material domains. If memory and memories are grasped through sets of associations with material structures and objects, this is suggestive of broader social and cultural processes that link persons or subjects with material domains. The materials of memory, whether in the form of texts, visual images, objects or bodies, hinge upon and acquire their significance through conceptual linkages between personhood and the material world. If personhood and social identity are fashioned through the body and the material objects with which this body is associated, then it is through that body and these objects (either directly or via associations with further bodies and objects) that the deceased are kept within memory. While these connections provide material resources for memory we need to explore the social and cultural configurations that situate the body, variously understood as a site of social being and subjectivity, in relation to its broader material environment.

As we have seen, prevailing metaphors represent the capacity of memory and the specificities of memories as material forms which exist internal and external to the body. To a certain extent, versions of memory as internal material structures and objects are consistent with notions of the body as permeable and receptive: the body embraces or enfolds the material world in the making of memories in that certain material forms are incorporated into and held within the body. So, for example, Carruthers highlights the somatic qualities of medieval memory that involved the internal physical storage of material and the registering of memories as bodily imprints. This was a form of memory that involved material transactions that took place across or at the boundaries of the body. Memories of the dead, which marked the bodies of the living and shaped the embodied actions of the bereaved, were conveyed through the powerful force of metaphor. An account from Florence, which represents a fathers' reaction to his son's death, illustrates this process:

> Months have passed since his death, but neither I nor his mother can forget him. His image is constantly before our eyes, reminding us of all his ways and habits, his words, his gestures. We see him day and night, lunching, dining, inside the house and out, sleeping and awake, in our villa in Florence. Whatever we do, it is like a knife that tears into our hearts . . . For more than a year I have not been able to enter his room, for no reason other than my extreme grief. (quoted in Braunstein, 1988: 616)

The knife, the torn heart and the disused chamber articulate the interconnection of objects, bodies and spaces that registered memories of the deceased. The dead boy continued to live as a material presence in the form of a memory image that possessed an expressive, articulate and mobile body. Here the metaphorical slides into the literal as this memory image was received as physical impact upon the living bodies of the bereaved, which constrained their spaces of habitation. As Braunstein states in relation to the medieval period, '[t]he invisible itself was rooted in the corporeal, and the community of the dead and of spirits prolonged its earthly existence by at times mingling with the living'

(1988: 630). In this context, the boundaries between the interior and exterior of the body, the intangible and the material, and the living and the dead were far from stable. Instead, these domains were inter-related so that each affected and shaped the other.

Understanding the body as a process that incorporates aspects of the material world can be seen as a central aspect of late medieval Euro-pean folk culture. According to Bakhtin, the predominant aesthetic in this cultural sphere was one of grotesque realism which emphasised a positive 'material bodily principle' (1984: 19). This aesthetic reached its fullest expression in festive action such as carnival and in the shared spaces of the marketplace, finding its way into literary forms especially in the work of Rabelais. Images of the grotesque body provided a 'logic' or 'system of images', producing a conception of the body as open or in the continuous 'act of becoming' (1984: 317). The grotesque body was not separated from other bodies or from material aspects of the world as they were easily incorporated through the pronounced orifices and openings of the body: 'The unfinished and open body (dying, bringing forth and being born) is not separated from the world by clearly defined boundaries; it is blended with the world, with animals, with objects' (1984: 27).

The grotesque body, as represented in folk culture, was situated in a particular relation to death, which was not seen as an end point in bodily life but as a phase in cycles of communal reproduction. As Bakhtin claims '[t]he grotesque image reflects a phenomenon in transformation, an as yet unfinished metamorphosis, of death and birth, growth and becoming' (1984: 24). Any clear opposition of life and death does not apply as: 'death is not a negation of life seen as the great body of all the people but part of life as a whole – its indispensable component, the condition of its constant renewal and rejuvenation. Death is here always related to birth; the grave is related to the earth's life giving womb' (Bakhtin 1984: 50). The interpenetration of life and death was expressed in the grotesque image of the double body or a single body that combines two – one living and one dying – as in images of old, pregnant women that 'combine a senile, decaying and deformed flesh with the flesh of new life' (1984: 26). The living and the dead body were thus interlinked. While the stress on the incomplete body or the points at which the body transgressed its own limits were characteristic of the grotesque, emphasis was also placed upon the bodily interior so that the depths of the body were often expressed in 'architectural terms' (for example as subterranean passages) (1984: 318). Furthermore, the inner body was rendered visible as '[t]he outward and inward features are often merged into one' (1984: 318). This conception of the body as one that was linked to other bodies, material objects and landscapes, or one that acted as a site at which internal/external transactions took place, can be seen as receptive to memory as the bodily incorporation of material. Ultimately, as Bakhtin states, the grotesque body 'swallows the world and is itself swallowed by the world', providing an all-embracing view of the materiality of the body caught in cycles of death and renewal (1984: 317). By embracing death as part of life, the grotesque image of the body provided a social continuum, which arguably did not face or fear loss. In other words this body, as process, was memory in that it retained and incorporated the lived material world.

The predominant features of the grotesque body, as discussed by Bakhtin, were eroded and displaced by a different conception of the body that emerged throughout the sixteenth and seventieth centuries, re-situating the body in relation to its material environment. The classical canon provided an aesthetic of beauty that was elevated above the grotesque, while the latter was progressively defined in negative terms as disgusting and degrading. Emphasizing the bounded individual, the classical body was maintained at a distance from the 'exterior nonbodily world' (1984: 29). Bakhtin outlines the key features of the classical body:

> the body was first of all a strictly completed, finished product. Furthermore, it was isolated, alone, fenced off from all other bodies. All signs of its unfinished character, of its growth and proliferation were eliminated . . . its apertures closed. The ever unfinished nature of the body was hidden, kept secret; conception, pregnancy, childbirth, death throes, were almost never shown . . . The accent was placed on the completed, self-sufficient individuality of the given body . . . the borderlines dividing the body from the outside world were sharply defined. The inner processes of absorbing and ejecting were not revealed. (1984: 29)

Thus, we arrive at a conception of the body as a completed, detached individual unit that must resist contamination in the breaching of its newly defined boundaries. The classical body was to provide a significant image through which dominant values, identities and sensibilities were projected. Stallybrass and White (1986: 21) analyse this 'finished' body as a central tenet of 'high' discourse and bourgeois individualist subjectivity. The epitome of this body was the classical Renaissance statue which was 'always mounted on a plinth' so that it was 'elevated, static and monumental'. The contours of the classical body were defined through difference and distance in relation to the grotesque and these divisions were established through the definition of acceptable (central) and unacceptable (marginal) bodies, spaces and social groups. Thus, Stallybrass and White assert that 'the bourgeois subject continuously defined and re-defined itself through the exclusion of what it marked out as "low" – as dirty, repulsive, noisy, contaminating' (1986: 191). This was a civilizing process that required bodily regimes and regulation as expressed, for instance, in codes of conduct which were recommended from the sixteenth century onwards as characteristic of civility. Connerton points to the impact of Erasmus' treatise (1530) in its definition of appropriate bodily conduct, including posture, gesture, facial expression and dress, as representative of the inner person (1989: 82). Rules of self-control and restraint were to reach into everyday practices as their extension to table manners would demonstrate. The discipline of the body was apparent in the distancing of the body from its material environment. The requirements of table etiquette, for instance, lead to the use of implements that interrupted contact between the body and food. The implications of this conception of the body and its boundaries were twofold. Codes of conduct, which encouraged internalized restraints, necessitated a 'mnemonics of the body' through which appropriate behaviour (in public and private) was reproduced (Connerton 1989: 84). Furthermore, these mnemonics placed emphasis on the bounded body, shifting emphasis away from the material transactions that moved substances across the boundaries of the body and ultimately denying the 'crudely material reality of things' (Connerton 1989: 84).

We can note the effects of the classical conception of the body in terms of the treatment of the dead and the materials through which they were remembered. It is significant that the emphasis on the integrity of bodily boundaries was also reiterated at the level of topographical boundaries. For example, Roach describes the changing spatial location of the dead from the medieval period, when the deceased were 'omnipresent' both spiritually (spirits continued to occupy the spaces of the living) and materially (when places of burial were also used for trade), to the eighteenth and nineteenth centuries, when the living and the dead were increasingly segregated. As Roach argues:

> Under a regime of newly segregationist taxonomies of behaviour in several related fields of manners and bodily administration, the dead were compelled to withdraw from the spaces of the living: . . . their bodies removed to newly dedicated and isolated cemeteries . . . As custom increasingly defined human remains as unhygienic, new practices of

interment evolved, eventually including cremation, to ensure the perpetual separation of the dead and to reduce or more strictly circumscribe the spaces they occupied. As the place of burial was removed from local churchyard to distant park, the dead were more likely to be remembered (and forgotten) by monuments than by continued observances in which their spirits were invoked. (Roach 1996: 50)

This account represents dominant 'segregationist taxonomies' where the bodies of the living and the dead are securely located in separate spaces and the favoured material object of memory is the static monument. The marginalization and containment of the dead, reinforces the concept of the living body as detached and removed from problematic matter. However, this process of differentiation and separation is rather more complex. As Roach moves on to argue, in certain contexts '[t]he living defy the segregation of the dead' especially in the ritual performances of marginalized social groups which mobilize forms of 'countermemory' (1996: 61). Furthermore, Stallybrass and White outline a broader theoretical position that points to the complex nature of 'the demarcating imperative' that divides up the domains of society, topography and the body. They suggest that where boundaries are erected in order to exclude what is seen as disgusting and dirty the social identity that is produced in opposition does, nevertheless, retain a connection with what is negated: 'disgust always bears the imprint of desire. These low domains, apparently expelled as "Other", return as the object of nostalgia, longing and fascination' (Stallybrass and White 1986: 191). Thus, while the bodies of the dead may be coded as 'other' and distanced in relation to the social identities of those with a living body, significant connections between self and other are maintained. We can see this operating through the use of fragments of the dead body (for example hair) as treasured memory objects or the keeping of other material objects that evoke the embodied person of those who have died.

Despite the apparent detachment of the early modern classical body from exterior material domains, social identity was expressed through connections with selected material objects and spaces. Items of clothing carried signs of social status, certain material objects were exchanged to express social bonds and certain architectural spaces were designated as sites of personal introspection and remembrance, for example the deathbed (see Chapters 6 and 7). These connections between bodies, spaces and objects articulated the inner dimensions of the individual and symbolized their social relations. Relationships between the body and material objects were, for instance, powerfully expressed in the exchange of souvenirs: 'throughout this period the boundary line between the body literally preserved and its sign or souvenir was surprisingly fluid. No doubt Norbert Elias was right to stress man's growing estrangement from his body, but the body remained present in the intimate souvenir' (Ranum, 1989: 234).

If the body was to retain its embeddedness within networks of material objects and spaces (themselves materials that, by association with the body, were infused with a degree of subjectivity) it is to these relations that we must attend if we are to appreciate the ways in which memories come to reside within the material domain. Parkin outlines anthropological approaches to these issues in the twentieth century stating that 'we have long become used to the idea of the lives of persons and objects as becoming mutually constituted, not in an organic but in a phenomenological sense through the use of metaphor and through perception' (1999: 314). Rather than conceiving of personhood as a static 'essence', it is understood as emergent through social interaction and association with particular material objects. Thus, it is via social engagement and networks of socio-cultural relations that persons and their identities are produced. Emphasizing the significance of material domains in this process of construction, Parkin describes the extension of personhood 'beyond the individual's biological body' and into meaningful objects – a process that he refers to as 'socio-material prosthesis' (1999: 303–4). Preserving connections between persons and objects becomes more urgent in conditions of distress and trauma brought about, for example, by the forced relocation of communities from home to unfamiliar territories. As noted above, displaced individuals and families in such crisis situations will seize upon objects which resonate with personal meanings (such as clothing, jewellery and photographs) prior to their departure and later a person will 'invest emotionally . . . in accessible objects, ideas and dreams rather than in the living people' who inhabit their new environment (1999: 308).

This mutually constituting interaction of bodies and material objects is not confined to times of crisis. As Lupton argues, in consumer societies, objects such as clothing are commodities that, once acquired, become part of the projection of self identity and are incorporated within our 'sense of subjectivity' (1998: 138). Mass-produced objects, as well as being 'functional, in many instances are infused with emotive capacities not only through advertising but also when objects become enmeshed in their owners' everyday lived world of relationships, work, housekeeping and leisure. It is through the incorporation of an object into routines that it becomes personally meaningful and it is this appropriation that defines the 'dynamic and inter-relational nature of the subject-object encounter' (Lupton 1998: 143). Lupton cites the example of shoes that are transformed through embodied use from an impersonal commodity to a decommodified aspect of the self; through repeated wearing the shoes 'become singularized, bearing the stamp of individuality and everyday experience of their owner, and move more towards the ontological state of "self" (subject) than of "other" (object)' (1998: 144). In addition to the acquisition of subject status, a vast array of objects with which we routinely interact can become 'tangible records' of relationships, events and feelings – thus forming personalized 'repositories of memory' (Lupton: 1998, 148). In contemporary Western societies, then, the material resources through which the deceased might retain a physical presence amongst the living become increasingly diverse and flexible.

Here we can differentiate between social and biological death in that the social lives of persons might persist beyond biological death, in the form of the material objects with which they are metaphorically or metonymically associated in social processes of memory making. If, as Lupton argues, material objects can generate emotional responses, then they are possessed of a certain agency or capacity to act within and shape social relations and perceptions. Social interaction with and through material forms tends to destabilize subject/object boundaries such that material objects can become extensions of the body and therefore of personhood. It is this production of personalized material environments that prepares the ground for the memory-making strategies of those facing the traumas of death.

Furthermore, as Connerton (1989) argues, it is the body itself that can provide a memory resource. Connerton identifies embodied or 'incorporated' habit memories, which occur through desires or compulsions that can override deliberate decision making. This form of memory resides in gestures, actions and movements, is often rhythmic and is reproduced in routine performance. Embodied memories of the dead, which are produced in the actions of the living, can emerge as habitual repetitions of bodily interactions developed through prior interactions with the deceased – thus loved ones might continue their presence through the bodies of those who survive them. For instance, death can heighten awareness of previous bodily proximity and engagement with a child or partner – bringing home a painful sense of loss. Equally, comfort might be found as the survivor re-enacts memories of a parent's smile, their way of holding wool and knitting needles, their predictable responses in conversations (Hallam, Hockey and Howarth 1999: 149–51).

Alternatively, experiences of embodied interactions with those dying in considerable physical suffering and pain might be rejected as intolerable memories. Lawton (2000), for example, has documented the interactions of hospice patients with relatives during the final phases of life, which tend to break down in situations where patients have suffered the distressing collapse of bodily functions and boundaries. Both patients and relatives reach a threshold at which they can no longer accept that the disintegrating body is the person they once knew. These dying bodies, in this contemporary context, unavoidably violate all current bodily ideals regarding cleanliness and control. From the relatives' point of view, they can no longer bear to visit the patient (sometimes regarding her as having 'already left' or died), and from the patient's perspective her reaction is to 'switch off mentally', to stop speaking and eating (Lawton 2000: 113, 130) This rupture in social interaction and communication can amount to social death prior to the event of biological death. Thus in situations where the physical body is no longer associated with a person (or is no longer perceived as the self that it once was) it can slide into object, or even abject, status: 'such patients constitute "body-objects" in the most extreme form' (Lawton 2000: 113). And it is this passage of body into object that, in this case, severely reduces recourse to the body in its final phases of life as a memory resource for bereaved relatives.

In identifying the contemporary potential for highly personalized memory making, we stress the social dimensions of this process. Individual biographies and collective histories merge and interact in perceptions of the lifecourse, as Harris (1987) has shown, so that wider social environments inflect individuals' memories. Following Halbwach's work between the 1920s and 1950s on the social dimensions of memory, Connerton asserts that 'the idea of an individual memory, absolutely separate from social memory, is an abstraction almost devoid of meaning' (1989: 37). Once this is recognized certain analytical problems are highlighted, namely, how are the complex relationships between the individual and the social, which constitute memory, to be grasped and examined? Lambek and Antze encapsulate this question when they ask 'how the memory of the individual – precisely that which is often taken to epitomise individuality – draws upon collective idioms and mechanisms' (1996: xiii). Here we have advanced the argument that it is in terms of socially resonant metaphors and materials that memory and memories relating to death are formulated, experienced and expressed. Other anthropologists have developed sophisticated and convincing perspectives on the construction of personally meaningful memories through socially shared and collectively sanctioned narratives that draw upon commonly valued cultural conventions and images (Skultans 1998). Throughout this study we place emphasis on the materiality of memory and the ways in which this is forged, elaborated and refined in conjunction with embodied actions, spoken words, written texts and visual images.

This chapter's comparative historical account of memory-making practices highlights the role of metaphors in the figuring of memory. The absences and loss introduced into human experience by death render the task of materializing memory all the more urgent. By attending to the cultural devices that have been used to map and communicate memories, we delineate the diversity of processes through which the past seems recoverable – and death itself is called to mind. As the metaphors and materials discussed throughout this chapter suggest, these processes not only vary across time and between places, but might also form sites of contestation in the face of competing claims as to what and how to remember. Whether intensely private or overtly public, remembering is a social practice that makes apparent the shared cultural images through which personal and social identity is produced. Notions such as containment – articulated in metaphors of boxes or storerooms – testify to the sense of memory as otherwise fleeting or ephemeral. Furthermore, the human body has been experienced as a site at which memories can most powerfully be inscribed or evoked – indeed we have noted the persistent metaphorical linkeage of memory, material domains and the body. As described, medieval figurings of memory took on the complexity of an imagined architecture within which recollections might be placed – thus providing a mnemonic system that acted to mobilize emotion and the imagination. Via the cultural devices of memory, form, order and meaning have been brought to the unpredictable, often chaotic, dispersal of individuals and objects at the time of individual deaths – and indeed the destruction of communities in war. Furthermore, while visual and spatial metaphors of memory are pronounced in Western contexts, repetition is often a feature of memory making that can lend a sense of continuity and connection with persons deceased. The discussion of materials presented in this chapter suggests that memories, as cultural forms, emerge and operate within wider social, epistemological and technological contexts. As the chapters to follow argue, the deliberate and strategic fashioning of memories, whether personal or collective, needs to be set alongside those all too painful recollections stimulated by material objects and places seemingly possessed of their own agency. While a memory might be sensed as either a 'scar' or obsession, a pleasurable journey or an arresting sensation, remembering in relation to death is a crucial social process in which metaphorical and material dimensions are profoundly significant.

Note

1. This is an extract from Jenning's poem originally published in Elizabeth Jenning (1967) Collected Poems, London: Macmillan.

Time, Death and Memory

In 1972 Fabian stated that anthropological studies of death were marked by a 'fascination with the curious, the violent and the exotic' that reinforced conceptions of a non-Western, primitive 'other' – a category further distanced by its projection into the (barbaric) 'past' (1991 [1972]: 178–9). If we look at historical patterns of cultural production in *Western* material cultures of death and memory, we do find the fascination that Fabian alludes to – not, however, as part of the construction of non-Western 'otherness', but as an aspect of the exploration of self, the material limits of embodied life and the possibilities of memory. The dead body, as represented in European memorial and memento mori imagery, became temporally distant and 'other' by virtue of its material disintegration. But the visibility of this 'otherness', its recovery within the present, was a significant feature of memory objects in medieval and early modern systems of memory making, which were also used to offer moralizing commentaries upon the transience of the material domain. Situating the 'otherness' of the dead body in relation to the living body of the self, memory objects were used to sustain connections between life and death.

In this chapter we extend our exploration of material cultures of death as they impinge upon memory over the long term in Northern Europe. In particular, we analyse materials associated with death, from the medieval period to the later twentieth century, which have been produced, collected and displayed in different social contexts, mainly in England. In attempting to contextualize this diverse range of death-related materials in terms of its memory effects we point to issues of consumption, appropriation and the cultural recoding of objects and images over time. We trace materials of memory as they shift within changing frameworks for understanding the world – from religious systems of belief through the 'secularizing' processes of enlightenment. Time is explored here as a dimension that feeds into the significance of memories and as an important aspect of the symbolism operative within material cultures of death.

Material and visual cultures of death in England have been linked to rituals surrounding death in studies that explore objects and images in the context of ritualized practices, especially funerals and periods of mourning (for example Llewellyn 1991). Here we provide an historical perspective that suggests that the domain of death-related objects tends to exceed and disrupt clearly demarcated ritual phases. The potency of these objects is not necessarily confined to the time of specific ritual performances; rather their temporal reach extends within longer term memory processes. The objects and images to which we attend are characterized by their dispersal across social times and spaces as they have been incorporated into the fabric of everyday life in domestic interiors or displayed in public arenas such as cathedrals and museums. We examine, for example, memorials and memento mori (objects that act as reminders of death for the living) in the form of effigies, transi tombs, printed images, sculpted miniatures and photographs. These have been used in collective ritual and personal remembrance or contemplation and their social circulation and consumption is evident at elite and popular levels.

The perceived duration of an object – its capacity to endure time and to operate across time by encoding aspects of the past or future in the present moment – is crucial to its memory function. In relation to memory and death, the issues of preservation as opposed to decay and loss are pertinent and find their expression both in the materials and the symbolism of death-related objects. For instance, objects constructed in stone, wax, ivory, paper or flowers to represent the body and flesh, have been associated with varying degrees of endurance such that material substances are seen in terms of their particular temporal qualities. What is lasting or ephemeral is conveyed through the perceived physical properties of the object. The materiality of memory objects often alludes directly to the bodily processes of dying, death and decay and such objects maintain tensions between physical presence and the threat of disintegration and absence. Thus death-related objects are often made to highlight their temporal capacities and limitations in ways that allow them to act powerfully within memory.

This chapter opens with a discussion of anthropological perspectives on memory and time as articulated through material object domains. The following sections examine the related issues of temporal stasis (in the case of memorial effigies), process (in the case of macabre imagery), the temporal dimensions of memento mori, the interplay of preservation and decomposition in memory objects, aspects of their fragmentation and display, the imagery of darkness and light as well as images of instruments used in the measurement of time. Each of these are analysed in terms of their significance within Western material cultures of death and memory.

Memory and Temporality: Material Dimensions

The ways in which memory operates through time, involving either continuities or disruptions of concepts, ideas and sensations, are crucially fashioned by prevailing material cultures. Social experiences of time and perceptions of the past are mediated by cultural forms including texts, visual images and objects. The latter all possess material dimensions that are animated and assigned meanings through embodied social practice. Lambek and Antze highlight memory as a temporal process. However, they point out that the metaphors used to describe memory, for instance in psychoanalytic discourses, tend to 'transform the temporal into the spatial and are intensely visual' (1996: xii). From this perspective, '[l]ayers are excavated, veils lifted, screens removed' in the processes through which subjects access memories which are always mediated by fantasies (1996: xii). Fabian has traced the deep historical roots in relationships between memory, objects and spaces in the Western tradition. To aid memory in Greek and Roman oration, parts of a speech would be mentally linked to visually arresting objects, such as statues, in an imaginary building and while speaking, the orator would mentally move through this architectural structure (see Chapter 2). Thus the 'temporal flux of live speech' was presented as a 'spatial topography of points and arguments', a strategy that was foundational in the 'spatialization of time' (Fabian 1983: 111). The spatialization of time here refers to the process by which notions of time are conveyed in terms of visualized places or a topography comprising distinctive objects and spaces.

Memory processes, temporality and material objects are, then, interwoven and these persist in long-term historical traditions that continue to register in the twentieth century. As Forty (1999) observes, Western conceptions of memory (derived from Aristotle) have assumed that material objects can hold and preserve memories, ensuring their continuity over time. Indeed, the values assigned to objects may arise out of their perceived capacity to physically endure time, as in the case of stone or marble sculpture. Furthermore, Seremetakis suggests that even the most mundane object can be 'laden with perceptual recall', in that it can act as a 'temporal conduit' by carrying socially shared meanings and histories through time and space (1994: 10–11). From this perspective, objects build up layered meanings over time to form histories of social events, relations and emotions that can be reanimated, denied or otherwise manipulated, depending upon the context of the object's use. Thus, it is not only the cultural production of the object and its physical properties that are significant, but also the unfolding social life of the object as it moves through time absorbing, or having impressed upon it, traces of its own history. Therefore, Seremetakis proposes that attending to the reception of objects in embodied social performances is crucial in attempts to understand material cultures and the memory/sensory processes that are enmeshed in them.

Once we acknowledge that objects can be inscribed with different meanings over time, the spectrum of material cultural forms associated with death becomes at once immensely broad and more complex in temporal terms. We can, however, identify a spectrum of materials which range from *dedicated* to *emergent* memory objects. Material cultures of death comprise, at one end of this spectrum, objects that have been intentionally produced as memorials and mementoes for the dead: objects that might persist or dissolve in their memory functions over time. At the other end of the spectrum we find objects that have had their varied uses in everyday social life but, as a result of their social relations and personal associations, come to act within memory processes as potent reminders of the deceased. In the latter category, for instance, is the clothing of lost relatives. During bereavement, the 'iconography of garments' can produce an 'aesthetic of absence': the look, feel, colour and texture of garments that remain after a death might evoke the past proximity of their owners and thereby highlight their absence in the present (Ash 1996: 219). Ash argues that '[a] collection of ties may not have the same effects on the spectator as do painting, sculpture or music, but "memory objects" can and do, have powerful repercussions in terms of visual and emotional affectivity' (Ash 1996: 219). The impact of personal mementoes of this type rests upon their connections with the life histories of their past owners and hence their capacity to retain fragments of the past within the present. While we can see, then, that mundane objects can be made to preserve past times, they are also linked to processes of change. A personal memento connected with a rite of passage such as death, provides a 'material sign of an abstract referent: transformation of status' (Stewart 1998: 139). So, for example, clusters of mementos kept in the form of

scrapbooks, memory quilts and photograph albums register transformations and changes that punctuate the life course (Stewart 1998: 139).

Thus, from a contemporary perspective, we arrive at a conception of
material cultures of death composed of historically shifting objects,
which might now be designated as 'high art' or 'low cultural form'
and whose temporal duration (in both physical presence and cultural
resonance) fluctuates according to specific social contexts of production
and reception. All such objects, however, are able to condense different
times through their aesthetic, sensual or material properties. In further
chapters we attend to material objects that enter into social circulation
and only later (especially after a death) become foci for memory, but
in the following sections of this chapter we examine dedicated objects
that have been produced specifically to address the themes of death
and time from the medieval period to the present day. We look at the
ways in which certain images have been repeatedly explored and
modified, namely those focusing on the human body and its transformations in life and death. The passage of time has been represented,
in memorials and memento mori, through images of the body, but it
is also visualized in an iconography that registers the flow of time in a
material environment of flowers, trees, earthly creatures and the
alternation of light and darkness. In addition, devices dedicated to the
measurement of time, including hourglasses, watches and clocks have
been incorporated into memento mori and memorial objects. The
double certainties of the passage of time and the arrival of death are
explored through these objects that dwell upon what remains at the
end of a life, what death destroys and what kinds of material traces it
is possible to retain as forms of memory. What makes these objects so
distinctive, and arguably so potent, is their perceived ability to articulate
tensions between stasis and change, preservation and decay; between
the recognizable and the radically unfamiliar aspects of the self and
other that emerge through dying, grief and mourning.

Static Bodies: Memorial Effigies

One central feature of monuments is their claim to permanence and
stability over time. The capacity of a memorial to physically endure
time, or its apparent resistance to the effects of time, are equated with
the persistence of living memory. It is, however, the physical body,
limited in its temporal duration, which has provided some of the central
iconography of medieval and early modern monuments. The effigy
provided a means by which the impermanence of the flesh could be

counteracted to ensure the future presence of the dead amongst the living. In the context of medieval Northern Europe, the display of the dead through human effigies on tombs could represent an 'arrestation of time in showing the body in a "steady state", dressed and alert as in life' (Binski 1996: 71). Effigies, as three-dimensional renderings of the body on tombs, emerged as a cultural form, maintaining spiritual and social relationships between the living and the dead, from the eleventh century. Tombs were the sites at which prayers for the dead would be performed and thus they functioned as points of contact between the living and the dead. Prayers for the dead were essential for the afterlife of the deceased as well as the future spiritual condition of the living as time in purgatory could be reduced in exchange for such prayers. This meant that tombs were oriented towards the future for both the living and the dead within the Christian worldview, as well as serving to maintain the social presence of the dead within the present. Tombs functioned to commemorate persons but did so by locating them within a social and spiritual system, working to display their social and political rank. Effigies conveyed a sense of permanence, and for elites, this provided a continuity of authority and social position symbolized in their sculpted costume together with signs of kin and family affiliation. Double effigies, representing husband and wife, sometimes linked in a hand clasp, from the thirteenth century reinforced the capacity of the tomb in the preservation of continuing relationships with the dead – here the bonds of marriage and the strength of family identity were displayed.

The use of effigies as a means to represent the past life of the deceased and to create their future social reputation continued in the early modern period when they also operated to exemplify virtues:

> As the natural body decayed, the ritualised monumental body prevented the social body from being overwhelmed by a similar fate. The monumental body was to be set up at the place of burial to mark its site and was designed to stand for ever as a replacement for the social body. As a subsidiary function, it also acted as a reminder of the living form of the natural body. (Llewellyn, 1991: 101)

While the effigy masked the decaying natural body which would inevitably disappear, it also created a stable social body that was assured continuity. The material, design, symbolic features, inscriptions and physical location of monuments all worked to reinforce this continuity. Monuments would occupy particular spaces within parish churches –

Figure 3.1 Monument to Sir Moyle Finch (1551–1614) and Elizabeth Countess of Winchilsea (1556–1634). This was displayed in the parish church of St Mary Eastwell in Kent after the death of Sir Moyle Finch but before that of his wife. It is now exhibited at the Victoria and Albert Museum, London. The V & A Picture Library.

spaces that carried associations of local authority, while the height and size of the monument (in relation to other monuments) would also be taken as an indication of social status. For example, the Monument to Sir Moyle Finch (1551–1614) and Elizabeth Countess of Winchelsea (1556–1634), displays the principle of continuity sought by the effigy: the deceased appears in a life-like posture, almost sleeping, with the signs of social status marked through his attire – his social body preserved in marble and alabaster (Figure 3.1). This monument was erected after the death of Sir Moyle Finch, but before that of his widow, in the parish church of St Mary Eastwell in Kent. At the time, this meant that the widow would have looked upon her own open-eyed memorial fixed alongside that of her husband. Here, the double effigy aspires to continuity and preservation of memory by freezing a moment in time, arresting bodily decay and maintaining the social life of the deceased.

Bodies in Process: Memory and the Macabre

If the effigy secured its place within memory processes by masking the effects of time, a different form of memorial – the transi – achieved the same by demonstrating, in stone, the toll of time upon the body. Transi tombs were a manifestation of macabre imagery that was characterized, from the thirteenth to the fifteenth century in northern Europe, by a concentration upon the breakup or decay of the physical body, which inspired 'shock, fascination' self-reflection and moral contemplation amongst the living (Binski 1996: 134). During the fifteenth century, transi tombs comprised representations of the dead in the form of two bodies: one dead, yet 'lifelike' or 'alert'; one dead and in a state of decomposition. These two states were represented though the codes of dress and posture so that the former body appeared in full attire, carrying the signs of social rank and status, while the latter appeared as a naked or shrouded corpse with decaying flesh. The two bodies set up a tension between the 'timeless' social body and the 'time-bound' natural body in death (Binski 1996: 139). For example, the tombs of Richard Fleming (d.1431) in Lincoln Cathedral and Archbishop Henry Chichele (d.1443) in Canterbury Cathedral, display the deceased as both a body intact and as a body in the process of decay (Figure 3.2).

The dramatic contrast between on the one hand, the static body and on the other, the body in process produced a memorial which also provided a wider commentary upon the nature of material life within the Christian spiritual framework. The imagery of decomposition conveyed notions regarding the body as a mirror of the soul – decay referred to inner sin, suffering and the corruption of the flesh. The body (and by implication the material world) is visualized as impermanent and unstable as the body's surface, the skin, breaks away to reveal a rotting interior. As the skull and bones are exposed, further disintegration of the flesh is suggested by the presence of toads, worms and snakes, which are woven into the body. The transi mobilizes the extremes of beauty and ugliness, dignity and vileness, which allude to the present human condition and to its future state. Transi tombs, then, functioned as memento mori – as objects that provided for the living powerful reminders of their own death, and prompted self-reflection. They drew upon macabre imagery, which featured death, as a corpse,

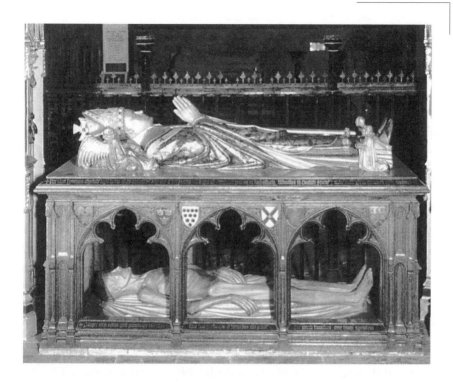

Figure 3.2 The tomb of Archbishop Henry Chichele (d. 1443) in Canterbury Cathedral, Kent. Canterbury Cathedral Archive and Library.

inviting the living to consider the transient nature of life and its vanities, and thereby encouraging the living to focus on their spiritual rather than their debased material dimensions. Death, figured as a cadaver, comes forward into the present to reveal the future state of the self and serves, in Binski's analysis, to represent 'the doubled self as other' or what the self will inevitably become (1996: 134). This condition of simultaneously living (having a stable material presence) and dying (when material substance disintegrates) is powerfully represented in the transi tomb where both states are dramatically juxtaposed.

Forty (1999) has proposed that when objects holding memories decay this indicates forgetting and, furthermore, that an important effect of memorial artefacts is to create a distinction between what should be remembered and what is to be forgotten. He suggests that this feature of separation is made visible in transi tombs where the decaying body is marked out as matter which will be left to wither and disappear (Forty,

1999: 8). We would argue, however, that rather than signalling a process of forgetting, the dimensions of decay visualized through the transi tomb are precisely those that constitute a powerfully memorable and memory-invoking object. We find that the distinctive macabre imagery of the transi, which fuses representations of life and death, persists in other cultural forms associated with memory. It is to these forms, their characteristics and persistence within religious and, later, 'secularized' discourses and practices that we turn in the following sections of this chapter.

Memento Mori: Remembering to Die

The imagery of death and time, displayed in the form of three-dimensional effigies and transi tombs, was also activated in more ephemeral printed materials which functioned as memento mori and were disseminated at the popular level in England during the sixteenth and seventeenth centuries. Printed ballads formed memento mori in that they served as reminders of death for the living and emphasized that the earthly world was 'but a vanitie' that fades away. They achieved this with the use of mnemonic devices that set up associations between death and actions as well as material objects in everyday life. For instance, ballads recommended that man should think about his bed as a grave or the morning crow of a cock as the last trumpet or the night bell of the watchman as the bell that would announce his own death (Watt 1996: 113). Each of these metaphors construed the daily marking of time as reminders of death. Reminders of death, within the Christian worldview, were integrated into spiritual instruction directed towards the living although, as we will see, the imagery of memento mori also inhabits the materials of memory dedicated to deceased persons.

In printed ballads and broadsides (single printed sheets), then, the conjuncture of time, death and memory was common. As Watt argues, 'the exhortation to "remember" was extremely pervasive, most often coupled with the word "death"' (1991: 251). Woodcuts of Time with a scythe and an hourglass and Death with an arrow, together with images of skeletons, and corpses ask the viewer to 'remember to die' (Figure 3.3). 'The map of mortalitie' (1604), a broadside, is composed of various images and textual components focusing on the passage of time and located around a skull, representing death (Figure 3.4). Here the objects depicted carry inscriptions so that the word 'Earthe' is written on a skull, which is accompanied by calls to 'Prepare for death but feare not

Figure 3.3 'Memento mori. Remember to die' (c. 1640). Folger Shakespeare Library, Washington DC (STC 17816.5).

death. Remember thine end.' Immediately below the skull, a book carries further textual reminders of the fate of the body: 'All flesh as grasse doth passe and come to nought. Gods word most pure aye doth endure not chang'd in ought.' Below the book, a corpse prepared for burial at a grave, reveals that 'A shroude to grave men only have' – the shroud is the only possession that will accompany man after death. The images thus play on the transience of the earthly body and material things in contrast to the endurance of God's word. These themes are elaborated in the detailed text which runs alongside the skull, book and grave. Metaphors of earth, water and dust again convey the future state of the body:

> Dust will to dust, as though art once were we:
> worldes vainglorie doth to nothing fade.

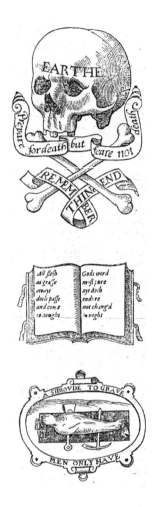

Figure 3.4 Detail from 'The map of mortalitie' (1604). Huntington Library, California (RB 18319).

Man doth consume as water spilt on sande.
Like lightenings flash, his life is seene and gone . . .

The swift passage of life, or life as a short flash of light, is made to contrast later with death as the birth of man's eternity with God. Just as the flesh is 'fraile' and becomes 'nothing' in death, the text states that the 'worldes best pleasures' such as 'beautie, strength and wit' will disappear. Death is represented as night and sleep but is also personified as a 'pale, ouglie' 'shape' that may appear at anytime 'sodiane, soone or late'. Death is, in temporal terms, constantly present and therefore, man should constantly think about it:

> Youth well to live, age well to die should care:
> In life, for death: in death for life prepare.

These printed materials thus acted upon memory, calling death into life and creating metaphorical connections that associated the passage of time in life with the inevitability of death. In the context of early modern literacies, when the printed word could not be read, the visual image supplied memento mori messages and such printed forms were also possessed of a certain valued materiality in themselves. They were viewed as objects to be carried about the person or attached to walls and these prints should be considered, therefore, as part of their spatial settings, acknowledging their connections with other visual media which dealt with death and acted as memento mori: 'These paper mementos performed the same function as a skull on the desk, a gruesome corpse on the back of a mirror, or the effigy of a cadaver on a tomb' (Watt 1991: 252).

The display of texts in domestic settings is evident in memento mori inscriptions on the interior walls of a manor houses that have survived from the later sixteenth century. One such text, from a house in East Sussex elaborates upon time and death as unavoidable aspects of life:

> In lyfe theare ys no suer staye
> For fleashe as flower dothe vade awaye
> this carcas made of slyme and claye
> must taste of deathe theare ys no waye.
> while we have tyme then lette us praye
> to god for grace bothe night and daye.
> (c. 1580, cited in Watt, 1991, 219)

The inscription represents the passage of time and the inevitable process of dying. The effects of time upon the body are likened to the fading of flowers, while the corpse decomposes into 'slyme'. The transition from life to death is also linked to the repetition of day and night, during which the living are called to enter into regular prayers that act as constant reminders of their mortality. These forms of memento mori worked through their constant visibility and alluded to patterns of daily repetition which linked death and time with material aspects of the body and the physical environment.

Preservation and Decomposition

The interplay of images concerned with preservation and physical decomposition evident in the material cultures of death, through effigies, transi tombs and memento mori, can be seen as an important means by which time and death were represented. This imagery captured the central effects of death in terms of the threat of loss implied by material disintegration and acted as a potent metaphor for the possibilities of memory. Binski has argued that the transi tomb ensured that the dimension of time was embedded in representations of death and it also marked the corpse as an 'object of aestheticised interest' (1996: 150). In their display of the body in a condition of physical crisis and as a manifestation of the macabre, transis can be linked to medieval conceptions of memory making in that they are 'about extremes, the moments of passage from intactness to decay, and from decay to annihilation' (Binski 1996: 152). A treatise on memory from c.1335 noted that memory images 'should be wondrous and intense, because such things are impressed in the memory more deeply and are better retained. However, such things are for the most part not average but extremes, as the most beautiful or ugly, joyous or sad . . . a thing of great dignity or vileness' (quoted in Binski 1996: 152). The antithesis of physical preservation and decay brings extremes of the body into view, moving between the ideal of beauty and the horror of decomposition.

Alongside transi and effigy tombs a wide variety of memento mori objects had been in circulation in Europe, deploying the imagery of death and intending to 'inspire humility and virtuous action in the living' (Cohen 1973: 84). Such objects included statuettes of skeletons and small ivory skulls that could be worn as jewellery and they often represented the boundary between life and death by showing a living figure on one side with a corresponding dead and decaying form on the other. The symbols of time and the end of material life are again incorporated. For instance, Cohen notes Erasmus's statement in 1519 regarding his medal, which displayed an image of the god Terminus (representing the end): 'He who looks upon death as the boundary of life and keeps the ultimate end of life in view may well take Terminus as his emblem, for he refuses to place his temporal welfare higher than his eternal one' (quoted in Cohen 1973: 52). Memento mori therefore

acted as objects that alluded to the cessation of earthly (material) life
and the beginning of the afterlife. But they were also objects positioned
on the very boundary between life and death, allowing the living to
gesture towards the after life and providing a medium through which
the dead addressed the living. Thus, objects that mobilized boundary
imagery contained within them possibilities for transcending the
domains of the living and the deceased – in other words they were
perfected as memory objects. The exploration of bodily (and temporal)
oppositions and extremes is a characteristic of death-related objects
which persists into the seventeenth and eighteenth centuries. Aspects
of the imagery of memorial tombs were not confined to sacred spaces
of remembrance in churches and cathedrals. Rather, they were reworked
in fragmented or miniaturized form and resituated in different display
contexts including cabinets of curiosities and museums.

Fragmentation and Display

Miniaturized skulls and skeletons in the memento mori tradition
survive today in museum collections. In the stores of the Science
Museum in London, for instance, intricately carved wooden and ivory
heads and busts appear as smaller versions of transis, representing the
body as a fragment rather than in full but with features that are half
preserved as living and half in a state of decay. These were used as
miniature memorials of particular persons and as memento mori
showing idealized male or female features. One of these shows woman
as Eve biting the apple from the tree of knowledge with a serpent coiled
into her plaited hair (Figures 3.5a, 3.5b). The head is divided laterally
into two – a split image of woman that is at once present in the flesh,
with hair, skin and an open eye, but is also deceased and reduced to
bone. The figure thus incorporates elements of biblical and macabre
imagery to operate as a memento mori but also as a moralizing commentary upon woman's sins and transgressions.

Deploying a language of decay, the miniature can be viewed in terms
of the visual codes of sixteenth and seventeenth century still life
painting. Attending to the sensuous detail of the material domain to
celebrate its riches whilst underlining its inherent fragility, death moved
through still life compositions. In these paintings

> candles flicker, pipe smoke curls away, music fades, flowers wither,
> butterflies flutter for the last time, glasses fall and are shattered, bread
> grows stale, weapons rust, all things decay. New objects are introduced,

Figure 3.5(a) Memento mori: miniaturised wooden model of a female head - half living, half dead (16.5cm). Front view.

Figure 3.5(b) Memento mori: miniaturised wooden model of a female head - half living, half dead (16.5cm). Back view. Science Museum/ Science and Society Picture Library.

and these provide the key: the skull (often in association with the portrait), the watch (sometimes in pieces – it no longer tells the time), the hourglass. The symbols spell out the message: death lies within all living things. (Aries, 1985: 193)

Death resonated in and through the visible world comprised of a multitude of objects, including skulls, jewellery, books, ornamental sculpture and luxuriant fabrics, all of which appealed to the senses and appeared simultaneously as beautiful and subject to decay. The high degree of visual accuracy deployed in still life painting highlighted the transitory nature of material life, reiterating the message of memento mori – that the earthly world was a vanity. Furthermore, the importance of visibility as a means of knowing, or possessing a knowledge of the world was celebrated in seventeenth century still life and as Alpers argues, this asserts a deep concern with the visual properties of objects (1989). Modes of seeing implied by this work dwell upon detail or render 'everything as a visible surface by slicing across or through to make a section . . . or by opening something up to expose the innards to reveal how it is made' (Alpers 1989: 84). Offering numerous views of the same object, including skulls, to reveal the sides, back and underneath within the same frame, this approach intensifies interest in the object and is, in Alpers view, a 'fragmenting approach', in which detailed, closely observed segments were valued for their beauty as a 'function of infinite attentive glances' (Alpers 1989: 85).

The possibilities for viewing miniature memento mori, rendered as fragments imaging the preserved and the decaying body, were thus opened up as multiple and repetitive. The small female head (Figure 3.5a, 3.5b), mounted on a stand and executed in minute detail is carved in the round, inviting close inspection from all angles. Held in the hand and rotated, the object transforms life into death and death into life, a circular motion reflected in the spiral of snake and hair suspended at the back of the figure. Such memento mori did not require the entire monumental body to visualize death; rather, they relied upon concentrated richness of detail which paid intimate attention to both the 'living' surface and the deathly interior of the body part. While Stewart suggests that the scale of the miniature presents for the viewer 'an illusion of mastery' (1998: 172), for early modern eyes, the possession of miniature portraits, as Ranum argues, expressed a 'desire for intimacy, for bodily contact, no less significant than the desire to be buried along with the beloved' (1989: 250).

But miniatures were also to become sources of fascination often incorporated into cabinets of curiosities (MacGregor 1985) – a process which tended to disrupt their resonance as reminders of death or of deceased persons. Stafford lists memento mori and miniature sculpted busts among the eclectic items such as shells, coral, gems, carved ivory, fossils, 'pickled monsters', petrified reptiles, and crucifixes displayed in cabinets during the eighteenth century (1994: 238, 242). Increasingly presented for public consumption in London, Paris, Berlin and Vienna, cabinets of curiosities visually juxtaposed a mass of 'grotesque' material for the purposes of entertainment and education (Stafford 1994). Cardinal suggests that such cabinets were related to Renaissance memory systems in that they provided a 'physical matrix for the placement and articulation of mental properties' and acted as material spaces for the 'linkage of images, objects and concepts' (Cardinal 1995: 80–1). Objects placed within cabinets were valued for their stimulating visual appearance and as part of collections they were also regarded as embodiments of ideas which condensed knowledge about the world (1995: 80–1). However, Kemp emphasizes that cabinets of curiosities were compelling above all because they displayed 'objects of wonder' that defied clear classificatory boundaries. Indeed, Kemp's interpretation of objects gathered into cabinets emphasises their movement as 'cultural migrators' (1995 179): 'They journey between religious and secular, Catholic and Protestant, godliness and vanity. They cross boundaries between public and private, the secret and the accessible, artisan and noble, high and vulgar taste, functional and decorative . . . centre and periphery, domestic and exotic' (1995: 181). Through this process of boundary crossing, the memento mori could be endlessly shuffled so that its functions once residing within the sphere of memory could be over-ridden and replaced with other social and cultural meanings. The visual spectacle of these cabinets, once considered marvellous and rare, was increasingly devalued as 'idiosyncratic' and 'irregular' with enlightenment emphases on systematic collecting, rational classification and orderly display (Stafford 1994).

Bodily Interiors

If the memento mori was miniaturized, fragmented and passed into cabinets of curiosities, it was also realised and fleshed out in further techniques of body modelling. A memento mori object from the eighteenth century, rendered in coloured wax and cloth to represent a life-sized female head, is again simultaneously preserved and decaying

(Figure 3.6). The head is positioned at the extremes of life and death, these being powerfully conveyed through the use of materials resembling the textures and tones of skin, hair and bone. The head rests between two hands, one in a fleshy and one in a skeletal form. Life is represented in the perfect complexion, the styled hair, the gazing eye, the red lips and the decorative bracelet secured around the wrist. Death is manifest below the skin where the skull is infested with insects including worms and a snail. A reference to Eve is made through the apple positioned below the living hand, which also gestures towards a wax label holding the inscription 'Vanitas Vanitatum et omnia Vanitas Ecc: Chap 1 V 2' ('Vanity of vanities, all is vanity' Eccles 1:2, Holy Bible, King James Version). Through these words and the imagery of decay, this object is situated within the material world understood as a vanity, resonating with the symbolism of transience which characterized sixteenth- and seventeenth-century still life painting.

The memento mori continued to resonate through the inscription and the physical structure of this eighteenth century wax model but we can also link it with the replication of the body in anatomical modelling. The interpenetration of memento mori and medical illustration was already evident in illustrated books of anatomy from the Renaissance (Sawday 1995: 112–15). In northern Europe, memento mori objects, in the form of skeletons carved in ivory, were often produced by the same craftsmen who sculpted miniature anatomical manikins for use as 'instructive tools' by doctors in medical training (Hansen and Porter 1999: 54). The wax model of the female head (Figure 3.6) points again to the movement of the memento mori into the material cultures of science, in that the modelling of the body in anatomical investigation appropriated the memento mori's visual codes. And furthermore, as the wax model fashions the female head as a double which is both 'static' and in a state of 'decay' we can detect traces of the transi: the anatomical model resonates with funerary sculpture (see Figure 3.2). As noted above, this wax model plays upon the opposition of life and death, preservation and decay represented in the reduction to bone and the presence of insects, but this time worked in scale and material that simulate the 'real' body. Fusing anatomical realism with the symbols of the memento mori, the object is ambivalent in that it can be viewed as both an instrument of empirical instruction and a focus for spiritual contemplation.

This model would also have been viewed from behind glass, separated from the viewer by its own cabinet (coffin), which allowed visual access from the front and both sides. The distance created by the cabinet might

Figure 3.6 Wax model of a female head, half living, half dead, eighteenth century. Science Museum/ Science and Society Picture Library.

also suggest its uses for observation only – rather than investigation through touch. Bronfen (1992) has pointed out that the uses of wax models during the eighteenth century by anatomy students provided access to the 'body' without requiring contact with the repellent realities of decaying flesh: 'Producing a substitute of the corrupt and putrefied dead body that would mask death, these models are endemic to a general cultural effort to eliminate the impure state of mutability and decay by replacing it with a pure and immutable wax body double' (Bronfen 1992: 99). The elimination of signs of physical decay, such as insects, (and biblical reference) from these replicas of the body is evident in nineteenth-century wax models. For instance one model of the male head and body (Figure 3.7), in the Anatomy Museum at Aberdeen University (c. 1890), retains the half living/ half dead structure so reminiscent of the memento mori – but this time the body is modelled as half intact/half dissected and the deceased 'flesh' is preserved – it is not withered to the bone or occupied by other creatures. In addition,

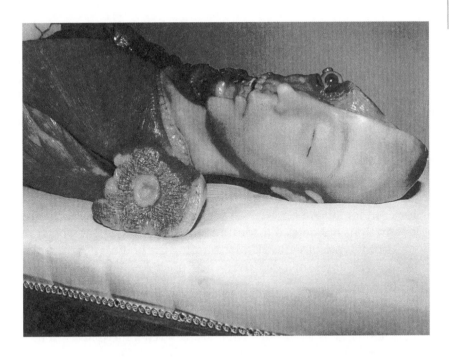

Figure 3.7 Wax model of human anatomy, c. 1890. The model is inscribed with the name of its maker, bearing the words: Dr. R. Weisker, Leipzig. Anatomy Museum, University of Aberdeen. Photograph: Norman Little.

it is the dissected half of this body that fixes its gaze upon the world, while the 'living' half sleeps, blissfully unaware of its fate. This shift in the role and positioning of the eye perhaps speaks to a 'secularised' conception of the mortal body – from 'religious art' to 'anatomical study' (see Bronfen 1992: 99). In Figure 3.6 the open eye of the living face suggests an awareness of inevitable mortality and physical decay viewed within a Christian system of belief but in Figure 3.7 it is the 'dead' who are awakened to the preserved intricacies of their internal anatomical composition. By the later nineteenth century, drawing the body into the spheres of science was to situate it within an increasingly secularized discourse.

Again, the prioritizing of the 'fixed' body modelled in wax, as opposed to a 'real' body in the process of decay, can be read as a detachment from time which stabilized the body and its visible interior. But unlike the static marble bodies rendered as memorial effigies dedicated to identifiable persons, anatomical waxes were models of anonymous bodies used to provoke a different kind of remembering. Wax models were bodies without lived histories or identities in that they retained no distinctive traces of the deceased persons from whose physical components they had been fashioned. Thus, it is not *persons* that were being 'fixed' in memory, rather it was a generalized knowledge of human anatomy that was being imparted in an educational context. (This is reinforced by the model's inscription, which imprints the name of the model's maker rather than providing any reference to the person deceased.) The static bodies of anatomical models would therefore serve the purposes of memory understood as an accumulation of empirically observable knowledge about the human form.

However, Jordanova (1997: 102) suggests ways in which anatomical representations of bodies did continue to register time by establishing them within 'types of series'. Understanding the body as a form which changed over time, included the visual tracking of species through different stages of the life cycle, the exploration of anatomical depth (for example the progressive unveiling of the womb) and furthermore:

> [t]he most obvious series that anatomists see, even if they rarely record it, is the progressive decay of flesh following death. This is, implicitly, a moral process, because death raises questions about an afterlife and about the quality of the life that has been lived. Just deserts. Even in a secular age, people reflect constantly, one might say obsessively on the theme of mortality . . . For many centuries, when it came to pictures, the skeleton was the conventional motif through which such issues were raised. Hence figures that are half skeleton and half flesh, are also series – they evoke the passage from life to death, a particular form of time sequence, which is morally charged. And, to extend the point, highly realistic depictions, whether two/ or three/dimensional (especially wax), which simulate life, by that very token, serve as reminders of death. (Jordanova 1997: 104–6)

Here Jordanova detects the presence of memento mori in the secular imaging of the body. Even if dimensions of decay, which animate the memento mori, are masked or denied they cannot be absolutely absented. Instead they return in forms acceptable to the aesthetics and sensibilities of particular historical settings. Physical decay, as a sign of the passage of time, retains its resonance precisely because it invokes the anxieties, tensions and uncomfortable intensities of Western memory processes surrounding death.

Darkness and Light

The iconography of death and time has drawn upon a rich imagery of darkness and light. In the printed memento mori of the seventeenth century life is likened to 'lightenings flash', it is 'seen and gone' (see above). Life and death were mapped on to day and night as waking and sleep were linked to the beginning and the end of the body's life cycle. The imagery of light and darkness during this period was developed through religious instruction where God was the ultimate source of light, which would banish darkness from the universe. Thus the world of human mortality and sin was linked to darkness. However, this darkness was ambivalent in that the material culture of mourning also deployed the symbolism of black and dullness as an expression of loss and modesty. To express modesty and maintain decorum during bereavement, through the medium of dark dress, was particularly important for women who were expected to wear veils and cover the hair (Llewellyn 1991: 89). As Llewellyn (1991: 90–1) has shown, the time of mourning was marked through the wearing of public and private costume, which was coded to convey the social status and rank of the bereaved. Here there was a transfer of emphasis from the body of the deceased to the social body of those in mourning: 'By this stage in the death ritual the natural body was virtually forgotten and culture's concern was to support the accumulation of meanings attributed to the social body' (Llewellyn 1991: 93). Thus the 'natural' time of death conveyed through the decaying body was displaced by the social time of mourning registered through the living body, its attire and adornment.

The proximity of women to death and the weight they would bear in terms of the work of mourning and remembrance were represented in visual images of the eighteenth and nineteenth century. In paintings and engravings of the female body, darkness and death were brought together at the site of the grave so that the intensity of grief and memory became most acute at night time. Indeed, the association of night with the emotions of grief had been implicit in nocturnal burials during the seventeenth century. Figure 3.8 shows an image dating from 1836 in which the veiled body of a woman lies upon a grave accompanied by her dog – a sign of faithfulness. Deepening tones of black centre upon the living, female body of the mourner which, in its dark coverings, signifies nothing but loss in its attempt to maintain contact with the dead. The positioning of the living (shrouded) body on top of the grave mirrors the corpse below – a doubling of the body that might provide a remote reference to the transi tomb. In such images,

Figure 3.8 A young woman wearing a veil and black clothing mourning at a tombstone, with her dog accompanying her. Mezzotint by H. Quilley after a painting by C. Hancock, 1836. Lettering: The mother's grave. Wellcome Institute Library, London.

the memory of the dead is most powerful at the grave – the grave stone replaces the body of the deceased and the grave is overlayed by the female form suggesting that it is through her living body that memories are mediated. But the 'natural' decaying body is not forgotten, rather it is recalled as the earthly underside of woman to which she reaches in the act of memory.

Women's nocturnal visits to graveyards as potent gestures towards the memory of the dead were also disseminated through printed images. Figure 3.9 shows an engraving of mourning during the night published in *The Lady's Magazine,* and accompanied by lettering: 'Beneath a pining yew-tree lonely sitt'st. To feast thine anguish on a daughter's tomb.' At night women enter the time of the dead, their bodies spatially aligned with those of the deceased to invoke their memory. By the later eighteenth century, metaphors of light and darkness conveyed not so much the notion of God as light, but reason as light so that darkness

Figure 3.9 A woman sitting next to a skull in a cemetery. Engraving by R. L. Wright. Wellcome Institute Library, London.

and therefore death came to express realms of fear and the unknown. Exploring the cultural representations of the eighteenth century (especially Gothic literature), Botting maintains that 'Darkness, metaphorically, threatened the light of reason with what it did not know. Gloom cast perceptions of formal order and unified design into obscurity; its uncertainty generated both a sense of mystery and passions and emotions alien to reason. Night gave free reign to imagination's unnatural and marvellous creatures, while ruins testified to a temporality that exceeded rational understanding and human finitude' (1996: 32; see also Reichardt 1998). The internal space of death-related memories could become as dark, gaping and threatening as unmapped zones without light: fear, disorientation and otherness became characteristic of the realms of the dead. If night gave women access to the dead and nourished memory it also provided a symbolism of the irrational, the superstitious and the emotional.

Instruments of Measurement

Memento mori, memorials and images of memory drew upon a symbolism of time and tense through an iconography of the body and further metaphorical linkages with flowers, trees, earth and its creatures, and the alternating rhythms of light and dark. The experience of memory conveyed through the registering of time upon the physical body was, however, complemented by further cultural devices dedicated to the demarcation of time. Instruments of measurement including hourglasses, watches and clocks were deployed as a means to capture and focus the processes of memory, which were seemingly more urgent when death was near. In sixteenth century cheap prints, death in the form of a skeleton carried an hourglass – signalling the end of mortal time and the beginning of eternal spiritual time. The marking of time's passage at the deathbed in the early seventeenth century was conducted through the ritualized turning of the hourglass by deathbed attendants and the provision of daily meals and timely seasonal fruits (Hallam 1996). Memento mori objects such as the silver pocket watch reconfigured bodily remains so that time was encased inside the skull (Figure 3.10). Worn about the body and also given as gifts, such material objects acted as constant reminders of mortality. Modelling and miniaturizing the body fragment, their form and their aesthetic interest were amplified and framed for closer inspection in nineteenth-century pictorial depictions. Figure 3.11 shows an etching of a memento mori watch given by Mary Queen of Scots (1542–87) to Mary Seaton. The skull is decorated with biblical images of Adam and Eve, including the serpent – a reference to original sin and the female root of human mortality.

The memento mori watch, in the form of an anonymous skull, held time to remind its owner of inevitable future death. In nineteenth century memorial photography images of the technologies of time were used to remind viewers of particular individuals. For example, a photograph from c.1890 shows the head, the bodily fragment understood as the site of personal identity, framed by the face of time (Figure 3.12). This print is a post-mortem photograph of a woman positioned inside a stopped clock. Both time and bodily decay are arrested by the photograph intended for domestic display to sustain family memories (see Chapter 6). Post-mortem photographs made by commercial companies were often framed with imitation flowers (Burns 1990), connecting the image of a person with funerary wreaths. In this instance, the clock as frame could thus potentially refer to frames of preserved flowers. Furthermore, Stewart proposes that 'The photograph

Figure 3.10 Pocket watch. Silver model of a human skull which opens up to show a watch inside. Science Museum/ Science and Society Picture Library.

Figure 3.11 Nineteenth century etching of the memento mori watch given by Mary Queen of Scots (1542-87) to Mary Seaton. Etching by Charles John Smith. Wellcome Institute Library, London.

Figure 3.12 'Woman's face superimposed on clock': Anonymous; Silver Print;
c. 1890. Photograph from: S. Burns (1990) *Sleeping Beauty: Memorial
photography in America*, Altadena: Twelvetrees Press. Photographs from this
volume are from the collection of Stanley Burns.

as souvenir is a logical extension of the pressed flower, the preservation
of an instant in time through a reduction of physical dimensions' (1998:
138). The relationship posited here between the photograph and
preserved flowers resonates with the symbolic connections established
within the field of the memento mori: flesh, like a flower, is destined
to decay and both, like a watch, display time. The nineteenth-century
rendering of this relation seeks to counteract this process by registering

and freezing the 'end' of a particular life. The photographic portrait is ambiguous in that the woman it captures could be alive or dead, except that her face is partly obscured by shadows – we cannot see whether her eyes are open or closed and we cannot read her expression. The portrait preserves a moment of partial visibility and there is just enough light here to recognize distinctive characteristics, while the remainder of the face dissolves into an unknown darkness. Just as the stopped watch is an image of arrested time (or an image of frozen memory), the photograph also gestures towards a movement or passage between lightness and shadows, life and death.

Enduring Time

The central message of the memento mori is that the material of life, including the body and all worldly possessions, will inevitably decay. By registering this message in diverse material objects, images and texts, memento mori have persisted and transformed over time. The interplay of imagery concerned with preservation and decay, fixity and mobility, appears to capture the antagonisms and boundary tensions that characterize death. The memento mori and its cultural derivatives have been mobilized in the form of the monumental body and the body fragment, in the materials of stone and wax, carved in wood and ivory (animal remains) or printed on paper, executed in paint and captured through photography, seen in flesh and replicated in flowers. The memento mori has occupied the zones of the spiritual, the curious and the secular, yet still in the later twentieth century its distinctive imagery resonates within materials dedicated to the remembering the dead. This appropriation can be detected in, for instance, media images dedicated to public figures. For example, one 'photomosaic' of Diana Princess of Wales, by Robert Silvers, reproduced in the *Independent* (one year after her death, 29 August 1998), represented her face in the form of a multitude of miniaturized photographs of fresh, vibrant flowers from all of the seasons. Her distinctive features are composed of innumerable petals in photographic form which supply the realistic colouring, from pale pink to deeper reds and blue/lilacs, of her smiling face and shiny eyes. This draws upon memento mori images in its implicit reference to the inevitable withering of flesh substituted here by flowers. However, these flowers (unlike the wall of bouquets left for her by mourners at the gates of Kensington Palace) claim permanence in their photographic form. The composite photograph mobilizes a visual language of emotion, where the gestures of grief, in the giving of flowers, are translated into an 'eternal' wreath or memory portrait. Yet, the image could be read as a death mask – Diana's features are recognizably hers, while alive, but they are rendered through materials (flowers) associated with fragility, transience and funerary gestures. The composition of the memorial image also conveys a 'passing away' or a process of disappearance: from a distance the image can be identified as Diana's 'living' face but as the viewer draws closer to it, her features disintegrate into the photographic fragments of flowers from which they are fashioned – once the flowers come into focus, we lose sight of her face. Furthermore, the image was published in a medium that is notoriously ephemeral – a daily newspaper that attracts attention long enough for the printers to produce the next splash of sensation.

We began this chapter by noting Fabian's critical reading of anthropological representations that have exaggerated the 'exotic', 'violent' or 'curious' aspects of non-Western death ways. Our analysis has, rather, highlighted aspects of 'otherness' that have been registered through European material cultures of death since the medieval period. The effects of time and death upon the body and identity have been figured in terms of what is 'vile', strange and abhorrent to the living – and sometimes inflected by gender difference. The imagery of the transi and the memento mori embraced 'otherness' represented in the form of insects and serpents and, indeed, through the use of materials derived from animals, such as ivory. Objects and images materialized death as temporal distance and this was conveyed through the imagery of decay. Maintaining tensions between fixity and disintegration, these objects encapsulate the oscillation of presence and loss, a process that characterizes memory processes. While the imagery of decay was tolerable and meaningful within frameworks of Christian belief, it was progressively dispersed and masked during the eighteenth century. Stewart has observed 'the body of lived experience is subject to change, transformation, and, most importantly, death. The idealized body implicitly denies the possibility of death – it attempts to present a realm of transcendence and immortality, a realm of the classic' (1998: 133). This would suggest that once the dominant body ideal was formulated as classical, safely bounded and static, and with the erosion of communities of belief that understood the spiritual messages of decay, the aesthetics of memory objects placed increasing emphasis on preservation. However, as we have seen, the memento mori continues to haunt the materials and imagery of memory objects.

f o u r

Spaces of Death and Memory

This chapter traces the relations between memory, spaces and material cultures of death. Memory processes have been imagined and communicated through a variety of spatial and visual metaphors that construct an architecture of internal memory places. Here we examine the relationships between *internal* states that configure memories and the material spaces of *external* lived environments, with particular reference to connections maintained between the living and the deceased. By approaching memory as a social and cultural practice, located in social space and mobilizing a range of material forms or objects, we analyse the nexus of space/body/object in acts of remembrance. How are the living and the dead provided with shared spaces through efforts of memory? How are the social meanings of spaces and objects associated with death constituted in social practice? How are material objects and the spaces they occupy pressed into the service of memory? Space, whether public or private, can be regarded as a cultural representation that is socially produced – its meanings are negotiated through social action. Over time, spatial relations, which are simultaneously material and metaphorical, tend to shape everyday social practices including those involved in the management of death and the making of memories. To interpret material cultures of death we need to attend to the social spaces in which objects are located, used, stored and displayed.

Within public spaces, the meanings and cultural values assigned to objects are informed by their spatial location; for example, when displayed within museums. The positioning of an object beside others in a cabinet and its location within a gallery – plus features such as lighting and labelling – will inform the public reception of objects. Conversely, the public placement of an object, such as a memorial sculpture, may transform its spatial setting and the social practices which take place within this, lending different meanings and associations

(Rowlands 1999; A. King 1998, 1999). Thus the spatial contexts of objects, together with spatially located social practices, are important interrelated dimensions in the formation of lived material cultures. A similar approach can be adopted when considering objects located within domestic or private spaces (Miller 1998).

The division and demarcation of social space is also a key aspect of identity formation – for the living and for the dead – therefore carrying further implications for processes of memory. Historically, the emergence of spaces of intimacy and privacy developed alongside the concept of the individual in Europe. With regard to the sixteenth century through to the eighteenth century, Ranum states that social relations of intimacy were shaped by 'the places and objects in which human emotions and feelings were embodied' (1989: 207). Ranum argues that:

> in the past the individual identified most intimately with certain particular places – an identification effected by means of emotions, actions, prayers and dreams. The souvenir-space (walled garden, bedroom, ruelle, study or oratory) and the souvenir object (book, flower, clothing, ring, ribbon, portrait, or letter) were quite private, having been possessed by an individual unique in time and space. (1989: 207)

While Ranum stresses the private nature of these spaces and objects, in that they were the focus of personal, sometimes secret, thoughts, yet their meanings were socially shared. Combs, mirrors and jewels, for example, appeared in portraits as part of bodily decoration and spiritual contemplation. Signing or marking objects such as rings, writing desks, tombstones and bookbindings, allowed personal identity to be asserted. Writing memoirs in notebooks, themselves regarded as objects, linked material forms to inner lives. Ranum (1989: 206–210) refers to these materials as 'relic-objects' – objects that were connected to the body and thus possessed a potency to evoke the qualities of their owners, acting as mementoes of love and friendship. Such objects were also associated with private sites and spaces considered to be conducive to inner contemplation or intimate communication with another person. For instance, walled gardens containing flowers, trees and lawns were sites of intimate or religious encounters, also providing private space for reading or reflecting upon love and death (Ranum, 1989: 213). Particular flowers carried associations, for example, roses with modesty, violets with humility, and a leafless tree might recall death and spirituality. As Ranum (1989: 213) argues 'the solitude of the garden, the passage of time and season, and the fading of flowers were reminders not only of life's fragility but of the death of Christ'. Secluded spaces were also marked out in the domestic interiors of middling to wealthy groups. Areas that had once been occupied by objects of furniture, such as bookshelves, became rooms designated as studies. Locked writing desks became locked writing rooms and Ranum (1989: 211) points out that '[f]rom here it was but a short step to the nineteenth-century bourgeois home, with its accumulation of objets d'art, papers, books and curiosities, always neatly ordered in glass cabinets and kept under lock and key'. These spatial arrangements resonate with the metaphor of memory as a chest or box, discussed in Chapter 2. Developments in the spatial organization of domestic relations, the possibilities of privacy and the fashioning of identity through material objects provided special sites and materials charged with personal associations and therefore rich as sources of individual memorialization.

Body, self and space, as Ranum indicates, have been increasingly linked with one another in acts of memory that privilege and attempt to sustain the unique character as well as the social status of the individual. Not only have individuals been associated with the spaces of their intimate lives, but also the embodied experience of objects and spatial locations are seen to encode values, beliefs and memories. Connerton shows how 'bodily automatisms' become the site of those cultural resources or generative schema which societies, groups and individuals 'are most anxious to conserve' (1989: 102). Repeatedly, the geological metaphor of sedimentation is used to describe how these spatially situated 'bodily automatisms' become imbued with meaning. Bachelard also uses this metaphor to describe the ways in which home can act as a place within which time's passage becomes fixed or condensed, where 'fossilized duration' is 'concretized' (1994: 9). Even after twenty years, the memory of the house where we were born can reanimate in us the feelings and gestures we knew at that time. 'Memories are motionless', he writes, 'and the more securely they are fixed in space, the sounder they are' (1994: 9). Bachelard (1994: 8) argues that 'the sites of our intimate lives' can be revisited imaginatively, just as the events of one's childhood are encountered during psychoanalysis. He argues that the passage of time is often resisted, and that revisiting space can allow the past to be reanimated as it was, in 'a sequence of fixations in the spaces of the being's stability.' In this way 'the finest specimens of fossilised duration' can be recaptured (1994: 9). However, Bachelard differentiates the remembered home from the lived-in home. To *remember* the home is to recover the intimacy experienced there, the thoughts, dreams and sensations that were particular to it – but not necessarily to recapture the home that actually existed. He is not simply describing a set of cognitions. Instead, he argues, 'the house we were born in is physically inscribed in us' (1994: 14). In our first house we therefore learn 'the hierarchy of the various functions of inhabiting' (1994: 15); gestures, muscular movements, orientations, subsequently repeated in the dwellings that follow. Bourdieu's analysis of the Kabyle house (1977: 90–1) also describes the divisions of domestic space and their correspondences in spheres such as gender relations, the elements, human/animal relations and times of the day and night. He describes 'the magic of a world of objects which is the product of the application of the same schemes to the most diverse domains, a world in which each thing speaks metaphorically of all the others' (1977: 91). Crucially, this 'application' occurs not through the operation of an externally located consciousness but through embodied, spatialized 'practices' and 'rites'. Meanings are therefore produced through sets of socially located practices (1977: 91).

Connerton's notion of 'habit memories' similarly describes the way memories are amassed or sedimented within the body (1989: 94). While Connerton argues for the power of habit, foregrounding the resemblance between 'bad' habits, desire and compulsion, for Bachelard '[t]he word habit is too worn a word to express this passionate liaison of our bodies, which do not forget, with an unforgettable house' (1994: 15). Drawing on these approaches, we argue that embodied practice is crucial to understanding how spaces and objects evoke memories of the dead and of death itself. We therefore address the experiential dimensions of material objects and practices as spatially located means of generating memories – the uses of cemeteries, the performance of commemorative speech, the scattering of ashes. By foregrounding embodiment, we show how a focus on the movement of the bodies of the living and the dead, in space, allows access to the sensual, imaginative and emotive aspects of death and memory in the twentieth century. An account of the spatializing of death and the dead therefore involves attention to embodied practice within space as, during the later twentieth century, we witness specific memory acts that invest particular zones with personalized associations. This chapter begins with theoretical discussions of space as socially constituted and then, in the later sections, we focus on case studies to explore the memory practices that contribute to a 'postmodern revival of death'. This refers to processes whereby expert discourses, such as curative medicine and grief counselling, give way to diverse innovations such as highly personalized funerals and the placement of memorial flowers at the sites of accidents (Walter,

1994). As the case study material indicates, some of these innovations may be located within institutionalized spaces of death, where persons nonetheless lay claim to memories through their own personally meaningful gestures.

Making Sense of Space

Moore's analysis of the structuring of social space privileges the neglected experiences of subordinated groups such as women (1996: 80). Her focus on spatially or materially grounded practices reveals the way spaces acquire social meanings and draws upon Bourdieu's (1977) account of how the house, for example, acts as the ground for generative schema that inform social action. In this view, the social divisions of space operate as motivating schema that shape social action, rather than simply reflecting rigid rules. Although individuals may be unable to articulate the system within which they operate, the competent individual possesses 'practical mastery', the ability to draw upon a spatially located mnemonic – but according to their own agendas (Bourdieu 1977). Through and within repeated practice, space acquires and generates meaning, but lacks fixed, autonomous meanings.

Moore also shows how spatialized meaning resonates out from the space of practice, through the operation of metaphor, to give meaning to other domains of thought and practice. Her ethnography of the Marakwet of Kenya demonstrates the way ambiguous meanings associated with ash articulate aspects of gender relations in sites as diverse as the disposal of refuse, burial practices, the cooking hearth and girls' strategies for avoiding an arranged marriage. As pointed out in Chapter 2, Lakoff and Johnson argue for the centrality of metaphor not only to conceptual systems but also to practice (1980) and we detailed the entailments of using the familiar experience of sleep to shape the material culture of death. Moore suggests that, '[a]ctors are not unaware of the meanings and values associated with the organization of space, and they are also in a position to choose how to invoke and reinterpret those meanings through their actions' (1996: 85). This chapter's case studies show similar invocations and reinterpretations of the meanings of space carried out through practice.

In elaborating the metaphoric process, Moore draws on the notions of literal and figurative meaning. She shows how cultural recognition of the primary literal meaning of objects, spaces and practices – for example, ash – is the precondition for their secondary, figurative meanings, realised through practice in other settings: metaphor 'proceeds from the literal to the figurative, and in so doing creates meaning' (1996: 82). If spatially located practice is viewed as text, the relationship between its internal elements and their literal, localized set of meanings can at once be distinguished from yet also related to the external fields into which their figurative reference carries. The meaning of objects and events in space is therefore expansive and open to reinterpretation in new domains.

Connerton's discussion of embodied spatialized memory provides a further perspective on practice as text. Rather than the inscribed texts, such as biblical and legal writings, which hermeneutic interpretation privileges, embodied texts represent a mnemonic that does not exist objectively, or independently of its performance (1989: 102) and they cannot therefore be scrutinized as discrete forms. As Connerton says, '[e]very group, then, will entrust to bodily automatisms the values and categories which they are most anxious to conserve. They will know how well the past can be kept in mind by a habitual memory sedimented in the body' (1989: 102).

The question of how the meanings of practice resonate beyond specific instances remains important: how can we understand their metaphoric operation? Moore explains that the shift from the sense meaning of space to its referential meaning involves its past and future meanings that attach or sediment themselves within the literal as it proceeds towards the figurative or referential: metaphor is a 'progression from the contextually defined meaning of an element towards a referential dimension, composed of all the meanings assimilated to that element in past and future contexts of invocation' (1996: 127). However actors' interpretations of the meaning of space do not simply draw on its immediate past. In a circular fashion, their interpretations are both the product and the source of particular versions of its historical antecedents.

By way of illustration, we can note the way in which public memorials held in honour of respected individuals work through the use of space, speech and embodied performance to create narratives that resonate in further social settings. An example can be cited in the posthumous celebration of the work of a distinguished academic and healthcare practitioner, which took place in 1999, at the annual conference of the British Society of Gerontology in Bournemouth. It reveals how spatially located action and speech produced an account of a woman's life and work. The location was the main hall, normally the site of the plenary sessions given by distinguished speakers. Key members of the academic community took the platform, their academic credentials being highlighted by the organizer. Their account not only fore-grounded the deceased's capacity for hard work, but portrayed her as sceptical if witty, caring but unwilling to suffer fools gladly. Produced at this location, this account celebrated an individual life whilst validating and reproducing the values to which her life in part conformed. Rank and file members of the audience were implicitly enjoined to emulate the woman's strenuous work schedule and her dedication to worthy causes. The sense meaning of these spatially located actions was the construction of a life history of someone who 'battled against prejudice', could 'galvanize others', for whom 'there was nothing she would not attempt', who was 'forthright in her condemnation of those who gave less than 100 per cent'. Their referential meanings, however, were realized in research centres, university offices and healthcare settings throughout Europe where the agenda for excellence implied in the keynote celebration impacted upon audience members' mundane work practices. It was in no sense the explicit edict of managers or training manuals. What the audience participated in was 'a particular and irreducible representation' (Moore, 1996: 94) of 'the professional life' as it ought to be lived.

This approach shows how death and the deceased are spatialized, whether at academic conferences or cemeteries, in hospital wards or bedroom wardrobes. These are sites that, through fleeting or permanent association with the dead, can evoke profound emotion by acting as potent reminders of particular persons and the condition of human mortality. Through the embodied experience of such spaces, one out of a range of possible meanings is produced. Thus as well as spaces of death, cemeteries are the site of jogging or sexual encounters; hospices are workplaces; a wardrobe of the deceased's clothes can be viewed as an economic resource for charities. Spaces are thus assigned a multiplicity of meaning and sites of death can often show characteristics of heterotopias, which Foucault (1986: 25) describes as follows: '[t]he heterotopia is capable of juxtaposing in a single real place several spaces, several sites which are themselves incompatible'. This layering or juxtaposing of spaces also has a temporal dimension and Foucault goes on to say, '[m]useums and libraries have become heterotopias in which time never stops building up and topping its own summit' (1986: 26). Located in everyday space – a roadside, a hotel, the top deck of a bus – heterotopias acquire extra layers of meaning as the abject and the ordinary are brought into an uneasy conjunction. The abject is often then either subject to 'erasure', managed through purification, or marked through practices such as laying bouquets of flowers. Set apart from the mundane world, spaces such as graveyards themselves attract other liminal or illicit activities. In both mundane and abject space, however, death has the power to create a heterotopia, that is, the layering of meanings at a single material site.

These spaces therefore encompass material objects associated with the living and the dead and with life and death, the body providing a key site at which they are conjoined. Sensory memory is a major focus for Seremetakis (1994) and Ash (1996) who show how 'everyday' objects appear to the senses and feed into memory. Seremetakis' work on 'sensory stasis' (1994), the 'resting point' in recollections of earlier sensory experience, echoes Bachelard's (1994 [1958]) conception of 'motionless' memories that can conjure up the memory or anticipation of sensory experiences and so enable us to 'know' time's passage. Without them, time remains an abstraction: 'We are unable to relive duration that has been destroyed . . . The finest specimens of fossilized duration concretized as a result of long sojourn, are to be found in and through space' (1994: 9). Spatial and temporal dimensions are therefore interrelated. Just as the spatializing of memory and death allows human mortality to be apprehended and given meaning, so the temporal reach of material spaces transcends the here and now, connecting with past and future lives and deaths. Seremetakis (1994) describes being away from home on a demanding research trip, when she felt an 'irresistible desire' to eat horta, the wild greens of her Greek homeland. As she cut the local grasses and herbs she experienced 'a resting point, a moment of stillness, where an entire past sensory landscape was translated into a present act' (1994: 16). Her memory is thus relocated in the present via an embodied experience of 'sensory stasis' that seems to arrest the passage of time and collapse the temporal interval between now and then.

Bodily sensation – the taste of food or the touch of clothing – therefore 'recovers' times past and stimulates memory. Ash (1996), for example, suggests that the clothes of the dead can allow an experience of the past to be translated into the present, yet carry an additional, paradoxical dimension. While such objects stimulate memories that remain motionless, they simultaneously evoke the passage of time. Clothing, Ash says, enfolds sequential memories and juxtaposes them with one another, another echo of Bachelard's (1994: 8) argument that we know ourselves not in time, but as 'a sequence of fixations in the spaces of the being's stability' (1994: 8). Describing the resonance of her dead husband's tie, Ash (1996: 221) reveals its implicit temporality; 'the simultaneously existing presence and absence of a person'. Memory, she says, knows the absence of someone yet within that knowledge there is 'the assumed pre-existence of that person in their absence' (Ash 1996: 221). Past presence and present absence are condensed into the spatially located object, her dead husband's tie. Its materiality feeds memory, to construct a sense of the absent person which is relevant to the survivor's present situation. Materialized traces of the human body have also been explored in contemporary art displayed in public spaces. We might note the sculptures of the artist Miroslav Balka, whose father was a carver of gravestones. In a review of an exhibition of his work it is observed that he no longer makes sculptures of figures, yet the plywood sheets and spirals of steel that face visitors to the gallery make it abundantly clear that he remains 'preoccupied with the body, with human presences, human habitations, rites and rituals' (*Guardian*, 16 December 1997). In these material forms and spatial enclosures from which 'the figure has escaped' we find traces, measurements and models of the body and its plight. Through embodied engagement with such objects, and the spaces they inhabit, the presence of absence comes to be produced.

The Dead Differentiated

The multiple and ambiguous meanings that we find inscribed in space, place and objects, although diverse, all share a fundamental role in creating and sustaining temporally located relationships between the living and the dead – and further situate the living in relation to their mortality. The embodied experience of space and objects allows these dimensions of social life to be realized.

Among Traveller Gypsies, the dead are feared and their threat to the living is managed by pinning them down in the non-gypsy space of the churchyard, a strategy that differentiates them from the living, nomadic gypsy community (Okely 1983). This exemplifies the power that can accrue to the dead, a quality that is well documented within the anthropological literature. For example, the ancestors of the Sherbro people of Sierra Leone have the power to bless and curse the living (McCormack 1985). As people approach death their status increases. Those whose speech grows 'incoherent' as a result of what Western medicine would term 'Alzheimer's disease' are understood to be in direct communication with the ancestors. Accessing a key source of power, elderly people receive care and respect from younger family members. In Western contexts, within the framework of Christian beliefs, the relationship between the living and the dead can involve delayed gratification – a future-oriented bond that has eventual reunification in the afterlife as its goal. The living and the dead are separated, briefly, in their respective earthly and heavenly locations. Henry Scott Holland, at the turn of the nineteenth century, articulated this: 'Death is nothing at all . . . I have only slipped away into the next room. I am I and you are you . . . I am waiting for you for an interval, somewhere very near, just around the corner' (cited in Whitaker 1984). Here, spatial metaphors of the home allowed the relationship between the living and the dead to be imaged.

We can note, however, that these spatialized relationships might emphasize both proximity and distance. In a study of later twentieth-century experiences of bereavement, a widow in her fifties described the objects in her home as a point of contact with her dead husband. Anticipating reunion with him after death, she felt his presence in the here-and-now (Hockey 1990: 52). On the other hand, unexpected 'visits' by the dead, beliefs associated with which are documented by Walter (1990: 232–42; 1994: 116–19), can be frightening, even when perceived as benign. Such fears may be explained in terms of secularized Western conceptions that tend to oppose the domains of the living and the dead – or at least posit a boundary that manages their interaction. During an interview, an Anglican minister described a woman's response to a visit from her dead father: 'I looked up and there, framed in the doorway, was my father and I was absolutely shattered. Nice to see him . . . but shattered' (Hallam, Hockey and Howarth 1999: 167). 'Unexpected' appearances of the dead can thus threaten perceptions of material reality as understood within the West.

While perceptions of the dead might locate them in different times and spaces, the departed are also made to share time with the living to the extent that they 'remain with us in memory'. Contemporary fictional writing amplifies this notion, where physical loss is explored through the ways in which it is registered in domestic spaces. Arundhati Roy's novel, *The God of Small Things* (1997), is an account of the return in adulthood of a twin sister, Rahel, to the home in Kerala, southwest India, in which she and her brother grew up – and in which they were implicated in the drowning of their childhood cousin, Sophie Mol. There Rahel discovers the memory of her cousin's traumatic death inhabiting the spaces and objects through which the lives of her extended family have subsequently unfolded – while Sophie Mol herself becomes a remote and shadowy figure. The absence of the child is therefore enmeshed in the continued presence of death via the material objects associated with her. Returning twenty-three years after the event,

Rahel finds that:

> The Loss of Sophie Mol stepped softly around the Ayemenem House like a quiet thing in socks. It hid in books and food. In Mammachi's violin case. In the scabs of the sores on Chacko's shins that he constantly worried. In his slack, womanish legs. (1997: 15–16)

Roy goes on:

> It is curious how sometimes the memory of death lived on for so much longer than the memory of the life it purloined. Over the years, as the memory of Sophie Mol . . . slowly faded, the Loss of Sophie Mol grew robust and alive. It was always there. Like a fruit in the season. Every season . . . (1997: 16)

In the absence of the child, therefore, memory takes on a mediating role, substituting the sustained horror of her untimely death for the brief years that made up her life.

The following examples, derived from contemporary Western contexts, describe other instances of spatialized memory making that retain deceased individuals within the social lives of their survivors. They are testimony to the potency of memories of the dead, located in spaces with meanings that are produced in specific ways, sometimes the province of just one survivor. However, their social nature should not be overlooked. Churchyards tend to maintain a spiritual 'community' of members, yet contemporary cemeteries are also the site of personal communications between the bereaved. An ethnographic study among people visiting graves in six London cemeteries (Francis, Kelleher and Neophytou 2000) highlights the social dimensions of this practice, both as interaction between the living and between the living and the dead. Common practices include: 'examining/washing/cleaning the memorial; tidying the space around the grave; saying prayers and partaking of rituals' (2000: 43). In addition flowers are set in place, whether cut or planted; the wording on gravestones is read and survivors spend time remembering the deceased (see Chapter 6). Through these embodied practices, located in spaces to which some visitors undertook lengthy journeys, the living created memory links between their preceding generation and their grandchildren who have never met their forebears.

Late twentieth-century children's graves in a Norwich cemetery reveal the social categorization of the dead into age-specific groupings. Infants are buried in a space dedicated to those who have died in childhood.

The break with traditionally restrained planting and, instead, the arrangement of colourful toys on the graves further emphasizes the poignant nature of the deaths which they mark (Figure 4.1). Such ritualized placement of objects maintains the material culture of childhood as though the children were still alive (see Chapter 6). The space of burial is partly recoded as the domestic nursery through the careful display of these objects, while, perhaps, the now empty nurseries in parents' houses may acquire intensely painful significance. Riches and Dawson note that, 'for many parents in this position, the only significant connection remaining is with the emptiness the child once occupied – at the table, in their bedroom . . .' (2000: 109). This movement of objects from the nursery to the grave, which maintains contact between the deceased child and their domestic material environment might form an echo of nineteenth century post-mortem photography of children with their toys – for example rocking horses, balls and dolls (see Burns 1990) (Figure 4.2). Klass also 'demonstrate[s] some of the ways that bereaved parents continue to develop their relationships with dead children through joining bereavement self-help

Figure 4.1 Children's graves in a Norwich cemetery, 1999. Photograph: Dr Nigel Norris.

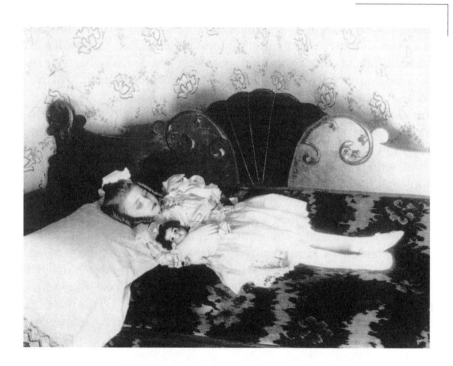

Figure 4.2 'Young girl on couch with her doll' post-mortem photograph: Anonymous; Silver Print; c. 1895. The photograph does not show any materials associated with death (e.g. flowers or a casket), but the girl is wearing a funeral dress. Photograph from: S. Burns (1990) *Sleeping Beauty: Memorial photography in America,* Altadena: Twelvetrees Press. Photographs from this volume are from the collection of Stanley Burns.

groups' (Riches and Dawson 2000: 172). Parents bereaved of their children collectively remember them, through talk, within mutual help groups such as the Compassionate Friends. At the group's annual conference 'the entire wall . . . is covered with photographs, newspaper cuttings, poems and other mementoes of their chidren's lives' (Riches and Dawson 2000: 173).

While communities of commemoration construct highly differentiated social identities for the dead, the threat that the dead body will be reduced to an anonymous materiality remains a disturbing prospect. This is evidenced in public controversies regarding the treatment and placement of corpses in medical institutions. When a photograph of bodies temporarily stored on the floor of a hospital chapel (Bedford, England) was published in national newspapers in January 2001 (for example, the *Guardian*, 16 January 2001), it signalled and provoked anxieties about the assimilation of individual persons into a collective mass of bodies – in this hospital space they were now 'objects' denied their subjectivity. The bodies of the First World War dead, which lay far from their homes, damaged beyond recognition, also became institutional property. Bourke notes that '[i]n death, white soldiers turned blackish and black Senegalese solders turned whitish' (1996: 214), indicating their loss of perceived ethnic identities. Unable to finance the return of bodies, families could not stage funerals in their homes and local communities. Other bodies were buried in mass graves, which register large-scale physical losses. The Grave of the Unknown Soldier was a gesture of reparation for their loss. It honoured the placeless dead, a heterotopic site at which the multiple memories of parents, fiancees and widows could be located.

Memorialization therefore facilitates relationships between the living and the dead. Highly volatile, it encompasses the power and vulnerability of the dead who are both revered and protected. This power not only demands responses from the living but can also be appropriated by them. The political struggles surrounding the death of Diana, Princess of Wales, show families making claims not only over their relative's body but also the narrative of her life and death. Earl Spencer's publicly broadcast speech at the funeral service challenged the Royal Family by alluding to tensions between his sister and her royal relatives. Davie and Martin ask whether this was 'an unforgivable exploitation of a privileged moment, made worse by the presence of the two Princes themselves?' (1999: 192). However, while the materializing memories of the dead might grant them a social presence, this presence is far from stable and can become problematic. The deceased members of some (socially subordinated) groups, while desperately mourned, can become 'invisible'. Their potent names are silenced and their photographs concealed. A parent bereaved of their child said, 'I used to try to talk about John . . . but it seemed to make them feel awkward' (Riches and Dawson 1996: 153). Tragic death and the deaths of those viewed as 'deviant' and 'worthless' can become socially invisible, the former omnipresent as a 'taboo' or an 'unmentionable' event; the deaths of the latter being 'unmarked' – for example, elderly people who are already 'socially dead' and subsequently die alone (Mulkay 1993).

Spaces of Memory

It is not only their relative visibility, but also the forms and media of their material markers that reveal the social status of the dead. The presence of material markers can work to define the locations they occupy as spaces of memory. These include body parts/substances, such as hair or ashes; and bodily attachments or appendages such as jewellery, rings, watches, clothing, diaries, letters, knives and handbags. Material markers may claim a 'static' form, such as the stone monument or they may become meaningful through use, being self-consciously reanimated in practice – for example, inherited domestic tools such as kitchen equipment and gardening tools. Other material markers held in archives may be regarded as 'information' by rationalized bureaucratic organizations, yet they might carry additional personal meanings: nineteenth-century orphanage records preserved the names of children in the public domain and these were to become the names of sought-after grandparents for elderly family genealogists in the late twentieth century. Mormon genealogical records allow Church members to baptize their relatives retrospectively, yet provide a key resource for family historians. Photographs and paintings of the dead similarly carry a multiplicity of meanings, depending upon their spatial location. Photographs of children inset into gravestones evoke the tension between the promise of life and the reality of death (see Chapter 6). Portraits of leading figures in board rooms may be viewed less as individualized memorials than embodiments of the values 'inherent' within organizations. In addition, references to the work of dead authors in academic writing locates them within the company of living scholars.

Despite the diversity of examples presented here, authors have described a sequestration of contemporary Western death (Mellor 1993). Differentiated 'death' spaces exist and are generally avoided unless specific visits are necessary: hospices, funeral directors' premises, cemeteries and graveyards, crematoria and public memorials. Yet these provide insufficient evidence of a sequestration of death. The 'taboo' nature of death has been fiercely contested and Walter cites Simpson's introduction to his English language bibliography of work on death: 'Death is a very badly kept secret; such an unmentionable topic that there are over 650 books now in print asserting that we are ignoring the subject'; Simpson also notes an additional 17,000 books on the topic of death and dying published between 1979 and 1986 (1991: 294). Walter explains this contradiction in terms of the fragmentation of death, a single instance being experienced through diverse frames, depending upon the survivor's perspective (lay, therapeutic, practical, bio-medical). Places associated with death therefore carry multiple meanings; their visibility and significance stem from the frame through which death is perceived.

If life crises such as death render the localized experience of space susceptible to processes of fragmentation, the places which unambiguously denote death are few. Objects and spaces such as bedrooms or clothing which unerringly evoke the dead can be closed off or destroyed. Survivors are often pressured to dispose of the belongings of the dead – having no further use, their storage may be read as evidence of pathological grief. The spectres of Queen Victoria, who laid out Albert's clothes every night, and Miss Haversham, who lived in the wreckage of her wedding feast, can be regarded as warnings for those who retain belongings beyond a culturally defined 'decent' interval (Littlewood 2000). Yet the dead are remembered and the materialities of their lives – clothing, household possessions, photographs, letters, diaries – often survive them as integrated and valued aspects of their relatives' domestic environments.

From a different perspective, the deliberate destruction, burning or locking away of such objects can further embed them within memory, despite the desire to escape painful recollections. If treasured mementoes are kept – photographs, a watch or jewellery – their emotive power can make it difficult to keep them constantly in view. Furthermore, it might become difficult to 'control' emotive objects as, for example, when elderly people destroy their partners' love letters lest they be accessed by strangers in the event of their own deaths. Rather than sequestration, therefore, an 'invisibility' of sorts sets in, items being dispersed or located within secular 'non-death' settings where their significance remains vital only for the bereaved.

Alongside reminders of the dead are objects, spaces and places traditionally associated with death itself; for example, the churchyard gravestone, the newspaper death announcement, the condolence or Mass card on the mantelpiece. Yet the decline of Christian practice and the growth of cremation (Davies 1997) make traditional sites such as graveyards memorials to a 'collective' past – or, alternatively, constitutive of living memory in a more individualized fashion. Ashes, for example, are often scattered in the deceased's favourite place – a playing field, a hillside, at sea, a rose garden. They are also left with funeral directors, families being unsure or divided over the appropriate method to be used for their disposal; or they may be stored or scattered at the crematorium. The 'marker' of the corpse may therefore be visible only to the bereaved – at, for instance, a particular tract of land or clifftop. In this more dispersed model, bodily integrity and a memorial form with discrete boundaries is less important, the ashes acquiring their own earth-, water- or wind-borne mobility. Their location exists for a limited rather than generalized category of 'survivors'. Links with the dead can even be confined to the privatized imaginations and memories of the bereaved.

Although cremation has allowed 'impromptu ritual in a radical invention of tradition' (Davies 1997: 28–9), this practice is largely undocumented. A study of the changed experience of public and private space among older widows and widowers in East Yorkshire (Hockey, Penhale and Sibley, 1999) revealed the example of Nancy, a widow of 72, who had created a spatialized memorial for her dead husband. It mapped on to their walk along a local lane and around the golf course:

> We would walk that, I think, two or three times a week. In fact that's where I scattered Peter's ashes, because he had a fear of being buried.

Nancy had kept his ashes in the urn provided by the funeral director on her mantelpiece for seven weeks. She said: 'I wasn't ready, wasn't ready . . . I used to sit, couldn't let him go.' When Nancy watched the funeral of Diana, Princess of Wales, on 6 September 1997 on television with a female friend and they 'cried and cried together'. She described how afterwards: 'I sat here and I knew then. I just said, "This is the day, Peter. We're going".' Viewing a state funeral had signalled an appropriate time to dispose of her own husband's ashes at a place that carried memories of their time together. Nancy said that her next thoughts were: 'Please don't let there be any young mothers pushing their babies in their prams, or anybody walking dogs – 'cos it's quite a popular walk'. To her relief the golf course was deserted. Nancy went on:

> I said, 'Thank you God' . . . and we went through the gate and I started at this tree and I talked to him – every handful – about what a lovely life we'd had. And now I walk down the lane every . . . once a week. I talk to him, by the grass verge and the trees. Sometimes I shout him and say 'Why did you have to leave me!' And then other times I thank God that he took Peter and not me because Peter would have never survived on his own.

Peter therefore has no collectively recognized marker, even though an accessible, public space has been claimed as his memorial. Nancy's disposal of his remains exemplifies the ritualized marking out of space in a way that confers personalized meanings upon a secular leisure facility . It evokes the treasured times of their shared lives, a natural setting of trees and grass in which she returned his body to the soil. The symbolism of Nancy's actions can be compared with early modern memento mori imagery, including the return of the flesh to the earth, and the transformation of the body into flowers and grass (see Chapter 3). But while early modern memento mori motifs of dust and soil were meant to convey messages regarding the transience of the material world in contrast with the everlasting, superior spiritual domain, the allusion to grass and trees in present-day memory practices aims to fuse the moment of disposal with the embodied life experiences of the deceased. Thus, references to trees and grass in Nancy's memorial act refers less to the inevitable decay of the material body and more to its continuity in the spaces she associated with her husband's life.

Nancy's discursive practice remains powerfully resilient in the preservation of memories. Continuing their once-shared walks and her ongoing dialogue she maintains their relationship rather than distancing him in a churchyard after an institutionalized ceremony of remembrance. This example contrasts with materially 'fixed' or dedicated locations of the dead. The case of Nancy, and those to follow, exemplify a publicly inconspicuous, yet personally evocative framing of the dead within the spaces of everyday life. The dead are sequestrated only in terms of their confinement to the private practices and memories of survivors – rather than their topographical location within the boundaries of shared, permanent memorials.

Nancy found the scattering of Peter's ashes irreconcilable with the mundane activities of dog walking and pram pushing. The public space of the golf course became sacred or set apart – differentiated from ordinary or profane usages – only when Nancy was able to privately 'personalize' it as her memorial. She continues her walks, a temporal strategy which counters the once-and-for-all rupture of their shared embodiment. Her shared 'secular' walks with living Peter are now repeatedly transformed into her 'sacred' walks with dead Peter. Her practice contributes to a postmodern revival of death that values individual choice; or what Walter describes as 'doing it my way' (1994). The following case studies also conform to Walter's definition of the postmodern and incorporate the notion of 'double coding'. He says '(it) is not a rejection of the modern and of the traditional, but a mixing of them at will, without any sense of inconsistency or shame (1994: 42). They show traditional death spaces being used as sites of individualized practice. Whilst traditions survive through reinvention not repetition (Roach 1996: 29), these acts of recreation or 'representation' vary. When traveller Gypsies bury their dead in a Christian churchyard, they do not simply repeat non-Gypsy ritual practices. Rather, they exploit ethnic difference, separating the inauspicious dead from the living by pinning them down in gorgio (non-gypsy) space – and setting themselves free to travel (Okely 1980). Thus they lay claim to particular ritual meanings within shared death space. Christian clergy's recent amendments to death ritual operate similarly. By allowing freemasons to participate in funerals and incorporating hymns to ancient deities, they help maintain the Christian funeral as an important ritual site. During a study among Sheffield clergy (Hockey 1992), an Anglo-Catholic minister said he would admit contributions from almost anyone but insisted on having 'the last word' (1992: 22), an observation that highlights the question of who is authorized to frame ritual events.

Private Practices in Public Spaces

As noted, 'the radical invention of tradition' enabled by cremation remains largely undocumented (Davies 1997: 28). As in other innovative work which anticipates the larger-scale gathering of data (Walter 1996), we draw on informal biographical and autobiographical material in these following case studies. They concern two sisters who have been lifelong friends of Jenny Hockey's and the personalized rituals she conducted herself when her father died. Some pseudonyms have been used.

Pauline

When Pauline's father died in the 1960s, he was buried in the municipal cemetery in Bedford where she grew up. Her mother, Maude, returned to her own birthplace in Scotland where she lived for over twenty years. Becoming frail she returned to the care of Pauline's sister in Leicester. When Maude died, her body was cremated and Pauline took the ashes to scatter on her father's grave in Bedford. When advised of a £10 charge for scattering ashes, she tipped them over the grave when no-one was looking – an illicit act that nonetheless drew on the institutional processes of memorialization and the concept of post-mortem reunification.

Jenny

Jenny's father, David, was born in Topsham, Devon during the First World War. His father – and Jenny's grandfather – had been killed in action and buried in northern France. David had neither met his own father, nor visited his grave. Spending his adult life in Cambridge, David died in a hospital in Hull where Jenny lives. His body was taken back to Cambridge for a funeral in the church where he had worshipped, attended by his friends and relatives. After cremation his ashes were returned to Hull, and intended for later interment in a churchyard at his birthplace, Topsham. During the interim period, however, Jenny had difficulty placing the ashes in the secular space of her home – she felt he could overhear her phone conversations. She therefore posted off the ashes to a Topsham funeral director ready for interment. However she then decided to inter some of the ashes in her grand-father's grave in northern France. She requested a portion to be sent back from the funeral director, went on holiday and found her grandfather's grave for the first time, scrabbled a hole in the earth and popped in a handful of ashes.

The war cemetery was therefore appropriated independently – and possibly illicitly – for a personal use. Being on holiday, Jenny's car boot contained secular or mundane objects – suitcases, bottles of water, spare cardigans – and a plastic carton of ashes, swathed in parcel tape. Just as Nancy found the contiguity of secular and sacred space on the golf course improper and disturbing, so Jenny felt shocked whenever she came upon her father's ashes whilst rummaging for a cardigan. The remaining ashes were later interred in the Topsham churchyard, the focus of a Christian memorial service. This traditional death site was not only her father's birthplace, but also an extension of his retirement in that the picturesque views from the churchyard had been a high spot of his holidays. Jenny has a picture of the churchyard hanging in her home, painted by her father during holidays spent revisiting his former home. At the site itself Jenny had a stone inscribed with the words 'Together in God's Care', followed by her parents' names. She had no marker of her mother's ashes after her cremation in Cambridge in the 1960s. Indeed she has no idea what became of them.

This account reflects the use of traditional or institutionalized death spaces and objects within highly individualized practices. Rather than making literal the metaphor of death as peaceful sleep, Jenny caused her father's remains to make seven separate journeys. By contrast with the emphasis placed on the integrity of the body found in burials, her practices divided his ashes and located them in different countries, neither site being close to where she lives. Jenny has friends whose father also died in the 1990s. Like her, they divided his ashes, between a Quaker cemetery, the garden of the house they all shared and the Lake District mountain he loved. While Jenny found the contiguity of ashes and holiday luggage in her car-boot disturbing, the accidental juxtaposition of the ashes of her friends' father with other parcels under the family Christmas tree provoked laughter. In both cases, however, the intimate conjunction of 'sacred' and 'profane' items stimulated a marked emotional response.

These case studies evidence many traditional beliefs and values: Jenny 'reunited' her father with her grandfather and her mother, using religious language and sites for this purpose. Her practice reflects the notions of an afterlife and a deity, the value of enduring family care and the 'sacred' quality of the remains of the body. Yet she has only hazy spiritual beliefs and a distanced relationships with her parents, neither of whom has left a painful void in her life. It was two years before she visited the stone set for her parents, having arranged its preparation by phone.

These memory practices can be understood in terms of the post-modern revival of death. By 'doing it her way', Jenny reconnected individuals who had predeceased her. Socially and geographically mobile, she adopted a materially grounded autobiographical strategy that fixed her relatives in memory and secured a familial context for her remembered past (Figure 4.3). Her imaginative resources were fleeting entries in her father's inherited diaries, his anecdotes and the photographs and First World War memorabilia stored in his old suitcases. They support a narrative – an inclusive family history – which was given material form through ritualized practices at key family sites in England and France.

This chapter has examined sites, places and objects through which death and the dead are remembered. This diversity links with a plethora of materially grounded cultural forms, often carrying highly contingent sets of meanings, a reflection of the 'postmodern revival of death'. The commemorative power of public objects and spaces such as war memorials, statues and street names is invoked in different ways by diverse social groups. Immediately after the First World War, political differences divided the nation in their choice of memorials, a conflict that had a provisional and precarious resolution. King argues that

> [i]f remembrance was to give retrospective meaning to death, it was bound to mean different things to different people. In the confusion of competing attitudes, they struggled to make the memory of the dead a right memory as they saw it. This entailed interpreting the symbols of remembrance in what seemed to each to be the correct manner, and arguing with others about their meaning. (1998: 210)

Figure 4.3 Display of memories in a living-room. Memorial objects and images 'encapsulate' a life-time, positioned within the confined space of a shelf. Photograph: Jenny Hockey.

It might be argued that, with regard to the twentieth century, it is not to death that we can refer, but rather to deaths, the meanings of which are negotiated from a diversity of perspectives. Rather than the sequestration of death and the dead in Western contexts, Richardson argues that representations of the dead proliferate in diverse spaces – either carved in stone or written into the names of buildings, institutes or avenues. She notes, though, that these can become 'invisible', in that they are often taken for granted or are passed unnoticed. We suggest that the memorializing potentiality of such materials is highly contextual. For academic and local historians they contribute to narratives of the past; for tourists they constitute part of the 'exotic' landscape of other cultures; for family genealogists they testify to forbears' acts of courage or citizenship; for the bereaved they are markers of their loss, 'sites of memory, sites of mourning' (Winter 1995).

Although layered or multiple meanings are encoded in memory spaces, memorializing *can* reflect and sustain collectivities. Some reveal a desire to connote a community's loss of a key individual. King (1997) documents the emotive resonance of Graceland, the home of Elvis Presley. Other public memorials commemorate deaths for a single cause and their shared impact within a community – for example, memorials that encompass the names of the war dead (Davies 1993). The scale of First World War bereavement produced a 'consensus' that a hard-won peace had to be protected in honour of the dead. King examines the degree of consensus thus: 'Although participants expressed different senses of the meaning of commemorative symbols, reflecting their differences of purpose, they retained sufficient sense of unity amongst themselves for remembrance of the dead to remain an almost universal public observance' (King 1998: 216). In contrast to emotionally fraught and controversial mass memorials stand dedications to individuals that might become 'neutralized' over time. With historical distance the 'peaceful' and 'timely' deaths of those who have been seen as a nation's or a city's worthies blend into a civic landscape that evokes order and predictability rather than emotional rupture. In these instances, the achievements of life rather than loss in death are being memorialized. Civic memorials conform more closely to 'the British way of grief' (Walter, 1997) and its characteristic emotional reserve. At funerals the bereaved 'perform' their grief quietly, merely betokening their private and 'authentic' emotional upheaval. Both an impassive face and noisy sobbing are inappropriate. Instead a performance of grief bridges the differentiated spheres of public and private emotionality.

However, we must also recognize changes in the boundary between public and private space during the twentieth century. Wouters (1992) highlights a growing relaxation of formal rules about the expression of emotion, a refusal of the social 'over-regulation' of emotion, which is seen to create problematic distance between external behaviours and individuals' 'inner' selves. Nonetheless, notions of appropriate emotional expressivity in late twentieth century Western society are subtle and contradictory (Lupton 1998: 169). While emotional experience vouchsafes 'feeling alive', intense emotions remain a focus for public concern in the West, particularly those seen as negative, such as rage. The informalization of emotional expression has nonetheless contributed to a more permeable public/private boundary. 'Bad' deaths (Bradbury 1993; 1996) in traffic accidents and collective disasters or the untimely deaths of the famous are increasingly made highly visible. Practices usually confined within cemetery walls spill out into public space as floral tributes are left at roadsides, football grounds, royal houses and schools. The media enhance their visibility disseminating

images of these 'newsworthy' acts. In these instances a public materialized language for the expression of private emotions has developed.

Our analysis has addressed the constitution of memory spaces
through networks of social and cultural relations comprising not only
the living and the dead but also the material objects that link them.
As Latour argues, the social environment cannot adequately be divided
into a natural/material and a social domain (1993). In his view society
comprises patterned networks of heterogeneous materials, only some
of which are people, while others are things. The assemblage of heterogeneous materials we have examined are interrelated social entities with
a capacity for social agency. Thus we resist privileging the living over
the dead as well as dividing the social world into distinct natural/
material categories and social actors. We therefore challenge the sequestration of keepsakes and mementoes to a private sphere of individual-
ised grief and address them within a broadly conceived network of
social relations and social spaces. To grasp the memory making potential
of spaces we need to observe the social actions and the placement of
material objects which occur within them. It is through the conjunction
of material spaces, bodies and objects that memories are variously
sustained and managed.

Memories Materializing: Restless Deaths

The articulation of memory through metaphor and relations between memories, the body, time and social spaces have been our central concerns up to this point. The perceived capacity of memories to counteract the loss of the past and to mediate the inexorable shift from bodily growth to organic decay is highlighted when we consider experiences of death. As we have suggested, memory making tends to require a material grounding when gestures of preservation and recovery are made. Yet, human memories remain precarious in their 'recovery' of the past. We have identified memory objects that, historically, have incorporated images of decay as well as permanence, whether in the form of the transi tomb or post-mortem photography. The tension between transition, or transformation, and continuity is a persistent cultural theme developed within material cultures of death and memory. While early modern images of bodily decay, which were once strongly linked to remembering, may have now been marginalized or incorporated into a cultural aesthetic that is more palatable (for example, the imagery of flowers), materialized memories remain foci of pain whilst simultaneously preserving relationships.

The tensions between continuity and change, which remain important aspects of grief in the late twentieth century, are often represented in bereavement literature as dualistic. In this context, the prospect of 'recovering' from grief may be felt to erode the 'continuing bonds' that many bereaved people wish to sustain with the dead (Klass et al. 1996) – hence memories of the dead are often described via oxymoronic adjectives such as 'bittersweet'. Similarly the modelling of grief as waves of pain that retain their intensity over time but become gradually less frequent captures the tension or oscillation between the loss and partial recovery of that which is absent (Parkes 1972: 57). A widow describes

101

this experience as follows: 'Mourning never ends. Only as time goes on, it erupts less frequently' (Bowlby, cited in Worden 1991: 18). Stroebe and Schut's dual process model of grief (1995), which identifies the need to look to the future as well as the past, to rebuild as well as to relinquish, reflects the possibility of somehow carrying the incorporated dead forward whilst simultaneously grieving their absence.

Memories are therefore crucially double edged, facilitating both the sensation of a recovery of whoever has been lost to the past but, simultaneously restimulating the painful feelings evoked by that loss. Further, as accounts of the enduringly visceral nature of grief suggest, memories do not simply call pain to mind along with lost presence; rather, they stimulate grief in the present for that which remains 'lost' to the past. Leys (1994: 637), for example, cites Claparede's argument that affect can only exist in the present. If previous emotional distress is recalled then it is either objectified and external to the individual or, as in the case of mourning, it produces emotional distress *in the present*. We can therefore distinguish between traumatic memories that produce a seeming repetition of the past and narrative memory that accounts for the past *as* the past. In narrative memory the past is abbreviated or condensed, and it is this kind of remembering which, from a therapeutic perspective, converts traumatic memories into an account which can be integrated into survivors' lives (Leys 1994: 647–8).

The first half of this volume has explored the ways in which memory and memories have been subject to change, in conception and material articulation. We noted, however, underlying continuities in the persistence, for instance, of spatial metaphors of memory – for example, memory as an archive or store. But, as the media culturally available for storage have changed, from the chest to the computer, so we have seen a comparable metaphoric adjustment in the way memory is imagined. It is from the perspective of memory as a cultural construct and process that we now move into the second section of this book to develop our discussion of various materials of memory – namely visual images, texts and embodied practices, including those that are ritualized. The effects of material that acts within and upon memories, making and breaking connections between the living and the dead, remain central concerns throughout. As our discussion thus far indicates, the ways in which memory is thought to operate are intertwined with the social and cultural devices discovered and made available for remembering and memorialization.

Memories materialize, through embodied practice and via lived, material environments that act as, or are made to provide, evocative stimuli. Furthermore, memory making constitutes a key aspect of cultural and social responses to death. We have examined the ways survivors experience and create relationships with the dead – and with death – via a range of material forms, where they place particular emphasis upon both the 'protection' of the dead from temporal erasure as well as the recreation of past intimacies. Our discussion, furthermore, has called attention to material forms and practices that are often seen as marginal in relation to culturally dominant means of memorializing the dead – the latter take such forms as, for example, large-scale public memorials or the performance of institutionalized state ceremonies. Less visible instances of the materialization of memory are often present in domestic spaces, belonging to highly personalized remembrance, which, nonetheless, draws upon socially recognizable conventions. Memories are often entrusted to the intimate spaces of domestic life, to form powerfully gendered memorials woven into the fabric of everyday practice; for example, in the care, storage and redistribution of the clothing associated with a deceased relative (see Chapter 8).

Focusing upon twentieth-century Western contexts, this chapter examines memories as forms of disturbance where the physicality of deaths and their associated material residues can lead to acknowledged rupture and unwelcome intrusions from the perspective of the bereaved. We explore the ways in which embodied encounters with scenes of death can infuse materialized memories with certain 'forces' that are difficult to control and manage. This leads into a discussion of the potency and perceived agency of particular death-related objects – and here we draw upon anthropological analyses of 'fetish' objects to elucidate the processes by which objects can make their marks within the field of memory. The 'otherness' of memories related to deaths and their apprehension by the living via evocative material objects is one of our central concerns here.

Material Disturbance

The materials enmeshed in the everyday lives of persons that survive after their deaths can evoke lost presence and present absence in potentially problematic ways. The tensions, ambiguities and contradictions integral to material environments that have undergone a form of 'trauma' or dislocation, can be worked out through further interactions with material objects in social practice. So precarious and unstable is the balance between recovering and relinquishing the dead, between achieving a comforting sense of continuity whilst repeatedly encountering the rupture of an earlier, embodied contiguity, that the nature of the materialities themselves and the ways in which survivors engage with them is crucial. Central to the following discussions of memories is therefore a concern not just with the way materialities enable remembering; but also with the way they animate disturbing memories and call for their management. In other words, material cultures do not simply operate as means through which memories may be retrieved and sustained so as to maintain continuities between past and present. Rather, images, texts and objects might stand as painfully isolated vestiges of those persons with whom they were once surrounded or associated. Surviving the people and places we love, these materials might highlight the passage of time. As Sontag observes with regard to photographs that continue to represent persons and place long after they have changed or perished: 'all photographs testify to time's relentless melt' (Sontag 1979: 15).

While there is, in Sheringam's view, a widely pervasive Western conception of memory as that which offers 'access to continuity, unity and permanence', he analyses modern French autobiographical texts to explore the 'conflict, doubt, ambivalence, pain or definitive loss' that characterize acts of remembering (1993: 289–90). Sheringham challenges the notion that autobiographical remembering is simply 'gathering and unification' (1993: 291). Memory might seem to provide a site of resistance to loss and the passage of time, but Sheringham is not persuaded that memories can simply create links between past and present and so provide the conditions for biographical continuity. Instead, he argues, to remember is to encounter the pastness of who or what once was – resulting in an awareness of the resilient difference that distinguishes the lived past from the perceived present. He alludes to Barthes' argument that a photograph not only testifies to the fact that something once *was*, but also 'underline(s) the absence of that very being or entity, manifesting the fact that it is not there now, that it is dead' (Sheringham 1993: 314). In the process, the instability of personal identity is highlighted.

Not only can remembering make us feel distant from the past but being inevitably incomplete, it can also frustrate the desire for continuity. Sheringham cites Stendhal's concern with 'memories' rather than 'Memory', an approach that points up the way emotionally charged 'fragments of the past', merely cast the remaining 'gaps and blanks' into starker relief (1993: 295). Vestiges of the past acquire resonance through their relation to something forgotten. By way of a material example: the less we can picture our dead mother's face the more evocative residual lipstick and cosmetic powder on her clothing may become. Memories that surface, whether in the form of a person's writings or other material fragments of a life, are traces of the past that demand reflection. Such a profusion of material forms can open up a 'vista' of the past, making it momentarily available for scrutiny in the present (see Sheringham, 1993: 296–7). Yet memories remain markers of disconnection – they stand as signals that the past has receded and thus the extent to which memories are perceived to overcome the distanciation of time remains both a focus of academic debate and an issue experienced at first hand in contemporary bereavement contexts.

Preceding chapters have focused on memory as a cultural process and outcome of social practices and, furthermore, Sheringham reminds us that memories are 'performative: when a memory comes to mind it exposes a desire or impulse, it has designs on us' (1993: 298). Memories can trouble us by surfacing unbidden in the form of private thoughts, sensations or dreams, sometimes stimulated *inadvertently* within the flow of our embodied encounters in the material world. As noted in Chapter 4, deliberate attempts to 'forget' unwelcome memories by hiding or destroying evocative material stimuli can cause the resulting gaps to act as even more potent reminders. While material objects can be used as vehicles for the deliberate recovery of memories – and wearing the deceased's clothing is a sensory experience that can evoke their embodied presence – there are aspects of material environments that are perceived as 'uncontrollable'. Unexpectedly finding an old garment at the back of a wardrobe yields an upsetting reminder that the person who once wore it has gone forever. Assailed by our memories, through material interactions, we might experience them as surges of sensations, mental images or physical reactions that occur and act upon us independently of our wishes. In such instances, the potency of material objects as suppliers of unwelcome memories exposes the shadow side of their domesticated role as malleable resources for more deliberate acts of memory making. When metaphorized *as* 'object' and materialized *in* objects, the effects of memories can be felt, as Sheringham points out, as 'violent disruption':

> To succumb to its [memory's] pull is to be dragged away from our moorings in the present. Memory breaks up the habitual routines of self-awareness and, rather than fostering unity, threatens everyday self-consistency. The unassimilable past lodges in the present like a foreign body. (Sheringham, 1993: 293)

To describe memory in this way is to afford it a degree of agency that affects routine perceptions of self. Sheringham examines this aspect of memory further with reference to Henry James' autobiography where James writes: 'I lose myself . . . under the whole pressure of the spring of memory . . . these things, at the pressure, flush together again, interweave their pattern, and quite thrust it at me' (cited in Sheringham 1993: 299). In James' writing, Sheringham finds representations of the agency of memory in its capacity to bring forth multitudes of particular details pertaining to past experiences and to forge connections between them. It seems that memory has the force to 'interrogate' James – to lead him to 'ponder' (Sheringham 1993: 299).

While analysing written texts, situated within the discursive field of autobiography, Sheringham is interested in those authors for whom memories remain at a distance or difficult to appropriate, and therefore require 'great effort' or work to render them meaningful in the present (1993: 301). In the following chapters, however, we focus on the material dimensions of memory processes (including written texts as material forms) in everyday and ritualized social contexts. We analyse perceptions of memories as possessed of the force that Sheringham identifies, but we also examine the social, cultural and material processes that unfold in attempts to manage or integrate the 'foreign body' of memory within the present. Throughout, we attend to the ways in which the materialities of death – which embrace the bodies of the living, the deceased and their associated material objects or traces – have been variously perceived and deployed in the production of memories.

In the following sections of this chapter we concentrate on the force of memories that have been encountered as part of experiences of death in twentieth century Western contexts. As we shall see, there are material aspects of death that continue to disturb and disrupt processes of recall such that their management becomes fraught with difficulty in personal, emotional and social terms. As outlined above, Sheringham has examined autobiographical texts revealing that memory has been apprehended as a form of agency. We will now explore this conception of memory's impacts as registered through material objects and the materialized aspects of deceased persons. The ways in which objects are felt to reverberate, to exude or transmit sensations, to reach into and affect the dispositions of the living, over time to ferment or fracture memories, needs to be recognized if we are to understand relationships between death, memory and material culture.

Here the human body – the materiality of persons – which, as indicated, may be dispersed across a field of objects with which bodies have come into contact, provides a key cultural arena through which the tensions of loss, recovery, memory and forgetting are worked out in relation to death. Encounters with the body after death may take place in expected or managed settings, such as chapels of rest, or in unanticipated, and therefore potentially more disturbing, situations when a death has just been discovered, such as sites of accidents or suicide. These encounters have lasting effects in terms of how memories of deceased persons later come to be experienced.

Discussing the working of the contemporary coroner's system, which investigates sudden deaths, Hallam, Hockey and Howarth (1999: 88–103) unpack the different meanings of the corpse for various participants in the proceedings. For families, 'the body continues to be a subject, a person' (1999: 89); 'the body is that of an intimate or an associate; it is a body replete with meaning and personal memories, it is a subject body' (1999: 97). Yet the dead body simultaneously attracts fears, a development that is often explained in terms of the professionalizing of disposal and the resulting unfamiliarity of lay people with this process (Aries 1981; Kellehear 1990). However these fears can also be linked with the centrality of the living body as a site of social identity, realized through the progressive 'enselvement' of the flesh across the life course (Turner 1998). Once recoded as corpse or cadaver, however, the dead body might exercise its own form of agency – in its perceived effects upon viewers it comes to stand not so much for the individual as for their loss and so forces acknowledgement of a death. The corpse thus makes a physical loss unmistakable, hence the contemporary therapeutic emphasis on 'viewing' the body as a way of encountering 'the reality of death' (Worden 1991; Hockey 1996). Parkes, for example, reporting his research among London widows, writes: 'some widows tried to convince themselves that there had been a mistake and it was not until they saw their husband's lifeless body that they were forced to believe him dead' (1972: 86).

The passage of time, the transitory nature of embodied relationships and the vulnerability of personal identity to erasure are thus evoked through exposure to the body that someone once *had* rather than the body that they once *were* (Nettleton 1998). In death the presence of the object body evokes the absence of the embodied person. Statements from bereaved relatives such as 'It just wasn't my father' or, as if viewing a portrait, 'That's Bill, isn't it!' (Hockey, unpublished field data) suggest that bereaved witnesses become aware of an unprecedented fracture of the embodied person they once recognized – the disjuncture of the object and the enselved body. Yet, after death, so inseparable are the object body and the embodied person that once the object body disappears from view at burial or cremation it may be difficult for the bereaved to recapture any recognisable mental image of that person. Those objects which had been intimately associated with that body – clothing and jewellery, for example – might then remain mere 'vestigial marks pointing to prior actions and presences' (Sheringham 1993: 296): following the encounter with the physical aspects of a persons death, memories can be shattered and dispersed.

The therapeutic literature on bereavement states that: 'it seems to take time for us to begin to recall "as a whole" people whose lives have been so close to our own that we have experienced them in a thousand fragmented parts' (Parkes 1972: 91). For C. S. Lewis, in the early days of his bereavement, even a photograph could not evoke his wife's enselved body: 'I have no photograph of her that's any good. I cannot even see her face distinctly in my imagination' (1961: 16). Thus it is often only with time that the habit memory of the embodied partner or child, who has shared the spaces of a survivor's life, can actually materialize and be held within the imagination. C. S. Lewis (1961: 37), for example, associated his eventual retrieval of memories of his wife with diminishing emotional pain: 'suddenly at the very moment when, so far, I mourned H. least, I remembered her best'.

It is the processes through which the shattered, displaced and troubled memory is apprehended and subjected to attempts at management (together with the materialities that this involves) that concerns us here. Rather than the presence of the enselved body in the present moment, the bereaved might access, and attempt to synthesize, a temporally scattered diversity of materialized memories relating to the deceased. For example, in the aftermath of a death, photographs and remaining personal possessions may be looked at, touched and talked about in the renegotiation of a meaningful biographical assemblage. This process is key to Walter's 'new model of grief'. Writing with reference to Western contexts, Walter (1996: 7) describes grief's purpose as the 'construction of a durable biography that enables the living to integrate the memory of the dead into their ongoing lives; the *process* by which this is achieved is principally conversation with others who knew the deceased'. If the memory of the deceased's enselved body is partially recovered it may thus take the form of a processual compilation of images and objects – a reconfiguration of materials temporarily drawn together from their scattering across the time of a life. 'Conversation', in Walter's view (1996), is the privileged Western practice through which this integration may be achieved. However, from our perspective the integration of memories of the dead is never a completed process in that there are materialized aspects of dying and death that remain, in their 'otherness', difficult to reconcile with the embodied person as known in life. Furthermore, we would argue that we need to attend to the ways in which memories are experienced via their materialized forms, rather than focusing exclusively on 'conversation' or verbal interaction, as the means by which memories following a death are negotiated.

The negotiation of relations between the object body (the dead body in the present) and the embodied person (the living body of the past) is a complex process. Parts of this process are enacted during the preparation and disposal of the corpse. This is a phase during which the object body may become a medium through which the enselved body, as in life, may be partially recovered. In contemporary Western societies, the corpse is often the material focus of practices such as embalming, suturing, cosmeticizing, dressing and positioning. Through these practices the body can become the site at which the social identity or personhood of the deceased may be encountered. As Howarth (1996) argues, this reconstruction of the social identity of the deceased is a performance to which practitioners and viewers alike give consent. It is not a denial of death; rather it is an encounter with the object body – but one that attempts a recreation of a previously enselved body as a basis for subsequent recollection (see Chapter 6).

However, the body that has so evidently passed over the threshold of life cannot, through viewing practices of this type, be perceived as equivalent to the body as it was perceived when living. As a materialized memory form, then, the dead body, however successfully staged as a version of the living person to instantiate a connection of recognition and familiarity, also intrudes upon present and subsequent memories as material evidence of the person's loss. Just as an autobiographical text, in Sheringham's terms, is fraught with fragmented memories that are not identical to past experiences, the staged and viewed body cannot fully recover past experiences of it. While the memory rituals surrounding this body might gesture towards biographical continuity, they cannot fully counteract the breach which is its death. There is a positioning of the corpse as a boundary 'being' – it is possessed of a residue of 'life' yet is also perceived as a physical marker of death. Again, we can allude to Sheringham's textual exploration of the 'border between the remembered and the forgotten' (Sheringham 1993: 295). He suggests that 'one sometimes feels that the vividly etched details of a scene are *residua* which owe their survival to proximity with emotional material which has vanished' (Sheringham 1993: 295). The powerful memory force of the familiar aspects of the staged corpse (such as the cosmetically aligned face or the hands wearing a recognizable wedding ring) become all the more potent in proximity to the 'other', remote dimensions of that deceased flesh prior to disposal – the motionless and cold body.

The Force of Memories

If the corpse in carefully managed and ritualized material settings has an impact upon memory, its agency might be felt in its capacity to demand both a reconfiguration of existing memories and to instil or lodge uncomfortable images and sensations within subsequent experiences of remembering. In each case, the bereaved may feel that they have no choice or control over this 'intrusion' into, and 'disorganization' of, their memory field. The turbulence of memories in their materialized forms can be further recognized in cases of sudden and unexpected death. In the event of accidents and suicides, the materiality of the body and its associated objects, such as the clothing worn, and notes written by the deceased become highly problematic and distressing foci of memories. Indeed in contemporary Western contexts we witness perceptions of those memories derived from the discovery of deaths as devastating and uncontrollable, and as echoes in spaces and material objects that come to 'possess' the recently bereaved or those who have moved through disturbing scenes of death.

Recent studies have documented the narratives of those survivors who bear the memories of relatives who have died as a result of suicide in Britain and America (Wertheimer 1991; Stimming and Stimming 1999). It is apparent from survivors' accounts that this form of death has particular repercussions in terms of their capacity for memory and the formulation of their memories. One man's written narrative described his retrospective apprehension of the day he was informed of his mother's suicide:

> The rest of that day was a blur. I was torn between doing what I had to do in order to join my family in Florida and wanting to crawl into a warm dark corner and cry until I had no tears left. I was paralysed by an inexplicable void, an overwhelming emptiness. I'm amazed that I was able to get everything done; I don't remember doing much of it. (Quoted in Stimming and Stimming 1999: 21.)

The destabilizing effects of a death are registered here as subsequent memory loss, as 'emptiness' or a 'void', experienced as 'overwhelming' and associated with physical restriction. The emptying out of memory appears as an involuntary occurrence, just as further narratives describe uninvited floodings with memories of suicide, in the following case through dreams:

> It's hard to remember a life without the dreams. They've become so much part of my nocturnal habits that I've come to accept their inevitability. (Quoted in Stimming and Stimming, 1999: 32.)

Here death-related memories enter at night, through sleep, their regular occurrence clouding the narrator's memories of his life prior to his mother's death – these memories have become so familiar that they seem to be part of the narrator's 'habits' but, at the same time, they are not entirely accepted in that they remain a source of waking distress. Wertheimer notes the ways in which relatives feel assaulted by memories, unable to block the flow of images of the death scene and also driven to consciously reconstruct the devastating event of the suicide in order to explain and account for it. Thus, '[m]emories of the scene are likely to remain with the survivor for many years to come, and may never disappear completely' (Wertheimer 1991: 18). This is especially the case with violent suicide where the resulting shock imprints persistent memory images which override other, less immediate, memories. In addition to these uninvited memories, which seem immune to erasure, relatives will commonly feel the need to recall and reinterpret the events leading up to the death in repeated attempts to make sense of it. It is here that the material objects associated with the deceased are regarded as particularly valuable in piecing together a retrospective, explanatory narrative of the death. Diaries, letters, photographs, personal documents, the deceased's house may be scoured for disparate clues or signs to help elucidate the death. It is in this way that material forms that might yield any previously concealed secrets will be interrogated.

Suicide notes are material forms that hold particular significance in this respect, although attitudes towards them are often ambivalent. They are seen as the last words written, the last pages touched by the deceased and therefore bear meaningful traces of those persons. However, as suicide currently calls for a legal investigation by police and coroners, material objects, items and notes that, from professionals' perspectives, pertain to the death are gathered and held as 'evidence' until after the formal inquest. It is, therefore, only after this extended process that notes, as a potential materials of memory, come into the possession of next of kin. Closely associated, as they are, with traumatic death, suicide notes as a memory objects might become sources of fear and obsession – they may be left with relatives or repeatedly handled. Thus, Wertheimer documents divergent treatments of them, from their destruction to their continuous reading and rereading.

The force of memories and their problematic materialities described here can be partly accounted for in terms of prevalent social attitudes and values that attend dying and death. In addition to the painful sense of loss, sudden, violent and self-inflicted deaths breach the expectations of a peaceful, dignified death, and also disrupt commonly held notions of life as precious and desirable. Wertheimer (1991) argues that spiritual and legal prohibitions, although now relaxed and repealed, still reinforce perceptions of suicide as transgression and a taboo subject. Jamison points out that '[d]eath by suicide is not a gentle deathbed gathering: it rips apart lives and beliefs, and sets survivors on a prolonged and devastating journey' (Jamison 1999: 295). Here the metaphor of the journey is suggestive of the restless renegotiation of memories, into which relatives, or friends feel compelled. A suicide is often particularly difficult to reconcile with memories of the deceased with the result that relatives are left with the ongoing task of rethinking both the life of the person lost and their own relationship with that person.

Strategies aimed at the eradication or control of unwanted, disturbing memories in this context are also drawn from collectively approved funerary rituals – and here we find a materialised language of the replacement and transformation of memories. In the narratives of those suffering from the onslaught of 'ugly' memories instilled through experiences violent suicide, Wertheimer notes attempts to produce meaningful counter-memories that are considered beautiful and welcome:

> Jean has some very positive memories of her daughter's funeral: I certainly like things [to be] beautiful and Anna would have wanted a beautiful ceremony and I'm sure a lot of people would tell you that it was extremely beautiful . . . its a good memory . . . and the flowers were fantastic. The house was filled with flowers, the crematorium was filled with flowers . . . her school friends sang beautifully . . . I think about it a lot. (Quoted in Wertheimer 1991: 98.)

Here the retrospective narrative focuses upon the creation of positive memories through the organization of and participation in funerary ritual, and especially the placement of flowers in the private and public spaces associated with the death. Such rituals offer a means to participate in and extend control over an event that is recognized as a potential source of future death-related memories. The material and embodied dimensions of the ritual (flowers and singing) are significant in attempts to generate lasting memory forms that overlay or dispel the threatening memories which are known to resurge and cause their havoc. Metaphors of depth and substance are commonly foregrounded in descriptions of this process.

Alongside the pleasures and the comforts of memory we therefore need to attend to the more problematic and troubling impacts of material objects, spaces, practices and images once a death has occurred. Memory is positioned within the social and cultural domain in a variety of ways, depending upon the role it has been made to play within institutionalized religion and political structures or within interpersonal relationships. Though the living may actively seek to maintain their relationships with the dead, through memory, we should not take this imperative as a given. As discussed in previous chapters, the dead have been positioned and afforded spaces in varying degrees of proximity to the living and, in addition, the devices and materials significant in the sustenance of relations between the living and the dead are also subject to change. In the contemporary context we can further note that the circumstances and perceived causes of deaths have implications for the materialised experiences of memory-making and management.

Material Objects, Memory and Agency

The cultural treatment of the body after death in contemporary Western contexts indicates that, alongside survivors' intentional use of material forms to construct an ongoing relationship with the dead, death-related memories appear to possess agency by virtue their association with loss and devastation. In accounting for the form of that agency – the sensation that memories, of their own accord, intrude or depart, or lead to dramatic shifts in perceptions of persons and their pasts – we look to the nexus of embodied social interactions and material objects as they register within processes of recall following death. From a social and cultural perspective, we need to examine who or what constitutes loci of agency in the formation of death-related memory experiences.

Agency is commonly regarded as part of the sphere of human social relationships and the notion that material objects possess forms of agency remains somewhat at odds with a prevalent Western distinction made between animate and inanimate entities. However, Gell's anthropological analysis of art redefines the operation of agency to include the domain of objects. Gell defines agency thus:

> [a]gency is attributable to those persons (and things) . . . who/which are seen as initiating causal sequences or a particular type, that is events caused by acts of mind or will or intention, rather than a mere concatenation of physical events. An agent is one who 'causes events to happen' in their vicinity. As a result of this exercise of agency, certain events transpire (not necessarily the specific events which were 'intended' by the agent). (Gell 1998: 16)

Throughout his study, Gell develops the notion that objects have significant effects within the social world – '[s]ocial agency can be exercised relative to "things" and social agency can be exercised by "things"' (1998: 17–18). Gell explains this assertion by stating that human agency is always enacted within material environments where, for instance, the human body and objects within the spaces of social action register that agency. Gell is keen to develop the argument that 'things' have agency, but he clarifies his position by stating that this agency is always 'relational and context-dependent'. Thus, in material, interactive situations an agent, for example a person, is recognized as having acted in relation to a 'patient' (the counterpart of an agent), for example a car, and a 'patient' comes into being in so far as there is 'an agent with respect to it' (Gell 1998: 22). The patient can also move into position as an agent, in Gell's example for instance, when the car breaks down causing the owner to walk home. But the car can only be regarded as an agent in the contexts of its use and in its relation to the owner as a patient and potential agent. By defining the agency of persons and things as relational Gell underlines his concerns with 'agent/patient relationships in the fleeting contexts and predicaments of social life, during which we certainly do, transactionally speaking, attribute agency to cars, images, buildings, and many other non-living, non-human, things' (1998: 22).

Here we can situate the social settings of death and subsequent remembrance as contexts in which material objects are attributed powerful, and often disturbing agency. To provide an example of this process we draw upon Carol Mara's account of her relationship to her son's clothing, which was returned to her nine months after his accidental death (Mara 1998) (see also Chapter 8). While Mara makes clear that clothing, for her, is an evocative source of memories and sensations linked to her life and family relationships, the resonance of clothing becomes particularly apparent after her son's fatal accident. She describes the way in which she took possession of the clothing her son had been wearing on the day that he died. The shorts, she writes, had been kept as 'forensic evidence' and 'the shirt I imagine cut from his body as he lay at the roadside' (1998: 59). A phone call from the police asking how she wanted the clothes disposed of prompted her reply '"I want them", I say. They are the objects which had last contact with his conscious body' (1998: 59).

Clearly clothes, in the context of a painful death, are regarded as a point of material contact with the body of a once-living person. They thus provide a means by which memories of that living body can be generated. The clothes are a memory material by virtue of their past physical proximity to the now deceased person. They are also a material extension of Mara's son's body – his personhood is recognized as residing within the clothes. While Mara describes taking the clothing home, touching and looking at the sock, shoes, trousers and watch – embodied, material transactions that are generative of memories of her son – there are aspects of these objects that are clearly unpleasant, yielding forth detailed memories of the accident and the sudden event of his death. So, gravel from the road embedded in the soles of the shoes, the 'black mark' on the trousers (which Mara sees as 'the place of first impact with the car') and the slit in a sock form materialized memories that are difficult to manage. Unable to retain the clothes within view but incapable of throwing them away, Mara describes how she placed them in a bag and then stored them in her son's bottom drawer. Writing about this, she states that these clothes 'carry an emotional power' and she anticipates (hopes for) a future time when they will 'no longer hold the terrible potency that they assumed one Saturday in September' (Mara 1998: 60).

In this woman's account we can detect the transactions, in Gell's terms, between the agency of persons and that of material objects. While Mara exercised her agency through the placement of materialized memories (the clothes) in a drawer, the clothes seemed to emanate an 'emotional power' or 'terrible potency' that took effect upon Mara such that she could not yet throw them away. These objects extend such a hold in this situation that Mara can only gesture toward a generalized future in which she intends to re-establish her control via their removal.

How are we to account for the push-and-pull involved in the negotiation of persons' and objects' agency in the shaping of materialized memories? In this instance, the clothing is so 'potent' because it is exists as material that is both familiar and other: it is a materialized extension of the embodied person and the material mark of their death. The clothing thus permits a desirable (physical) connection and demands the acknowledgement of a fatal disconnection. In this instance, fragments from the site of an accident are materialized in the domestic setting occupied by the bereaved – this is a materialization that, for the bereaved, ensures a surging forward of shattering memories.

'Other' Materialities

Studies that explore the potency of material objects and their capacities as agents have also questioned the prioritizing of human agency within sociological studies that assign only a derivative agency to the material world. We may acknowledge that things come to matter, and become imbued with meanings through their treatment and uses in social practice (Miller 1998), but contributors to Spyer's collection (1998) highlight the importance of approaches to materiality that do not over-privilege human agency. Spyer (1998: 5) highlights 'the powers that things have to entrance, raise hopes, generate fears, evoke losses, and delight' – powers that cannot be understood simply in terms of a stable person/object hierarchy . Yet, as Pels points out, dominant understandings of person/object relationships tend to define, 'those people who say that things talk back' as 'dangerously out of touch with reality' (Pels 1998: 94). Brown explains this negation when he suggests, 'the very convergence of our fear and our delight in things prompts us to disavow their activity and potency in everyday life' (1998: 949). Bataille's arguments are relevant here: 'in an "industrial society, based on the primacy and autonomy of commodities, of *things*, we find a contrary impulse to place what is essential – *what causes one to tremble with fear and delight* – outside the world of activity, the world of *things*"' (cited in Brown 1998: 949).

There are, however, debates about the power of materiality, or the animation possible within the 'world of things', which recover the undeniable effects of objects upon persons. Spyer et al. (1998) focus on those materials that have come under the rubric of the fetish – disparate and often heterogenous or hybrid objects that have shifted across territories and disrupted classificatory orders since early contacts between Europeans and 'others': 'the fetish continually oscillates between a Eurocentric and an Other dimension, between recognition and disavowal, absence and (negative) presence' (Spyer 1998: 3). Composite, heavily laden objects such as the African 'power figures', or *nkisi*, can be cited in this respect (Shelton 1995). Furthermore, clothing and materials such as gold, lace, fur and velvet enter into the realm of fetishism in that their materiality might, in certain historical circumstances, come to dominate persons as charged objects (Spyer 1998: 5) – they may generate intense desires whilst instilling anxieties.

Thus, such objects tend to be possessed of a materiality which exudes a distinctive force within human/material relationships. Pels refers to the ways in which 'the materiality of things can stand in the way of, and deflect, the course of human traffic' (1998: 95). Furthermore, Spyer alludes to the 'physicality of things' that have the capacity to 'strain' the 'human designs and constructions to which they are subject' (1998: 6). If this approach emphasizes the ways in which materialities cannot be easily domesticated by human agents, the fetish also 'threatens to overpower its subject, because – unlike our everyday matters – its lack of everyday use and value makes its materiality stand out, without much clue as to whether and how it can be controlled' (Pels 1998: 99). The difficulties and disturbances involved in the materiality of the fetish stem from its association with excess – as Shelton points out, the fetish does not simply transgress established systems of classification but actively spills out across the boundaries of the spaces which might be allocated to it (1995: 7).

Here we encounter the notion that certain objects, by virtue of their insistent materiality and their capacity to transgress 'orderly' systems of classification, become 'other' in relation to the pliable domain of unthreatening everyday things. Again, as Pels asserts, '"other" things' are those that 'disrupt everyday valuations, and thereby raise doubts about the ability of human beings to maintain control over their meaning' (1998, 99). We can apply this perspective on the 'otherness' of things, the breakdown of order and the instabilities of meaning, to the materialities that surround death – and here we are concerned with the implications of these 'other' objects in the formation of memories in contemporary Western contexts.

Recognizing the powers of 'other' objects allows us to gain insight into the twin dilemmas faced by the bereaved. On the one hand, their attempts to retrieve vanished presences and ruptured relationships involve engagement with material forms such as personal possessions, photographs, gravestones, all of these forming treasured objects that can be pressed into service as a focus for present and future remembering. The deliberate selection and management of these materials is achieved through the exercise of human agency. More perplexing, however are those material objects that somehow resist and disrupt processes of materialized memory making – seemingly exuding their own form of agency. We have already cited some instances of 'resistant', disturbing memory materials – the suicide note (in familiar handwriting but shaping, perhaps, shocking words), the clothing eventually returned from the site of an accident (recognizably part of a person but also the 'evidence' of their death), and, indeed the corpse (simultaneously a person and yet no longer that person). These 'objects' might come to have 'life' after death, situated on a border between the familiar and the radically unfamiliar. But beyond these borders, which are partly salvageable as memory forms, lie those materialities which seem irretrievably scattered, uncompromising in their ability to cause anguish and jarring in their evident lack of place within tolerable memories.

Take, for instance, the varied and unpredictable amassed materiality of a household which has to be dismantled following a person's death. Amidst the sheer bulk of this materiality, which in itself may become overwhelming, lie the potentially threatening material discoveries that the bereaved have difficulty associating with the lives of their deceased relatives. Thus, the act of intervening in the intimate material environments of the deceased may become a frightening excavation in an unknown territory – this is more likely to occur in situations where inheritance has not been organized through will making. The problems posed for the bereaved by the once functional and meaningful possessions of the deceased might be difficult to resolve. Initially there may be unwillingness to redistribute, destroy or even touch domestic assemblages that the deceased has so recently left 'intact'. With regard to the eighteenth century treatment of the house immediately following a death, there was an impulse to 'freeze' the domestic interior. Stopping clocks at the hour of the death, turning mirrors to the wall and draping black cloth over pictures and garden beehives (the beehive had formed a metaphor for the structure of memory, see Chapter 2), were gestures that arrested the movement of the house: 'Death is signified in these instances by a halting of motion and a stilling of context' (Stewart 1994: 212). At a remove and seemingly beyond the access of the living, the interior stands as an 'immobile' material surround, once part of a life and now difficult to interact with. This tendency to disengage domestic interiors from the actions of the living in attempts to enshrine the daily lives of the dead is evident in contemporary settings where the bereaved keep bedrooms 'just as they were' at the time their loved ones died.

This form of 'stasis' is often treated, however, as a temporary measure to counteract the distress involved in managing the material accumulation of a life that has 'ended' or, if it is allowed to persist, it may be perceived as a source of obsession and 'unnatural' investment. Thus, allowing materialities to 'settle' without their human counterparts might be regarded as an overly passive stance in relation to a charged, and difficult to disentangle configuration of material objects. We can argue that this difficulty arises partly out of the material 'burden' involved in interactions with collections of objects that have become anchored in the spaces of a past, yet stubbornly present, habitual domain – it might, consequently, be seen as a violation to move them. Furthermore, from the perspective of the bereaved, the undesirable prospect of counteracting, for the last time, the agency of the deceased expressed through the persisting arrangement of his/her personal possessions might also reinforce the 'weight' of these materialities.

Attempts to reorganize and dispose of the possessions of the deceased might also throw into relief the charge of individual material objects that are unexpectedly encountered or now, after the death, appear to disturb domestic spaces. Thus, for example, the discovery of photographs, clothing and personal items that have either been forgotten or have never been seen before by the bereaved might exercise powerful effects – they may be deeply inconsistent with memories of the deceased, his/her lived identity and personal relationships. Laurie Sieverts Snyder (1998) has described the contents of a box of photographs that she went through after her mother's death. Here she found an envelope, labelled by her mother, containing:

> snapshots of my father, looking very handsome, age 31, standing at the ship's rail with an attractive young woman. The photograph is labelled on the verso, in his hand writing, 'meine kleine Freundin, Patricia Hays' – this is not my mother. My mother was in Frankfurt, waiting to hear where they would go, and during that time she lost her third baby. (Snyder 1998: 82)

In Snyder's account of her mother's treasured belongings (see Chapter 7), the inherited material objects that she is now able to 'live with', and take pleasure in, contrast starkly with those buried photographs which fracture and disrupt memories of the past.

Personal, highly valued possessions are often recognized, by those facing death, as potentially problematic. We witness the concerted efforts of the dying in the disposal of their goods, or in easing their transition into the hands of others. Reaching the end of their lives, it is not uncommon for older people give their possessions to charity shops or to destroy them, buying one last item of clothing that will 'see them out' – this rather than face the prospect of them falling into the wrong people's hands (Hockey 1990: 135). With time to prepare for death through the distribution of property, the dying person will attempt to reduce the risks involved in the subsequent discovery of potentially disturbing materialities. Or, in exercising protection over what have become 'sacred' possessions (particularly highly eclectic and personalized collections), those anticipating their deaths might attempt to negotiate an inheritance strategy. It has been noted, however, that this is often a fraught process as family members find it distressing to talk about death and relatives may not be prepared to look after those objects that are so closely associated with the dying person (see Belk 1994).

Perhaps inevitably, we find material objects that 'escape' these forms of control and, again, these may be experienced by the bereaved as particularly upsetting. Objects left on the periphery of domestic life, perhaps already forgotten by the dying, perhaps too difficult for the dying to deal with, may be later encountered in their stark singularity by the bereaved. Contemporary accounts of these encounters (Hockey, unpublished field data) highlight the ways in which singular 'mundane' items, following a death become charged as sources of sorrow. Wellington boots left out in a vegetable plot, Christmas parcels wrapped and hidden on top of a wardrobe, a half-finished doctoral thesis that promised to transform its author's professional identity, personal items hidden in the office drawer of a previous owner and discovered by her successor are all objects in process, formerly integral to ongoing lives. They remain present yet 'lost' and drifting in the absence of the living body/self of their owners. In responding to these 'disengaged' objects, their enduring, melancholy qualities are accentuated. Moreover, their marks, impressions or effects can stimulate unease, invoking, as they might, the prospect of our own death. As such these residual objects can destabilize the values that we attach to our own material possessions once we imagine their unstable existence continuing in our final absence.

Alongside the treasured memories that are the product of desired or deliberate memory-making we can therefore situate those materialized memories that – whether chosen or not – make their mark upon survivors. Through their materiality objects often endure, obstinately, despite the loss of the individual for whom they held meaning, purpose and historical associations. Once bereft of their personalized context, such objects seem to acquire a form of agency. Akin to fetish objects in their powers of evocation – they are 'other', unsettling of familiarity, difficult to control, simultaneously fascinating and disturbing. Making sense of how material culture both produces and constrains memory making therefore involves attending to the shifting resonances of material forms across time. Surviving the mortal body, objects that awkwardly fit 'nowhere' move through the living/dying/mourning trajectory into states of categorical ambiguity. Their potency as materials of memory is therefore highly unstable and can give rise to different kinds of remembering at different points in time, some involuntary and some elected.

'Dead' Matter

So far, this chapter has focused on the more disturbing aspects of memory making after death, not simply to account for disruptive memories (and their relation to desired memories) but also to address some of the theoretical debates surrounding the social, cultural and personal significance of material cultures. While social scientists have acknowledged the material nature of human interaction, for many this seems to remain secondary to their core interests. Lupton cites Lunt and Livingstone's criticism of this approach: 'research in the social sciences has tended to be directed at the relationships people have with each other, or with social institutions, rather than with objects or things' (1998: 137). Similarly Miller questions the privileging of interaction between human beings and refers to material culture studies as 'the insistence that things matter' (1998: 3). Further to this, Pels, in his study referred to above, argues for a theoretical approach in which neither persons nor material objects are necessarily assumed to 'possess a predetermined primacy' (1998: 102). In order to advance his argument, Pels suggests that materiality is not simply a quality of objects; rather materiality resides in the sensuous processes of 'human interaction with things' (1998: 100). Thus he states: 'the "material" is not necessarily on the receiving end of plastic power, a tabula rasa on which signification is conferred by humans: Not only are humans as material as the material they mould, but humans are moulded, through their sensuousness, by the "dead" matter with which they are surrounded' (Pels 1998: 101).

These perspectives are highly pertinent to our present discussion of death and the materialities involved in the formation of memories. As we have argued, the materiality of deceased persons is often instrumental in the subsequent, embodied experiences of the living. The 'moulding' that Pels alludes to is witnessed, for instance, in contexts where insistent and disturbing material traces of persons who have died in violent circumstances might shatter memory experiences. Or the domestic material settings of the recently deceased might become a fearful and unpredictable terrain which restricts, or re-configures, embodied practices within it. Or, further to this, a death can cause the emergence of objects that are somehow 'excessive': fitting 'nowhere', difficult to place and calling into question the validity of systems of personalized meanings.

Pels' hedged allusion to 'dead' matter is meant to imply that matter is never devoid of signification and, furthermore, that signification here cannot simply be understood in the sense of meaning conferred by human agents. But how does the assertion that material objects always have a life and, sometimes an 'aggressive' life that seems to exceed human agency, work in the field of death-related materialities? As the previous sections of this chapter have argued, certain material dimensions of death and bereavement can cause unanticipated and difficult-to-control disturbances in social relations and in memory making. What emerges from these is the sensation that material objects can assert their own pressures upon destabilized human agents. We can argue that the force of these objects emanates from both their association with the past life of the deceased (the objects facilitating, therefore, the perceived extension of their agency) *and* from their association with an ultimately uncontrollable event – the event of death. Death and especially sudden death would, therefore, appear to animate material objects to such a degree that they are apprehended as 'beyond control'. As we have seen, however, there are multiple and varied cultural strategies through which attempts are nonetheless made by persons and social groups to counteract and neutralize the force of such objects. These strategies are often undertaken in awareness of the memory effects that material objects can exercise.

Taking a further example, we can attempt to assess Pels' argument that meanings are not simply inscribed upon objects by human agents and in so doing we explore an instance of memory making that has emerged via the dynamics of embodied human agency and the power of deathly materials. In a fatal train disaster at Gretna in May 1915, 210 officers and soldiers were killed. They were travelling to Liverpool where they would have boarded troopships embarking for Gallipoli during the First World War. In the aftermath of these deaths, a person (now unknown) was present at the site of the accident, perhaps helping

Figure 5.1 Damaged face of a watch. The museum label reads: 'Bracelet watch found in wreckage after troops train disaster at Gretna Green, 1915'. Displayed in the Encyclopaedia of the North Exhibition from 1990, Marischal Museum, University of Aberdeen. Marischal Museum, University of Aberdeen.

to retrieve the bodies (their purpose in being there is unknown). Amongst the rubble, this person's eye must have been drawn to a small, scarred and burnt object, for he or she salvaged it and took it to a museum in the north-east of Scotland. This object is the barely recognizable scorched and melted face of a wrist watch, its straps missing together with its hands (Figure 5.1). The object was then given a label and it has been on display in the North Gallery of Marischal Museum, Aberdeen, since 1990. The handwritten label carries the following inscription: 'Bracelet watch found in the wreckage after troops train disaster at Gretna Green 1915'.

The extraordinarily moving and evocative object, together with its placement in the museum speaks of the troubling materialized memories that we have been at pains to explore in this chapter. This watch is both recognizable as a personal possession and disturbing in its disfigured, melted condition. We do not know the person to whom it belonged, but we imagine the watch's uses as part of that person's life – keeping time, aiding his timely arrival at the train which, as he may have thought, would take him to his likely death at war. After the train disaster, however, the watch becomes other in its passage through a site of collective death. The impact of the disaster is materialized on the face of the watch – it is now both deficient – in its missing parts – and excessive – in its refusal or disruption of categories. Highly ambiguous, it has been part of 'wreckage', yet remains distinct from it; it was a personal possession yet it is no longer; it has shifted from its role as a personal item to become material evidence of a devastating collective experience. The watch is linked to a single death, yet it carries the weight of multiple deaths, not just at the site of the train disaster, but also those resulting from war.

The potency of this material object does not, however, operate necessarily to evoke or disturb personal memories. Rather it is arresting in its presence as materialized damage, accident and destruction that might resonate with the various experiences of death that museum visitors may bring to their viewing of the object. Furthermore, it is the object's label that amplifies its distressing material qualities, providing the link between the object and the site of death which generated it in its present form. Without the label, we sense through the object that harm has been done – the object has suffered damaging impact – it holds its form but it is broken. But with the label – its literal inscription, which is now tied to it – a deepening of the object's potency has occurred through the active preservation of its association with 'wreckage' and 'disaster' (death). The label provides a succinct, yet powerful narrative of salvage – the object was threatened by the prospect of loss, but it was 'found', retrieved and preserved in the Museum. Thus we can detect the interplay of 'forces' or agencies at work here. For the watch to have been 'found' at all, we imagine that it must have exercised some form of attraction at the point of initial discovery. For it to have been taken to the Museum, we suspect that it had no place within the possessions of the person who rescued it – was it somehow 'beyond' assimilation within a domestic space? We might speculate here about perceptions of the Museum as an appropriate repository of potentially disturbing death-related objects. Was the transportation of the watch to the Museum part of a strategy to 'contain' its potency? Once in the possession of the Museum, the object was made to submit to inscription – an insertion into a narrative that at once 'makes sense' of its very presence in the Museum, but also an act that ensures the persistence of its troubling qualities.

At work here is the dynamic interaction of an 'other' material object (made other through its presence and transformation at the site of accidental death) and the living human agents who have come into contact with it. And at stake is not necessarily a field of personal memories but, rather, the material relations through which past deaths are brought into the present. This analysis could be supplemented by an examination of the aesthetics of display and the nuances of viewers' responses – it so happens that this object is currently displayed in a cabinet alongside a human skull and other instruments of time measurement, including hourglasses (Figure 5.2). We might note, here, that museums have been associated with cemeteries (Pointon 1999: 40) and accused of 'executing' objects by inserting them into institutionalized classificatory orders, effectively deadening the resonances they held prior to collection. In the case of the burned watch, it is rather that its museum labelling and display enhanced its troubling presence and its evident passage through a site of destruction.

Figure 5.2 Cabinet displaying the damaged watch alongside clocks and other instruments of measurement. Encyclopaedia of the North Exhibition from 1990, Marischal Museum, University of Aberdeen. Marischal Museum, University of Aberdeen.

Strains of Memory

So far we have discussed the destabilizing effects of materialized memories that are marked by violent departures, unanticipated or accidental deaths. However, Sheringham has drawn upon work that suggests that all memories are 'other': they always relate to absence and by extension to death. With reference to Derrida he states:

> A memory is a memento: a memorial to remind us – for the future – of what is no longer; a material substitute in place of what is absent . . . To remember is to engage with what is already other. The act of remembrance merely disjoins our memories from 'us', turning them into foreign bodies, alien inscriptions. (Sheringham 1993: 313)

The argument, here, is that the marks, scars, signs, tokens and inscriptions that form the material traces through which past gestures reside in the present can be assigned meanings, but they cannot fully recover what has already gone – the distance between 'now' and 'then' 'can only be filled by the leap of interpretation' (Sheringham 1993: 313–14). Focusing on material domains, we have argued that such 'leaps' can be made through embodied sensations triggered by tactile objects associated with the deceased – sensations of both presence and absence. The materialities surrounding death, can also be perceived as 'foreign', disturbing persistence, indeed ineradicable substance, which brings back uninvited sensations and images of deaths – this is especially the case with material objects that are scarred, marked or otherwise metamorphosed at scenes of deaths. The argument here is that past deaths can seem to resurge (partially but powerfully) of their own accord, rather than requiring persons in the present to reach back for them. The unwelcome presence of death-related memories via deeply anchored and tenacious materials therefore places strains upon memories. It is not just that living persons struggle to recover memories of their dead, rather, it is also that the material residues of painful losses can constitute burdens which are difficult to situate in the present. From this perspective, the strains of memory are twofold: they are generated in desired attempts to regain what is irrecuperable and they also emerge with the unsought material insistence of loss.

Materialized Memories

Throughout this chapter we have examined various materialized memories that become lodged within domestic and institutional spaces.

In this final section we take up issues with regard to the ways in which these materialized sites have been conceptualized as memory forms. As discussed in Chapter 2, Nora has proposed that modern memory in Western contexts is located at material sites, such as museums, archives, libraries and national monuments rather than in bodily gestures that were once, in pre-modern or non-Western societies, important means of experiencing and transmitting memories. In 'spaces, gestures, images and objects' (Nora 1989: 9), groups and individuals once made embodied memories. Nora differentiates these, as aspects of 'true environments of memory', from the sites or 'lieux' of contemporary memory. The latter, he argues are 'remains' (1989: 12), edifices of memory that are distinctively and necessarily material, located in a relation of exteriority to the living subject. In the modern context then, we find materiality differentiated from human embodiment. Thus Nora argues that 'the less memory is experienced from the inside the more it exists only through its exterior scaffolding and outward signs' (1989: 13). In his view, if we are preoccupied by memory, this is because it is no longer the involuntary and collective repetition of customary and embodied traditions that it once was. 'True memory' has been replaced by history, the rational, dutiful recovery and recording of a distanced and often vast materially based memory site (Nora 1989).

However, if we conceive of materiality, not as a dimension of externally positioned objects, but rather, following Pels (1998), as an aspect of embodied persons' interactions with things, we can interpret sites of death-related memories in a different way. The materialities of death that we have discussed retain powerful connections, and, in some instances, stand as (problematic) extensions of embodied persons now deceased. These sites of memory cannot be maintained at a distance, divorced from the embodied persons who feel the troubling proximity of physical deaths as well as the persistent physicalities of the dead. If we are to acknowledge the perceived agency of material domains in contemporary experiences of these memories, then the embodiment of persons as enmeshed in sites of memory must be recognized. In the following chapters of this book we attend to dimensions of embodiment and its relation to materials of memory. These encompass visual and textual forms that, as we show, can become enmeshed with the bodies of the living and the dead in various processes of memory making which we explore from the early modern period to the present day.

Visualizing Death: Making Memories from Body to Image

Paintings, sculpture, clothing, and burial apparatus were integral to early modern English death rituals and were part of a rich and varied visual culture of death (see Llewellyn 1991). These are also visual images and material objects that have been culturally significant in the shaping of memory. This chapter focuses upon visual forms embedded within embodied social practices and material cultures, with specific reference to death and memory. We begin by considering the significance of the visual in the shaping of memory and then move on to analyse the linkage of death and memory, through the body and its imaging (see Chapter 2). Here we address the historical treatment and positioning of the corpse, attending to the ways in which the body has been visually apprehended and manipulated into materials of memory. Examining the visual aspects of memory in this context, we acknowledge the complex relations between immediate visual experience in lived social spaces, and the production of visual representations, which link the tangible present to other (past and future) remembered or imagined bodies, times and spaces. We consider the body itself – a body that has passed the threshold of life, a body that is no longer a living form but through death can be reanimated as a material of memory. We can discern this transformation of the body from a living form into a dead yet socially active memory 'object' in the uses of the corpse as relic and as a substance that has been deployed in mourning practices. The second part of this chapter is concerned with photographic images which centre around death. We examine nineteenth-century memorial photographs as well as present-day uses of this medium in domestic displays of lost loved ones and the incorporation of photographs at the grave. Central to this chapter is the relationship between visual images and materiality, so that we examine both the visual properties of material objects and the material dimensions of visual images as they impinge upon the issues of death and memory. Here we find complex relationships between image and matter, the bodies of the living and the dead, the subjects and objects of memory.

Visual Memory

The impact and significance of the visual in the making of memory has been recognized since at least the medieval period in Europe. As we noted in Chapter 2, the metaphors used to define memory have been predominantly visual and so sight has been understood as the primary sensual means by which memories are generated and maintained. Stewart (1999) comments upon deeply rooted philosophical debates regarding the senses from which a hierarchy has emerged, such that sight and hearing are prioritized above smell, taste and touch. She refers to an 'economy that ranks the senses and regulates the body's relation to the social world in a transformed and transforming way' (1999: 22). Yet, she points out that 'the body bears a somatic memory of its encounters with what is outside of it' (1999: 19) and this is not necessarily structured or restricted by dominant hierarchies of sensual experience. Thus, for instance, museums might be regarded as 'empires of sight' – as tightly organized spaces in which material objects are reserved only for visual appreciation. However, Stewart shows how the sense of touch was central to the sixteenth-century precursors of museums in the form of religious displays, namely the shrines of saints which held relics partially available for human contact. Eighteenth century sculptures displayed in French salons, invited physical contact and in the present day, Stewart states with regard to museum architecture and furnishings 'the museum retains a vestigial relation to touch as the primary sense for the apprehension of powerful matter or material' (1999: 28). To situate visual experience, as it informs memory, in the context of bodily practice and lived material environments, is to acknowledge the interaction between sight and other senses. As Seremetakis argues, '[m]emory is the horizon of sensory experience, storing and restoring the experience of each sensory dimension in another, as well as dispersing and finding sensory records outside the body in a surround of entangling objects and places' (1994: 9).

The memory-making capacity of visual experience is crucially dependent upon the social and cultural contexts in which images are received and interpreted. Thus, the interaction of visual images and other forms of cultural representation such as the written or spoken word are also significant in terms of the meanings assigned to particular visual encounters. Zelizer, for instance, notes that words can act to systematize and connect images in memory and she argues, further, that the materiality of images works to sustain them as distinctive 'vehicles of memory': 'materiality renders visual memory different from other kinds of remembering. Images help stabilise and anchor collective memory's transient and fluctuating nature in art, cinema, television, and photography, aiding recall to the extent that images often become an event's primary markers' (Zelizer 1998: 6). While the material dimensions of images, such as the card, frames and albums that comprise photographic forms, contribute to their 'stability' and endurance over time, we should also recognize that their significance and connotations are open to negotiation and strategic manipulation as they are produced, viewed and circulated in social practice. The material presence of an image may afford it an appearance of 'fixity', but its cultural associations tend to shift and transform. Images held in memory are similarly subject to transformation. As Melion and Küchler (1991: 4) argue, the model of memory as a 'place where visual data are stored to be tapped when necessary' is misleadingly static and we should attend, instead to a more 'active' notion of memory that recognizes the dynamic interplay between mnemonics and processes of representation. Melion and Küchler also acknowledge the role of bodily practices in the making and transmission of images which interact with memory. Thus they assert that 'mnemonic processes are indivisible from the material act of representation' (1991: 7). Here we arrive at a complex juncture of embodied practice, visual representation and materialized memory processes.

The Corpse as Memory 'Object'

The active, living body can be regarded as a site for the generation of memory in that embodied practices reproduce social relationships over time and produce durable cultural objects (including visual representations) through the manipulation of materials. If embodied practices are central in the mediation of memory, how does the dead body figure at the nexus of bodily practice and memory making? How are material fragments and traces of the dead animated in efforts to sustain relationships in the face of loss?

The capacity of the corpse to trigger and shape the memories of the living crucially depends upon the ways in which death is conceptualized as either a continuity, rebirth, or as the absolute end of life. In early modern England, for instance, the prevailing Christian notions about death as the release of the spiritual from the material body defined the corpse as matter that would fade away, in contrast to the continuity of the spirit that lived on. In this setting, the corpse was buried, while the social presence of the body could be maintained via a stone or marble funerary monument that provided a sculpted body as in life (see Chapter 3) (Figure 3.1). The corpse after disposal was allowed to recede, to return to dust, while the stone or marble image of the body, made visible for the purposes of memory, was one that marked a death while referring back to a 'life' – the personhood of the deceased was thus partially retained when visual signs of social belonging and status were deployed by, for example, displaying the deceased in sculpted clothing and jewellery. Funerary monuments of this type rest upon a precarious boundary somewhere between the status of a corpse and a socially 'living' body.

This tendency to refashion the corpse into a visual likeness of its previous living form can also be witnessed in the practices of contemporary undertakers and embalmers whose work with the dead body presents the deceased so that he or she is recognizable to relatives (see Chapter 5). Since dominant contemporary perceptions of death position it as the antithesis of life, and cultural values emphasize the 'healthy', 'fit' and active body in the realization of selfhood, the corpse then comes to represent 'disorder and dysfunction' (Hallam, Hockey, Howarth 1999: 126). The pollution and contamination that the dead body therefore signifies is contained and managed in medicalized settings and through expert practices that are seen to protect public health. The corpse is regarded as a material manifestation of death, a body devoid of a self and individuality, but for the short time allowed for bereaved relatives to remain in contact with it, the body is 'staged' and presented in an approximation of embodied 'life'. This is attempted through embalming, restoration, the application of cosmetics and the use of clothing that temporarily arrest decomposition, reinforce the physical boundaries of the body and transform its features to constitute a surface appearance of a person 'at rest'. The end result provides a 'memory picture' – the last compelling image of the deceased that may be retained by relatives (Hallam, Hockey, Howarth 1999). In this context, the socially or legally sanctioned disposal of the body after death impinges on the uses of this body as a memory form. Such treatment of the corpse prioritizes visual appearance and makes special appeal to the sense of sight. It is only at the level of visual experience that a 'life-like' memory picture of an inert body can be sustained. Though a departed relative may visually resemble the person they were in life, once touched or held in the context of viewing, they no longer *feel* like that person. For the living, the combined sense memory of that last encounter is thus deeply ambivalent – the dead person is simultaneously familiar and other in relation to that previous self.

The dead body is often represented, for the sake of tolerable memories, as a replica of the living body. The representation of the corpse as a living body, in for instance memorial sculpture and portraits, is a cultural translation that seeks to render invisible the material reality that is the dead body. As Bronfen argues, '[t]he translation into representation is one that permits a break with the material referent of the signifier' and this is necessary in 'an attempt to re-stabilise one's position in the world when faced with an event as destabilising as death' (1992: 45–6). Imagining the dead body, so that memories of it can be more readily facilitated, seems to necessarily involve degrees of masking that distance its unstable and disturbing materiality. In contemporary Western contexts the corpse is predominantly regarded as inert matter, or bodily substance without sensation. It is ultimately incapable of action, numb, and empty of the self that once inhabited and animated it. This is a body that is radically vulnerable: it is defenceless against decay and decomposition. These features of the dead body stand as reminders of the fate of all flesh, and they are abject in that they disrupt 'identity, system, order' (Kristeva 1982: 4). As such, the corpse becomes 'other' not only in relation to the living body that it once was, but also in terms of the threat that it poses to the broader social system. This passage into 'otherness' (seen in various historical periods as either a sign of sin, the instability of material as opposed to spiritual dimensions of life, or as the antithesis of the classical bodily ideal) engages memorial making that might, on the one hand, seek to represent the corpse as a perfected and stable body that refers back to the person in life, and on the other, attempts to portray the disappearance of the body in decomposition as, for example in transi tombs (see Chapter 3) (Figure 3.2). Both of these strategies of representation refigure the corpse according to culturally recognizable codes, conventions and styles, attempting to recover the corpse as that which otherwise threatens to be absolutely lost. Thus, acts of memory making, manifested in the fashioning of memorial bodies, draw the receding corpse back into the social system, in attempts to 'fix' it as a visible material likeness of self or other in a stabilized opposition. As explored in Chapter 3, materialized memory materials, such as flowers, are also used as aesthetically acceptable means of 'visualizing' the processes of physical decay which death unleashes.

Although, or perhaps because the material body after death can be experienced as disturbing, further memory practices have sought not to replicate the corpse, but to salvage and redeploy it directly. Rather than using materials such as stone, marble or ivory, to represent the body, it the flesh itself, or bodily substances such as bone, blood and hair that are regarded as powerful memory 'objects'. The corpse and fragments of it have been held within the social spaces of the living through rituals and techniques of preservation. While the corpse can been seen to pass into 'object' status, this designation is complex and ambivalent, given that the uses of the corpse in memory practices tend to sustain or reinscribe personhood via this object. Here we can cite the uses of the corpse in the form of relics and in memorial costume.

The physical remains of the dead can be regarded as the epitome of a memory 'object' as they stand, not only as a material reminder of the embodied, living person, but as a medium through which the dead might communicate directly with the living. Medieval transi tombs were often inscribed with messages from the dead encouraging the viewer to look upon the figure of the 'decaying corpse', which made conventional announcements such as: 'Stand, seeing in me, who is eaten by worms, what you will be. I, who was once young and beautiful to look on' (Cohen 1973: 18). That the corpse could speak back to the living through its 'body', afforded it a vestige of subjectivity that was compounded further when the living were invited to see themselves in the other. Memorial sculpture of this type represented the dead body as a site of contact and continued dialogue between the living and the deceased in ways that disturbed the subject/object boundary.

In this context the use of relics (bodily parts, clothing or personal items of saints or martyrs) also operated as memory forms that were simultaneously persons and things (Geary 1986). As Le Goff notes, popular memory focused upon the saints and the dead where the physical remains of saints (relics) not only provided sites of collective remembering but were also approached for assistance with the earthly problems of the living (1992). Within medieval popular belief, saints were afforded 'miraculous gifts' by God and could, therefore, work miracles for the benefit of the living. Thomas notes that by the early sixteenth century in England, the shrines of saints in churches or cathedrals had become widely recognized pilgrimage centres visited by many in search of cures. Placed at shrines were the saint's relics – bodily remains or appendages which were possessed of magical efficacy. As Thomas observes, 'Holy relics became wonder-working fetishes, believed to have the power to cure illness and to protect against danger'

(Thomas 1985). Relics could be mounted and displayed in elaborate, jewel-encrusted cases or reliquaries made of precious metals – sometimes in the shape of the human head and torso – with apertures so that relics could be touched to activate their powers. Such techniques of framing and visual display amplified the sacred charge of relics, and as Aston points out these three-dimensional anthropomorphic figures would have been seen by medieval viewers *as* the saint (not a replica) in that they 'housed a bodily presence' (1988: 25). Furthermore, there was 'some "practical identity" ' between the image and the imaged' so that the boundary between the representation (the reliquary/relic) and what was represented (the saint) was not clearly defined (Aston 1988: 35).

Relics were not, however, confined to shrines as they circulated as gifts or as commodities that were sold or stolen. For instance, Christ's blood was sold by the drop to be worn as protection against bodily harm (Thomas 1985: 34). As Geary points out, the value of relics was dependent upon the belief that they were the genuine remains of a saint. This was established through public rituals that transformed the corpse from 'mere human remains' to sacred relics 'emphasizing both the identity of the remains with those of a saint and the actual miraculous power exercised by that saint through those particular remains' (1986: 178). Once designated as sacred and powerful, relics were seen to assist in a range of problems including the settling of disputes and the finding of other lost objects. To achieve these ends the living entered into a system of exchange with the dead, extending veneration towards the relics as well as prayers and offerings in the form of candles, wax or wood votives, property or money (Geary 1986: 175). It is in this sense that during the medieval period, 'the sacred could be encountered through and within bodies' (Mellor and Shilling, 1997: 124). Relics as 'person-objects' were infused with the sacred, acting as memory forms in recalling saints but also as a channel for the curative or beneficial powers required by the living. Geary further highlights the transformation of relics, throughout their biographies, from persons to 'objects of commerce' as the 'boundaries between object and subject are culturally induced and semipermeable' (1986: 188). Such shifts from subject to object would carry implications for the degree of memory function exercised by the relic.

During the Protestant Reformation in England, relics were redefined as evidence of the corruption and excesses of the Catholic Church and its associated 'superstitions' and as such shrines were dismantled and destroyed (Thomas 1985). Aston argues that by the fifteenth century the proliferation of sacred images was coming to be regarded as a distraction from belief and as an incitement to idolatry and disrespect (1988: 26). Gold, ornament, and colour as well as elaborate ritual finery thus became suspect as erroneous visual access to the divine and were rejected by reformers who regarded the written word as the preferred means of finding God (Aston 1988: 45). Thus requirements that saints' relics and shrines be destroyed amounted to systematic attacks on what had been collective forms of memory making via bodily means. Ranum notes, however, that the preservation of body parts as materials of memory persisted at the level of personal social relations so that the 'body remained present in the intimate souvenir', for example locks of hair were treasured after a spouse or relative had died (1989: 234). Here Ranum points to a shift in the social spaces occupied by human material as a memory form: where once relics had accumulated in churches as mediators of collective memory, by the nineteenth century, material remains fashioned as mementoes sustaining family memories were located in the home. (A parallel movement of the relic/body part into cabinets of curiosities and museums of anatomy is discussed in Chapter 3.)

The potency of human remains as facilitators of personal memory is evident in the uses of hair jewellery sustained from the seventeenth to the nineteenth century in Northern Europe (Luthi 1998). Worked into brooches, lockets, rings, and bracelets (often with the use of precious metals and stones) human hair has extended memory connections through the powerful evocation of the person to whom it once belonged (Figures 6.1 and 6.2). Kwint notes that the 'dead margins of the self', including hair, have carried a 'charge' that is almost magical and that this is compounded by our sense of the inevitable transformation that takes place after death: the human subject ultimately becomes material object at the end of life (1999: 9). Human material that was regarded as 'dead' while the person was living, is thus transformed into a 'living' substance at death in the sense that it is reanimated as a possession capable of sustaining the deceased in close proximity to the bereaved. The physical durability of hair makes this possible as it stands in stark contrast to the instabilities of the fleshy body. The quality of endurance and the specificity of reference to a particular individual renders hair especially appropriate as a memory form.

Pointon observes that hair, as a human remain 'stages the death of its subject and simultaneously (as bodily substance that outlives the body) instantiates continuity and acts as a material figure for memory' (1999: 45). Severing a lock of hair from the recently departed is a gesture of separation that also initiates an unfolding process of recall through

Figure 6.1 Three small heart pendants. (Left) A tiny eighteenth century heart with a scene in hair on one side and hair initials on the back. (Centre) A crown and gold-wire cipher over hair and blue silk. (Right) A double-sided faceted crystal heart with gold wire ciphers over hair on both sides. Photograph: Alice Fowler for A. L. Luthi (1998) *Sentimental Jewellery: Antique jewels of love and sorrow,* Princes Risborough: Shire Publications.

the preservation of the body part. The wearing of hair jewellery connected the body of the deceased with that of the living, a function that was fulfilled in the sixteenth century by miniature portraits of loved ones framed by jewels and suspended about the neck. Miniatures were sometimes surrounded by the hair of the person depicted and Ranum highlights the potential complexity of this jewellery, describing one eighteenth-century locket that contained miniatures of two women, a mother and daughter, to which locks of their interwoven hair had been attached (1989: 250). Nineteenth-century miniature photographs were also framed with locks of hair and mounted in jet to be worn as pendants (Luthi 1998: 27). These sustained physical proximity and shared intimacy. Jewellery containing hair could carry family memory over generations, mobilizing the symbolizm of shared bodily substance woven together into inter-locking patterns. The significance of hair could be amplified through further embellishments as in the use of enamel carrying inscriptions on hair rings – such inscriptions sustained the linkage between the body fragment and

Figure 6.2 Hair bracelets were given as tokens of love as early as the seventeenth century. These are all nineteenth-century examples, showing different ways in which hair could be used. The bracelet with charms is American and made from the hair of five different members of the same family. Photograph: Alice Fowler for A. L. Luthi (1998) *Sentimental Jewellery: Antique jewels of love and sorrow,* Princes Risborough: Shire Publications.

particular persons. One late eighteenth century mourning ring, with plaited hair mounted in a gold band encapsulates memory across three generations of men – the black enamel edging referred to a grandfather, white for his son and a further inscription on the inside of the ring memorializes a grandchild (Figure 6.3) (see Luthi 1998).

As a form of materialized memory, hair was retrieved at the point of death and elaborated into culturally acceptable and meaningful body adornments. Pointon notes two predominant means by which hair was treated, both of which 'contain' the body part and shape its memory making potential. Firstly, hair was mounted within jewellery and kept in place beneath glass and, secondly, hair could be worked into tubes, ropes and bands intended to encircle the wrist. Both of

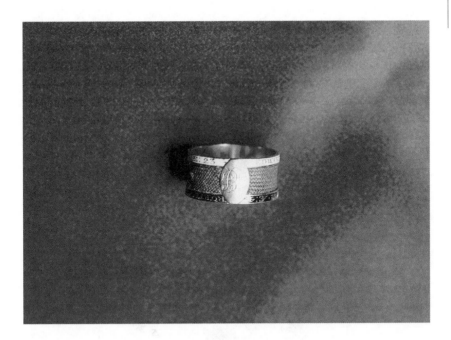

Figure 6.3 Mourning ring. Three generations of one family are commemorated in a mourning ring with plaited hair around the shank. The black enamel is for the grandfather, who died in 1791 aged forty-three. The white enamel is for his son, who died three months later and, and the shield and an inscription inside the shank are for his daughter's son who died in 1794 aged one year and twenty-two days. Photograph: Alice Fowler for A. L. Luthi (1998) *Sentimental Jewellery: Antique jewels of love and sorrow,* Princes Risborough: Shire Publications.

these play upon both the visual and the tactile aspects of the memory 'object', even if the dimension of touch is denied when hair was protected by glass. Hair work manuals published in the nineteenth century, provided instructions on how to make jewellery which would call to mind the deceased. They also offered for sale pictures that worked hair into motifs and scenes associated with rituals of death, for example flowers, headstones and cemetery scenes (Figure 6.4) (see Luthi 1998). Hair was thus positioned as a visual medium infused with special powers of recall, holding in view both a part of deceased persons and references to further objects and spaces dedicated to memory. Plaited into shapes akin to lace, hair jewellery also materialized the repetition and rejoining motions of memory processes. Pointon states that the preservation and

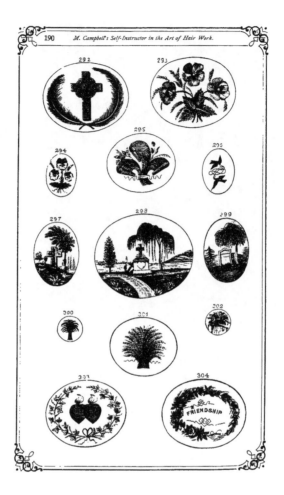

Figure 6.4 Examples of hairwork pictures offered for sale by Mark Cambell in his *Self-Instructor in the Art of Hair-Work*, published in America in 1875.

display of hair after the death of loved ones in the form of jewellery 'materializes grief as secular reliquary and micro-museum' (1999: 56). Hair retains reference to the relic in its status as a potent, if not 'sacred', fragment that inspires 'reverence, awe, fear' and readily evokes the human 'whole' from which it is derived (Pointon 1999: 43). Just as earlier relics were regarded as person-objects, materials that were at once a bodily remains and intimately tied up with the person of the saint, mourning jewellery consisted of and represented particular persons. These are memory materials which, as Pointon observes, are 'both objectified and incorporated (or united actually and/or meta-phorically with the subject's body)' (1999: 42). The physical self of the bereaved could also be built into such jewellery as, for instance, the tears shed in grief appeared in the form of pearls upon mourning jewels (Olalquiaga 1999: 284). Hair jewellery is also a 'personalised and minia-turized' form of memory that, once possessed, mounted and displayed about the living body of the bereaved, resembles the museum as a system of value and collection that acts as a 'defence against death' (Pointon 1999: 42).

While mourning jewellery came to occupy the personal space of the living body, domestic interiors of the nineteenth century in England expressed a 'preoccupation with death' and were 'closed atmospheres loaded with mortal reminiscences' in the form of highly personalized objects (Olalquiaga 1999: 282). Nineteenth-century photographs of the deceased were framed alongside careful arrangements of locks of hair (Figure 6.5). Hair from departed loved ones was kept in boxes, arranged and inscribed in a manner that, perhaps, formed miniaturized 'coffins' that could be unlocked and touched in domestic settings (Figure 6.6). Olalquiaga (1999) notes the relocation of cemeteries from within the city to its outer boundaries during the late eighteenth century, and the corresponding intensification of the home (especially in middle class circles) as a site of materialized memory. The accumulation of objects in domestic spaces – drapes, furnishings, family photographs and albums, dried flowers – developed alongside the impulse to collect and preserve specimens such as dead butterflies and fossilised shells that were systematically displayed in public museums of natural history (Olalquiaga 1999). Interiors were layered with objects to form private realms of safety, refuges of stillness which were highly conducive to personal reflection and remembering.

Body, Death and Memory in Photographs

Materials devoted to the preservation of memory exist in a cultural network of replacements and substitutions. Authors have pointed out that miniature painted portraits and hair lockets fell out of usage with the emergence of the photograph (Stewart 1998: 126; Olalquiaga 1999: 284). Photographs have operated as expressions of sentiment and in reducing the scale of the human body to its likeness in a miniature image or in salvaging a trace of the body, loved ones are sustained as treasured possessions. Warner notes the correspondences between the photo-graphic portrait and earlier Western forms of physical representation

Figure 6.5 Portrait photograph of a woman who died, aged twenty, in London c. 1880. The photograph was framed with an arrangement of her hair, mounted under glass and placed in a further frame for display in a domestic interior. Private Collection. Photograph: Nina Sparr.

that sought a powerful resemblance to the body. Saints' relics, death masks, wax figures and anatomical models of the human form belong, in Warner's view, to the same category in that they are 'neither dead nor alive' (1995: 41). Similarly, the photograph has the capacity to preserve, or maintain as living, aspects of that which has passed and those who have died: 'to enshrine identity, creating a memorial which pleads for deathlessness and issues a challenge to time – on behalf of someone' (Warner 1995: 41). Photographs, in this context, stand in a particular relation to the body – they do not comprise human flesh as

Figure 6.6 Hair, arranged and framed with a further plait of hair, mounted in a box under a sheet of glass which can be locked. The object is fixed with a hook at the back for hanging upon a wall. Dating to the nineteenth century, the box is also inscribed with the deceased woman's name. Private Collection.
Photograph: Elizabeth Hallam

in the case of relics, but they do rely upon physical proximity at the time the photograph is taken. It is this closeness, contact, or the shared physical space of camera and person that affords in the photograph a power to evoke sensations of intimacy with the departed.

As Edwards has observed, the photograph stands as a central medium infusing nineteenth- and twentieth-century memory. While carrying a visual image, a photograph's materiality is also important in sustaining its 'privileged position as a conduit of memory': here image and material object are fused (Edwards 1999: 221). Photographs are created with a view to the future – they are a means to preserve, in the form of a 'transparent' image, the present moment for later contemplation. To 'take' a photo, in current popular conceptions, is to freeze a fragment, not only of time and space, as Edwards points out, but also a selected aspect of experience, sensation and action. The instant recorded in the photographic image is seized in order to provide subsequent 'unmediated' access to the past. However, the material dimensions of photographs, including their styles of display and positioning in lived environments, inflect the ways in which they act as a form of memory making. Held in lockets, mounted in frames on walls, collected in albums, left in boxes in attics – these modes of treatment, which change over the course of a life in response to unfolding events and experiences, shape the manner in which the photograph interacts with memory. In this way, the photograph is more than an image – it is a tactile possession that engages not just vision, but also touch, and, as Edwards argues, other bodily senses such as smell. For example the handling of old, heavy family albums intensifies the experience of looking back (1999: 228).

The uses of photographs in relation to experiences of death are complex, especially when we note the changing sensibilities and rituals surrounding this life crisis. The practice of post-mortem photography in the late nineteenth and early twentieth century produced images of the deceased between the time of death and that of burial. Suspended in this liminal phase, subjects were photographed, framed and displayed for viewing in domestic interiors. Ruby (1995) situates post-mortem photography in relation to earlier European portraits that depicted a person after death for the purposes of memory. Typically undertaken, in the American context, by professionals employed by lower middle-class groups, the photographing of the recently deceased provided a means to memorialize persons at the final stage of life. It was to the living person that these photographs alluded in that the dead were arranged in a posture of restful sleep so that their final image, captured by the camera, was one of a still life-like presence.

Sleeping Beauty with 'Floating Roses', an anonymous print from c. 1910, demonstrates this principle whilst also alluding to the processes of post-mortem viewing and funerary ritual. The deceased woman is presented as though in a deep peaceful sleep, where the casket becomes her deathly bed (Figure 6.7). The title reference to the fairy tale in which the princess was reawakened is amplified by the living flowers representing resurrection (Burns 1990). The scene of this photograph is carefully staged and composed. The dense white satin worn by and surrounding the woman is arranged in thick folds, contrasting with the pattern of lace and wallpaper which frame the casket. Flowers in wreaths and bouquets have been brought to this room in gestures of love and sympathy while the woman holds a last single rose. The photograph freezes the flowers, which will later wither at the graveside. Above the 'sleeping' woman hangs a painting – perhaps her favourite scene – an object that might also have supplied memories of the departed relatives

Figure 6.7 *Sleeping Beauty with 'Floating Roses'*; Anonymous, Silver Print, c. 1910. Photograph from: S. Burns (1990) *Sleeping Beauty: Memorial photography in America*, Altadena: Twelvetrees Press. Photographs from this volume are from the collection of Stanley Burns.

who once owned it. Hung on the wall, directly above the women's face, is a further photograph of two small girls who smile out from a portrait. This may have been the woman many years earlier as a child, sat with her sister in the same chair and a matching white dress. The image works on a visual level in that it is meant to be looked at in future acts of remembrance. But it would also appeal to other senses in that it was a record of touch, of physical contact between persons and material objects, and perhaps even of smell – would those who gazed at this photograph have recalled the fragrance of flowers in the room that day? The memory functions of the photograph might also reach out to associated actions, sensations and emotions that are not directly visible within the image. It was taken at a certain point within a ritual process, in the domestic setting before funeral and the subsequent unfolding graveside rituals – so aspects of this later sequence may also have been evoked in the viewing of the photograph.

An important dimension of the way in which post-mortem photographs worked within memory was their display within the spaces occupied by the living. Ruby notes that a typical setting for post-mortem photographs to be taken was the parlour and it was in this space that the images would be visible to both family members and visitors to private houses. However, by the mid-twentieth century, as Ruby points out, people had become reluctant to employ professional photographers to produce these images and equally reluctant to reveal them to others outside of the family. Taking photographs of the departed became a private and largely concealed act and this was facilitated by the development and accessibility of cameras from the 1890s onwards (Ruby 1995). These images tended to be stored away in special albums, in a Bible or alongside private family documents which were only viewed by selected persons (Ruby 1995: 161).

Although the practice of taking photographs of the dead has continued, it is a form of memory making which is now much less visible, given the reluctance of people to reveal or talk about it. The seclusion of images of the dead body, betrays a current orientation towards physicality that prioritizes the living, healthy, active form (Hallam, Hockey and Howarth 1999). It is thus images of the living body that come into focus as a site for the generation of socially acceptable memories. In this respect, Ruby argues further: '[t]he movement away from death being represented primarily in a post-mortem photograph toward images of mourners and funerals can also be seen in the advent of graveside pictures where the deceased is represented only by the gravestone' (1995: 99). The shift towards the living, mourning body, within death related photography during the earlier twentieth century, records the postures, expressions and material culture of grief. Captured within the frame are the gestures, glances, tears, clothing and jewellery which register, on the surface of the living body, the internal sensations of loss, regret and longing. For the viewer, who had also participated in the scene, this would have opened up the visual recall of embodied emotional reactions to a death – it is the self experiencing the dislocation of a relationship that is depicted. In photographs where the grave occupies the frame and the gravestone replaces the body of the departed, it is the spaces and materials of memory making that are foregrounded. These are images which address a different phase in the continuing social life of the deceased. The transient flesh is no longer visible, rather, what is brought forward in the photograph is the site of the grave and the durable stone, attended and revisited by the living. Funeral and graveside photography represent the interplay of physical distance and proximity. They record or arrest moments of separation – the physical removal of the deceased via the funeral – and they register moments of contact – when the living return to the grave, to repeatedly touch the stone that has replaced the ones they have lost.

The association of the memorial stone with the departed body has been consolidated with the use of photographs. Ruby (1995) documents the incorporation of this media into the fabric and design of memorials from the 1840s to the present. Here it is the image of the deceased as they appeared when they were living that is commonly attached to the headstone alongside inscriptions of specific names, dates and relevant memorial words (see Chapter 7). The photographs tend to be fashioned as miniature, framed portraits. Further favourable photographs of the person are also fixed in frames that are placed upon (rather than being attached to) the headstone. Displaying a living likeness at the grave sustains a publicly visible face that has been selected as the preferred memory form by those involved in the rituals surrounding death. The material of the stone is effectively fused with (or closely linked to) the living bodily trace of the departed, thus establishing the headstone as a distinctive physical presence that 'lives'. There is a temporal complexity here that shapes memory making at the graveside. The now departed are 're-embodied' in that their physical disappearance gives way to a replacement image fixed at a previous time in their lives. The healthy, active and often happy looking person is brought into the present, obscuring the painful phases of dying and death.

This mobilization of the photograph, to establish a highly personalized living memorial, is now compounded by graveside practices that involve the relocation of 'everyday', mundane objects from the home to the cemetery. Over the last five or so years (since approximately 1995), visitors to one cemetery in Nottinghamshire, have increasingly brought gifts and personal possessions to the graves of their adult relatives and friends. Clustered around and expanding out from the headstones are potted plants and vases of flowers, letters and cards, toys and small ornaments, decorative windmills and wind chimes, poetry in small frames, lanterns and candle holders, a can of beer. While the majority of these objects are arranged at the head, there is a growing tendency to mark out and create displays around the entire boundary of the grave. The graves carry the appearance of domestic spaces – a hybrid mix of garden and living room display. Each arrangement is tailored to the interests, hobbies and personality of the deceased and incorporates objects treasured by the person while alive as well as new gifts consistent with their perceived preferences and desires (Figure 6.8).

Figure 6.8 Adults' graves in a Nottinghamshire cemetery, summer 2000. Headstones carry photographs of the deceased taken whilst living and photos are also kept at the graveside in small frames. Displays of material objects, notes, cards and flowers brought to the deceased, expand and contract throughout the year. Photograph: Elizabeth Hallam.

The visual appearance of the graves is highly eclectic – the sombre tones of the standard white, grey and black headstones standing in stark contrast to the rainbow colours of ornaments and flowers. The use of colour also differentiates the graves of adults and children. In a small section of the cemetery dedicated to infants, graves have been marked out and covered with coloured gravel in bright tones of pink and blue upon which flowers, teddies, small toys and drawings, cards and letters are placed (Figure 6.9).

Embellishing the graves in this manner is explained and assigned further meanings by visitors to a shared section of the cemetery. Regular attendants at graves relate stories to one another about the lives of their departed so that a common set of memories are transmitted and woven around the material objects as they are built up and rearranged. Anniversaries and holidays often intensify the tributes as presents are brought on birthdays of the deceased and at Christmas, lights and festive decorations are used. The treatment of the grave as a space for

Figure 6.9 Children's graves in a Nottinghamshire cemetery, summer 2000. Photograph: Elizabeth Hallam.

the departed yet still 'living', rather than the dead, is painfully apparent in a report that one family took food to one young man's burial place at Christmas. The graves of children and young adults who have died in accidents become particularly elaborate foci of gift giving at Christmas time. During Christmas 2000, children's graves were decorated with tinsel, Christmas wreaths, miniature Christmas trees, Santa Claus figures, snowmen and Christmas cards with personal messages (Figure 6.10). Graves of adults have received similar investments with Christmas wreaths and cards, while remarkable arrangements at the graves of two young women were clustered with holly, festive flowers, small

Figure 6.10 Child's grave in a Nottinghamshire cemetery, December 2000. Seasonal messages, cards and decorations are placed at the graveside. Photograph: Elizabeth Hallam.

plastic angels, cherubs, candles, glass globes with snow scenes (Figure 6.11). A nearby tree had been decorated with Christmas baubles and an angel in the manner of a Christmas tree.

The personal value of such material compositions was demonstrated in October 2000. The title deed holders of the graves were requested by the Council, through notices in the cemetery and letters to private residences, to remove their personal possessions. The Council's stated aim was to improve maintenance work, such as the mowing of grass, which it claimed was obstructed by these objects. According to a newspaper report, there had been strong protests against this request, which had triggered a certain amount of local unease. One widow was reported to have disclosed 'I was very distressed. It [the Council's letter] was very distasteful and has upset many people. My husband has only been gone six months and I have not come to terms with it yet. The only comfort I have is to go up there [to the cemetery]' (*Chronicle Advertiser*, 4 October 2000). The comfort referred to here is the continued material contact established at the grave, which is expressed through the process

Figure 6.11 Young woman's grave in a Nottinghamshire cemetery, December 2000. Detail showing messages and seasonal decorations brought to the grave and displayed around the headstone. Photograph: Elizabeth Hallam.

of gift giving or the assemblage of specific objects sustaining the 'everyday lives' of the departed.

The highly personalized graves of loved ones have been transformed into spaces in which the 'living' deceased reside and receive visitors and gifts – again memory practices infuse material objects with a high degree of subjectivity. The headstone is, in a sense, animated as the body of a person in that it is washed, cared for, gazed at, dressed with flowers, offered drinks, and surrounded by household and garden ornaments. These are acts of memory that are transformative and regenerating – while a headstone photograph stills time and depicts a person at a particular point in the past, its wider material surroundings reconstitute that person within the present in very tangible ways. Dealing with the trauma of death, people visiting the Nottinghamshire cemetery have mobilized commonly recognizable domestic materials and images to create, as one family spokeswoman was reported to have called it, 'a place of beauty' (*Chronicle Advertiser*, 4 October 2000). This beauty also resonates with a sacred charge when grave sites, with their elaborated 'living' displays, are described by local visitors as 'shrines' (*Chronicle Advertiser*, 4 October 2000). Again we find correspondences here between the photograph-headstone and the relic in that both form what Edwards (1999: 226) terms a 'focus of devotion'. Here the cemetery is not just a place that is visually pleasing and arresting – it has been shaped into a place to 'feel'. The personal, material investments which develop the basic or standardized gravestone into a sacred, increasingly individualized site have become, in the case of the Nottinghamshire cemetery, a publicly contested memory-making practice. As represented in the local press, the attitude of the Council is one that prioritizes the practicalities of cemetery work. The Head of environmental health had stated that 'A whole range of individual adjustments have been made to graves which have made maintenance almost impossible' (*Chronicle Advertiser*, 4 October 2000). Here the progressive accumulation of 'personal memorabilia' that reconstitutes the social lives of deceased individuals is seen to threaten the overall 'health' of the cemetery. Keen to re-establish order and control in the interests of a public memory ground, authorities are seeking to regulate the expansion of what visitors regard as their private space. By November 2000, the local press reported that the Council had agreed to 'permit "impermanent" memorials' placed at the headstones, 'provided items do not encroach on adjoining graves or prevent routine maintenance' (*Chronicle Advertiser*, 8 November 2000).

The current uses of photographs at the site of graves embeds them within an unfolding set of material relations and exchanges which sustain the dead as socially living persons. This is a cultural process which provides a means to maintain a physical proximity with the deceased – a sense of 'being with' a particular person now, rather than simply recalling what has passed. These graveside practices require intensive investment, a repetitive return to the site of burial to renew and update it with appropriate material objects as time passes. The positioning of memorial photographs in this context can be compared with the current domestic display of photographs that frame and preserve the dead in rather different ways. Again authors have noted the shrine-like aspects of photograph assemblages in the home (Edwards

1999) and the place of snapshots in ritual: as 'material traces of an irrecoverable past, [photographs] derive their power from their embeddedness in the fundamental rites of family life' (Hirsch 1997: 5). Family photographs are framed, assigned a special place on, for instance mantelpieces, shelves and dressers. Arranged in clusters, photos establish connections between family members – they might portray a certain togetherness in times and spaces occupied by persons now deceased and those still living. They might also connect those of different generations, visually linking members of a family spanning back over the last century. Such displays are a projection of collective identity which has historical roots. While these photographs bring bodily traces of the dead, as they once were when living, into the lived environment of their survivors, they also register loss: '[t]hey affirm the past's existence and, in their flat two dimensionality, they signal its unbridgeable distance' (Hirsch 1997: 23).

The significance of the visual in the making of memory is clearly pronounced in a range of historical and cultural contexts. Here we have focused on visual forms as enmeshed in embodied practices and cultural processes that are possessed of a powerful materiality. At the heart of this chapter we have focused on materials of memory that are linked to the bodies of the dead and the living in particular ways – as fragments of the body or as photographic traces which are constituted as 'living'. Thus uses of the corpse as a memory material with distinctive visual properties is dependent upon its place within wider systems of belief and ritualized practice. Hence the relics of saints and the locks of hair from the deceased were fashioned as memory forms that were once culturally acceptable. While the visual dimensions of these were often highly elaborated through devices of framing and the attachment of precious metals and gems, they also appealed to the sense of touch – and touching a relic or a lock of hair was important in unleashing the powers of these person-objects. The visual aspects of memory materials were thus one aspect in a nexus of embodied sensual apprehension which fed memories.

With the dominant repositioning and definition of these uses of the corpse – either through processes of Protestant reformation or through the increasing 'distancing' of the dead as 'unhygienic' or 'contaminating', relics and hair jewellery were viewed as either corrupting or distasteful. Nineteenth-century technological developments in photography provided further means to preserve physical traces of the dead within the domestic spaces of the living. Here we have argued that post-mortem photographs were visually compelling in their capacity to replicate 'real' scenes of death, replete with detail and texture. They could also appeal to sensual experience functioning as a record of touch, condensing the rich materiality of an interior and capturing last moments of physical proximity between the deceased and the living. Further uses of photographs at the site of graves in contemporary settings reveal a shift in focus from the dead to the 'living' bodies of those being remembered. Where photographs are fixed to headstones, or displayed in frames upon them, it is an image of the past (living) person that is preserved. In the examples discussed, the photograph, as a visual form, is inserted within a network of material objects that comprise the grave. The photograph in this context may stabilize an image of the deceased person as he or she once was, but the graveside practices in which it is placed are shifting and transformative. The continuously unfolding redisplay of the grave, as clusters of personally meaningful objects are brought, removed and reconfigured, positions the deceased within the present: the 'dead' are made to share the social time of the living. Again we note the conflicting attitudes towards these practices in one locality – the bereaved see these practices as essential to memory maintenance whereas the Council has become concerned about the overflow of 'untidy', 'impermanent' personal mementoes. To grasp the significance of the visual in the making of memories, then, we need to attend to its material dimensions, its positioning within wider fields of material objects and the embodied practices that orchestrate these 'entangled' relations over time.

Death Writing: Material Inscription and Memory

This chapter is concerned with the social and cultural significance of writing in memory processes relating to dying and death. It is widely acknowledged that writing, reading and the development of literacy have had major impacts upon memory and recollection (Ong 1982; Goody 1987) and at the same time, anthropologists emphasize the significance of the spoken word and oral narratives in the organization and communication of memories. While social practices involving written and oral dimensions are now recognized as interrelated (Street 1993), less attention has been paid to the intersections of writing, material culture and memory. We open this chapter with a discussion of memory and words, noting the significance of narratives (both spoken and written) and highlighting relationships between these and the material cultures or lived material environments in which they are enacted. In the sections that follow we explore the materiality of a range of writing techniques brought into play during the processes of dying and grieving. These forms of death writing possess powers of evocation, and work within memories, not simply as a function of their *content*, but by virtue of their form and execution in material terms. With particular reference to the ritualized aspects of death and memory, this chapter explores certain settings in which writing unfolds as embodied practice involving the manipulation of material substances and objects, including paper, wax and stone. We focus on the marking of paper as a means to record the will before the event of death, the inscription of words upon objects to retain aspects of the deceased and writing in the form of sculpted or sewn materials – all instances of memory practices that unfold at the juncture of material culture and inscription. As in the previous chapter, where we noted the fusion of visual image and materiality (including that of the body), writing at or after the point of death for the purposes of memory is often a matter situated at the interface between body and material object.

Memory in Words

Anthropologists have foregrounded the importance of words or narratives in the shaping of memory and identity and of particular relevance to our current study are the relationships they have posited between words and materiality. Narrative has come to be understood as a dynamic cultural process embracing both the written and the spoken word that emerges within social interactions and performative contexts. Tonkin asserts '[l]iterate or illiterate, we are our memories' and, with reference to Europe, America and especially Africa, she explores oral narratives as 'representations of pastness' that help to generate and reproduce social life (1995: 1, 97). The spoken word, in this context, is also a social action and a mode of communication. Furthermore, oral narratives are generated, received, repeated and modified in social settings through shared discursive conventions. In Tonkin's account of representations concerned with the past she focuses mostly, but not exclusively, on language, arguing that 'representations need not even be verbal, but as soon as a representation is communicated or interrogated, words enter in. And as "the present" is a perpetually disappearing moment, so all languages allow their speakers to refer back' (1995: 2). While language here facilitates memory, Tonkin moves on to suggest that 'material evidences' such as photographs, work tools, clothes and books also trigger memories and are woven into or provide recognizable points of departure, reference or anchorage for oral narratives. This is especially the case given that a person's identity or social role is often 'bound up' with material objects and, in turn, what 'humans recall is strongly connected to their identities' (Tonkin 1995: 94, 96).

Skultans, in her study of memory in post-Soviet Latvia, also focuses upon oral narratives as a means by which lives are remembered and made meaningful. Here, the rich connections between spoken narratives, literary themes and historical texts are testimony to the creative formation of stories which are socially shared in the aftermath of disrupted lives. Skultan's states that '[t]he breakdown of the everyday structures of living creates a need to reconstitute meaning in story telling' (1998: 26). In situations where people find it difficult to describe past experiences, for example the suffering of violence, they adopt themes or conventions from literature or from what they have 'read, heard or sung' (Skultans 1998: 48). Thus Skultans highlights the spoken

word as a complex cultural medium through which memories are represented and communicated. She does, however, also suggest important
connections between language and the materiality of social experience:

> Although language reaches out to its referents, including the past, it is,
> even less than I had supposed, a transparent medium offering unproblem-
> atic access. Rather, it is a dense medium which holds in suspension the
> residues of personal and social histories. To use a metaphor with Baltic
> connections, language is the amber which preserves relics of past feelings
> and ideas. (Skultans 1998: 24)

While metaphor might confer upon language a compelling 'material'
dimension, Skultans also emphasizes the relatedness of narrated
memories and the 'substance' of earlier experiences to which these
memories refer. For instance, the experience of exile leads to an
emphasis on the physicality of shared dwelling places in later recollections of the past (Skultans 1998: 31).

Oral narrative may form an important vehicle for memory, retaining
connections with the lived material world through its referents (and,
indeed, its embodied performance necessarily takes place within
material settings), but written texts physically occupy material surfaces
(such as paper) and spaces (for example books and shelves). The written
or printed word requires materials, implements, machines and bodily
actions for its inscription and these have important implications for
memory-making. So, for instance, Stewart compares speech and writing:

> Speech leaves no mark in space; like gesture, it exists in immediate context
> . . . but writing contaminates; writing leaves a trace, a trace beyond the
> mortality of the body. Our terror of the unmarked grave is a terror of the
> insignificance of a world without writing . . . Writing gives us a device
> for inscribing space, for inscribing nature: the lovers' names carved in
> bark, the slogans on the bridge, the strangely uniform and idiosyncratic
> hand that has tattooed the subways. (Stewart 1998: 31)

This appears to set up a rather misleading opposition between speech
and writing (and one that does not hold, as we argue later in this
chapter) but it does outline some of the material dimensions of writing
with which we are concerned: the life of the inscribed word might
overlap with, but may also extend beyond the physical body; materialized words become potent as markers that preserve identity after death;
the materials and spaces of writing are as diverse in form as they are in

function, articulating gestures of intimacy as well as public statements. Stewart also states that writing can be seen as both knowledge and object in that the book can be regarded as a set of ideas and as a material form – although there are cultural and economic factors that differentiate and accentuate these properties. For example, before the spread of print technologies, manuscript books requiring hours of work to copy by hand were highly valued, treasured for years, and, as Butor points out, they were like monuments and 'even more durable than a structure of bronze' (Butor 1961, quoted in Stewart 1998: 33). Here the materiality of the book was apparent and important whereas, by contrast, twentieth-century commercialized, mass-produced printed books tend to be consumed for their contents and then discarded so that the material of which they are comprised is not valued.

A further example links books as cultural artefacts closely to the body. Stewart cites instances of miniature books from the fifteenth to the early nineteenth century, which condensed texts of a certain magnitude, such as the bible or calendars, into tiny, jewel-like objects that could be attached to belts, rings or neck chains. They were crafted with considerable skill and care, and embellished sometimes with golden letters or metal pages. There are parallels between the miniature book and miniature portraits, which were also worn about the body to remind the wearer of loved ones. One silver miniature book, for example, had a coloured, enamelled pansy on the front and an engraved cobweb from which hung a pearl and ruby spider (Stewart 1998: 41). Stewart notes that the pansy was regarded as a flower with a 'human' face that, together with the spider making its home upon the book, had the capacity to invoke a significant other (either alive or departed) who had been connected to the owner through personal or domestic ties. Books as objects have been made to act as memory possessions linking persons, not only through the written words that they crystallized but also through their fabric, material embellishments, uses and spatial positioning in relation to the body and other material objects.

We can assert, then, that written words as forms of cultural representation have important material dimensions that reinforce their memory-making capacities. Indeed, we can approach the written word as a memory vehicle, embedded within material cultures and possessing strong visual qualities. So for instance, memory objects, such as headstones, might comprise textual as well as visual and tactile dimensions (see Chapter 6). The meshing of word and image can readily be seen at work during the early modern period, so that in Dutch painting, texts and associated writing implements were presented as visually stimulating objects (Alpers 1983). In still-life painting of the time, books, letters, rolled-up manuscripts, writing quills, and sealing wax were rendered in exact detail, which concentrated upon and amplified the materiality of the written word and its associated paraphernalia. The texture, colour, and play of light and shadow in these paintings highlighted written materials as things engaged with the senses and also as objects that were open to wear, tear and decay. These were objects that had a place in life, which were used and touched by the human hand and they were also, like all possessions within the mortal world, marked by their own transience. This was the central message of still-life paintings concerned with the vanitas theme: skulls, the often repeated vanitas motif, were depicted alongside inscriptions on paper and in stone which told of the inevitable withering of all worldly things revered as beautiful (see Chapter 3). Inscribed mottoes such as 'Everything decays with death/death is the final boundary of all things' (quoted in Latin in Barthel Bruyn the Elder's *Vanitas Still Life*, 1524) and the positioning of skulls on top of worn books, their words no longer legible (for example in Pieter Claesz' *Vanitas Still Life*, 1630) imbue the written word and its material manifestations with death and undermine notions of immortality suggested by the apparatus of the book. Here the drawing of writing into the worldly material domain accentuated its physical properties but did so in a manner that underlined its vulnerability in the face of time: just as the human body would inevitably be reduced to lifeless bone, so the paper and vellum of books would eventually become dusty, damaged fragments.

Conceptions of written words as performative materials and inscribed letters as infused with a degree of subjectivity stand in a difficult relation to notions of texts as carriers of objective information. As Stafford (1994) has suggested, cultures of enlightenment reinforced the status of certain written forms as means to systematize and provide direct access to knowledge – for example in the cataloguing and labelling of museum objects. As a result writing, in the contexts of enquiry, was further stripped of its status as a cultural object possessed of material and visual properties. Thus we witness an elevation of texts as primary bases of knowledge so that the domain of material things and of sensory experience was subordinated, as a means of knowing the world, to rational print-based language (see also Appadurai 1986). With reference to Ong's work on orality and literacy, it has been noted that in predominantly oral cultures, memory and knowledge are synonymous, whereas with the development of literacy the 'subjective' impressions of memory are separable from 'the idea of objective truths inscribed in

some transcendental archive' (Clark 2000: 242). However, this opposition of the written/printed word (objective knowledge) and oral/visual/
material world (subjective memory) is problematic. Authors have shown
that the printed word draws upon and operates in relation to co-existent
oral conventions and visual codes (Watt 1994) and, indeed, that literacy
practices in their social contexts are diverse and heterogeneous in their
configuration or mixing of different modes of communication, including written, oral and visual components (Street 1993).

Our aim is not to deny the potency or power of inscription that has
been afforded to written words in memory making, but to draw out
the persistent significance of their visual and material dimensions
situated within the social practices associated with dying and death.
The next two sections of this chapter explore these aspects in more
detail, focusing firstly on early modern will making and secondly on
memorial inscriptions rendered in stone.

Deathbed Memories Materialised: Words Written, Seen and Spoken

In the later sixteenth and early seventeenth centuries, the last wishes
of a dying person could be expressed through the spoken and the
written word and these intentions were expected to be confirmed at
the deathbed through ritualized practices of writing and speaking the
will. These involved socially and legally recognized codes of comport-
ment, gesture, speech, and action on the part of the dying person as
well as those who visited or attended the deathbed. Will making was
an act of memory performed by the dying as it involved certain
recollections of the past and it was also a means by which the deceased
was later remembered. Materialized memories produced through will
making should be understood in the context of early modern perceptions and expectations at the deathbed, and as articulations of relationships pertaining between the body, speech, writing and material objects.
Here our analysis is based upon the detailed descriptions provided by
witnesses, resident in the south-east of England (Kent) and recorded
by the Church courts in Canterbury, during legal action taken when
wills were disputed c. 1580–1640 (Hallam 1994). Those whose wishes
and intentions were documented by these courts came mainly, though
not exclusively, from the ranks of middling to wealthy householders.

The deathbed was an important site, in the early modern period,
which formed the domestic location in which dying people saw their
family, kin and friends, settled their estates through the making of wills

and attended to their spiritual condition before facing the final moment of life. The relationship between life and death was constructed, especially in religious belief, as a continuous process and reminders of human mortality were widely circulated (see Chapter 3). There was a keen awareness of the necessity to be properly prepared for death as a rite of passage into the afterlife. Cressy notes that '[d]ying was a process of sloughing of one's mortal coil, a process thought to begin at birth that accelerated in the final stages of illness or decrepitude. "Death" was the extinction of the flame of life, the moment when most Christians thought the soul departed the body' (1997: 379). The ringing of passing bells calling for prayers for the dying, funerals, graves, sermons, and memento mori in the form of paintings, printed images and objects all acted as reminders of death, encouraging contemplation of the fate that would come to all, regardless of social rank and status. Combined with a rich visual culture of death, texts disseminated since the fifteenth century in the form of advice literature describing the *ars moriendi*, or craft of dying, provided detailed instruction on conduct required at the deathbed. After the reformation, the Protestant emphasis on preparation for death continued to inform deathbed practices. The dying had a duty to examine their lives, seeking God's forgiveness for sins and, while forgiving others, to make sure that their family was materially and spiritually provided for (Houlbrooke 1998: 159–60). To achieve the ideal of the 'good death', Christians had to confirm their inner faith, express this externally through prayers and gestures and pass willingly into the hands of God (Houlbrooke 1998: 159–60). Visitors and attendants at the deathbed were expected to provide comfort, help and support in the active pursuit of these ends, participating in and witnessing the final performances of the dying.

Will writing was an important part of conduct at the deathbed – a performance or series of practices shaped by prevailing social, cultural and spiritual codes. These codes were inculcated and reproduced over time as the ritualized deathbed attendance of women and men would have been experienced repeatedly during the life course. As Houlbrooke points out, the ideal of the good death was modified in practice as the reformation progressively gave way to increased individual choices in modes of action prior to death (1998: 182). Cause of death and its occurrence at different times in the life cycle, the participation of medical and ecclesiastical specialists and the quality of relationships pertaining within households and kin networks could all affect conduct at the deathbed. Household and family tensions could be exacerbated during the phase of dying and these could lead to the neglect of or unsatisfactory performance of duties on the part of the dying and their attendants (Hallam 1994). In addition, factors such as social status, wealth, age and gender gave rise to a variety of deathbed experiences. Gender differences, for instance, informed the social practices surrounding the dying. From the formal legal perspective, women could not make wills without the permission of their husbands (see Houlbrooke, 1998: 84), and the gendered division of labour that organized the management of the deathbed tended to assign will-writing responsibilities to men (Hallam 1996). However, unmarried women and widows would make considerable efforts, through spoken interaction and by ordering the writing of their wills, to express their faith and also to direct the appropriate distribution of their material possessions. Women as servants, kin and friends, would also make valued contributions as diligent, often long-term, attendants at the beds of the dying (Hallam 1996).

The deathbed formed an important domestic space in the making of memories in that the social action within it, including speeches and gestures, was characterized by a heightened display of emotion and spirituality as well as the expression of moral and material concerns. The intersection of personal, familial and legal interests ensured that this site attracted a high degree of participation, on the part of relatives, neighbours, Church and legal representatives, in phases of mundane and ritualized action during the last months or days before a person's death. Gathering together to confirm personal bonds, and to hear last wishes and advice from the dying provided lasting memories for survivors. The numerous written accounts of deathbeds in diaries, letters, biographies and autobiographies (Houlbrooke 1998) are testimony to the significance of the deathbed as a narrative focus in the textual preservation of lives.

The framing of the deathbed in written texts as a scene of memory making was also reinforced through visual images of this space. Llewllyn cites examples of portraits which, showing particular individuals of high social status on their deathbeds, were viewed as a means to preserve memories of the deceased (1991: 32, 41). In 1633, Lady Veneta Digby, for instance, was represented in a deathly 'sleep', framed by the folds of her gown, bed linen and curtains. The portrait of Thomas Braithwaite (1607) shows the dying man sat in his bed, which is draped in black cloth. Accompanied by an attentive male figure, Braithwaite gazes down upon the will that he is writing. While the black fabric of his bed frames the pale paper upon which he writes, his upper body is supported and surrounded by pillows, which are also inscribed with words. The increasing dissemination of images during the sixteenth century, including those depicting death, provided visual access to deathbed scenes through the medium of print. The conventionalized arrangements of the domestic chambers, in which people lived the last of their days, were visualized as interiors organized around the dying person. Images of the deathbed, for example, those illustrating ballads in popular cheap print, typically showed the dying person surrounded by attendants and visitors at the bedside, bearing witness to the event and in gestures of prayer (see Hallam 1996). Later sixteenth- and seventeenth-century engraved versions of the deathbed, especially those associated with middling to wealthy social groups, also incorporated images of will making (see Cressy 1997). Figure 7.1 shows a deathbed scene in which a dying man is attended by three male figures – two men are involved in the writing of the will at a table, while a third sits weeping in a chair. In painting and in print, deathbed scenes integrated bodily gestures, material objects and written texts into the visual image, framing them as potent memory forms.

Figure 7.1 Engraving showing a deathbed scene where a will is being written, c. seventeenth-century. Wellcome Institute Library, London.

An important aspect of deathbed practices was the settlement of the dying person's estate through arrangements made in the transfer of property. The making of wills could begin some time before death was imminent, but the deathbed remained an important site for will writing, amendment and the confirmation of last wishes. At the deathbed a combination of spiritual and material concerns were brought into play. Material possessions, while significant in social and economic terms as markers of rank, status and privilege, were represented from the Christian perspective as ephemeral and transitory in comparison to the eternal nature of spiritual wealth. Just as in death the human body would be returned to the earth and reduced to dust, so all material acquisitions would eventually be destroyed through death and time. Detachment, at the point of death, from the material world was central to post-reformation Christian notions about the separation of the body and the soul – the soul would pass into eternal life with God, whereas the body would be left dead, bereft of action and senses, and subject to decay (Cressy 1997). Within the requirements of the good death, concentration on the spiritual dimensions of life was highlighted, yet Houlbrooke notes the varied worldly concerns expressed at the deathbed throughout the sixteenth and seventeenth centuries. The spiritual gifts offered by the dying to their kin, in the form of blessings or advice regarding faith in God and duty towards family, might be balanced by concerns expressed about the material security and provision to be made for surviving relatives (Houlbrooke 1998: 189, 191).

The process of will making operated in a context in which the transfer of property was interpreted as a communicative event: the giving of gifts made statements about past, present and future relationships and was, therefore, implicated in the reproduction of relationships beyond the grave. At the deathbed the domain of the material was conceived, not just in terms of the Christian worldview (as a sphere of temporary trappings to be left behind by the spirit), nor just as property governed by customs of inheritance but as sets of belongings charged with a diversity of social and personal meanings. Material objects were infused with significance beyond their material existence or monetary value, consolidating their status as memory objects that had the potential to retain aspects of the deceased within the social lives of the bereaved. An awareness of the memory functions of objects was apparent at the deathbed, informing the decisions made at this point with regard to gift giving and the transmission of belongings.

Certain material objects had the capacity to represent social relationships, retaining them in memory, because they had come to be associated with the person, body and identity of their owners and once given to another they could operate as indicators of intimacy. To be given such an object was to be afforded a token of physical proximity with a loved one even after death. Pertinent here is Ranum's definition of such tokens as 'relic-objects' – forms that were regarded as a fusion of body fragment and material object, and possessed of emotive charge: '[w]ords of love were given concrete embodiment in certain relic-objects: notes, letters, perhaps even a single word in the handwriting of the beloved ... Favourite love tokens included women's combs, ribbons, rings, bracelets, handkerchiefs, gorgeoires (bodice covers), mirrors, pearl necklaces, belts, garters' (1989: 246).

Material tokens of intimacy exchanged during courtship and marriage, including those made of paper and marked with ink, were assembled into a 'language' of affection and sentiment. The expressive potential of tokens was considerable in that they conveyed subtle and nuanced messages about the qualities of persons and their relationships. O'Hara has provided a detailed account of the 'language of tokens' in early modern England (Kent), which she describes as a 'vital, sustained code of popular practice', involving a diverse range of gifts, each with their own symbolic associations, given in the formation of marital relationships (O'Hara 1992). The giving of tokens articulated varying degrees of attachment, commitment and intention on the part of men, although women, especially widows, would reciprocate by giving in return. Hundreds of different types of tokens were mobilized including money, clothing and textiles (predominantly gloves), metal objects (mostly rings), animals and food, letters and books, the precise meanings of which were assigned in specific contexts of giving and receipt. Words spoken during the act of giving or inscribed upon the object would further delineate the object's personal meanings (O'Hara 1992) and thus words were bound up with the material, tactile dimensions of embodied social interaction and exchange. Such gifts were not only meaningful during the time of courtship; they were also given in order to sustain memories over the life course as indicated, for example by inscriptions on rings that invited the recipient to 'Were this for a remembrance' (O'Hara 1992: 27). Tokens of this type would be retained and others brought into play as a means to express enduring affection at the deathbed.

Will making and the giving of tokens at the deathbed in early modern England was an important part of the social practice of memory. The making of a will, especially for social groups concerned with the careful distribution of property, involved recollections of past events and relationships as well as anticipation of future situations. Decisions about the contents of a will would depend upon the quality of relationships between family, kin and friends. These relationships were often recalled at the deathbed through memories of significant gestures, attitudes, words and actions in the past. Thus, will making entailed reflection upon lives, and it involved assessment of the conduct of others in relation to prevailing codes of conduct, respectability, honesty, kindness and love. For example, when, in 1626, Joyce Knowler declared that her sister should have her rings, linen, a silver spoon and her bible, she also stated that her brother 'was a naughty boy and that he should have nothing of hers but her pewter cupp'.[1] Here the pewter cup given to Knowler's brother would have acted as a negative comment upon his behaviour, providing a material reminder of the moral assessments made by his sister prior to her death. Furthermore, the bequests made through wills and the act of giving gifts at the deathbed would have a significant impact on the ways in which the deceased was subsequently remembered. When in 1590 Elizabeth Wills, who lay 'extreme[ly] sick' in a 'lowe chamber' in her bed, declared that she wanted to give a 'stock of bees' to one Thomas Harlowe, her gift not only promised to nourish her friend's memories – it potentially spoke to the medieval metaphor of the bee hive as a structure for memory[2] (see Chapter 2).

To be of 'good' memory (associated with a settled bodily state) was a necessary prerequisite for successful will making. Witnesses called to the Church courts to give evidence in cases where wills were disputed often provided descriptions of the dying, their physical condition and their capacity for memory as demonstrated according to the criteria of appropriate speech, gesture and action expected at the deathbed. The account provided by Jane White of Canterbury in 1631 reveals the ways in which the memory capacities of her dying sister, Elizabeth White, were assessed. An hour before her death and accompanied by various female kin and her brothers, who had been requested to write her will, Elizabeth White had declared her last wishes. Jane White later stated in court that the testatrix 'were in truth of very good memory and had her understanding as sound and perfect during the [time] as ever she had it in her health, as her sensible speeches and other her actions at that time plainly showed'.[3]

The capacity for good memory exhibited during the making of wills was, according to Houlbrooke, commonly taken as an indicator of sound 'mental health' (1998: 89), but memory was not just the internal mental state of individuals; rather, it was a socially negotiated property that was assigned through the interpretation of words and gestures.

Furthermore memory, as perceived at the deathbed, was also articulated through the careful distribution of material tokens consistent with the social expectations associated with particular personal relationships. When John Hailes of Canterbury lay on his deathbed in 1602 he requested that the desk containing his written will be brought to his bed. The will was read before witnesses to confirm its contents as Haile's last wishes and the event was marked with the giving of tokens:

> out of his desk the testator delivered tokens to those present – Mrs Sprackling his sister two pieces of gold and also two showell abourds (as he termed them) for Luke Sprackling her husband and to his wifes sister Mrs Osbourne a little box which he said was his mothers and to this deponent (William Symmes) the testator gave an amber bead and two pieces of gold and to his the testators wife he said prithie Mill let mr Symes take his chiose of my books – all of these actions showed the testator to be of perfect mind and memory.[4]

Thus the written will relied upon its reading and witnessing for validity and the occasion of reading was underlined by the handing over of material objects. In this case it is notable that John Hailes had within his possession a small box that had once belonged to his mother. Already a carrier of her memory he had then passed it to his sister-in-law so that it accumulated layers of family memories. And again, we see books as possessions that, through the gesture of giving, would act as reminders of a person deceased.

Scenes of writing were often recalled by witnesses describing the deathbed and if we turn our attention to the physical act of inscription we can note significant phases of this ritualized process. The writing of wills was the preserve of men in their capacities as notaries, gentlemen, and officials of the Church. In proximity to the dying person, men would transfer the wishes and intentions of the dying onto paper (in draft and fair copies), the text would be read out, checked, amended, confirmed as the final will, signed or marked (with a personal sign) in ink by witnesses and the dying person, then sealed. The accounts of gentlemen who witnessed the final confirmation of William Nutt's will testified to the sacred status of the document, completed and displayed in a gesture of prayer: taking the will in his hand, 'he the said testator [William Nutt] kneling downe uppon his knees gave god thankes very hartely that he had gyven him such good tyme and opportunyty to finishe his will so well according to his mynde. And then caused the same to be rouled up and sealed up with three seals'.[5] Seals made of wax and imprinted with a sign associated with a particular person indicated property ownership but also attached traces of personal identity to the document. This was further reinforced when the seal was worn in the form of a ring with a shape or image cut into it. One further notable dimension here is the symbolic status afforded the hand as the agent of writing and a site for the display of identity: '[h]and-writing acquires a special weight as indicative of 'character' . . . The signature effectively becomes a substitute for the person . . . also an assertion of truth or of consent' (Goody 1986: 152). The will, as constituted through ritualized actions, was the bearer of not only the future intentions of the dying person but also a highly charged material form that carried the imprint of their body. Once finalized, will documents were often kept in boxes and chests, a facility enjoyed particularly by men of high status. Locked away and protected within material enclosures, the will as materialized memory was again resonant with medieval metaphors of memory as a wax tablet or a strong box (see Chapter 2), but this time imbued with the stamp of the 'individual' and concealed within private, domestic spaces.

Writing after Death: Memory in Stone

We have seen that speaking and writing, in the ritualized spaces of the early modern deathbed, not only conveyed the last wishes of the dying but also transferred the embodied identity of persons onto a material 'object' – the written will. The scene of speech/writing in this context involved bodily gestures and the giving of gifts which would inflect subsequent memories of the deceased. Thus, the material dimensions of writing were significant in memory making. Writing or the construction of a text that outlives the dying, was recognized as a precarious process in that all aspects of the material world were open to decay. However, materialized memorial writing has taken many forms in the pursuit of elusive permanence so that words have been fashioned in a variety of media – in stone and in thread or fabric. Each of these materials might come to be valued in terms of their varying degrees of durability. Such materials also acquire symbolic associations and have been used to memorialize in a range of different ways, encompassing personal meanings and public statements. While the writing of early modern wills was conducted in relative privacy before the death of a person, the next section of this chapter explores writing that is dedicated to the public memories of lives past. The form, content and context of memorial inscriptions has a profound effect upon the ways in which a (materialized) text works within memory. Here we examine individual and collective memorials from the eighteenth and twentieth centuries in England and America, teasing out the work of words of which they are composed.

Memorials, fashioned in durable substances such as stone and marble are used as markers of the site of burial and they often derive their memory-invoking capacities from their proximity to the bodily remains of the deceased. As noted in Chapter 6, memorials might also be regarded as a replacement for the vulnerable body or come to be treated, through graveside practices, as though they *are* a body – this accrual of identity and subjectivity normally associated with the living body occurs through the use of particular visual images/material objects. The inscription of words, however, is often crucial in establishing relationships between the memory object (for example, a memorial stone) and the subject to be remembered. Again culturally and historically specific codes and conventions of representation impinge upon the formation of memorial writing – from the materials in which it is executed and the language it deploys, to its positioning in relation to visual and sculpted imagery.

Aries has described the historical variability of practices that marked and made tombs visible or recovered them from anonymity after the eleventh century as part of a 'desire for commemoration' of ordinary persons as well as those regarded as great. He notes that medieval epitaphs, asserting the identity of the dead, developed alongside religious obligations to make wills (Aries 1983). Until the fourteenth century, epitaphs could establish the name, date of death, words of praise for the deceased and their profession, thereby also marking rank and status. At this point prayers to God for the soul were also inscribed, encouraging a 'dialogue between dead writer and living reader' (Aries 1983: 218). By the fifteenth century inscriptions linked family members with one another and two centuries later the epitaph was used as a biographical account – a condensed series of pointers used to sustain memories of a lifetime's merits and achievements. Material inscriptions are highly complex in their content, format and spatial location as well as the relation they sustain with the body of the deceased. Below we discuss two examples, involving individual and collective memory making, to explore the materiality of words which have mediated the living and the dead.

One eighteenth-century memorial, dedicated to Anna Rhodes (1764–96) was erected in St James church, London. The church was later demolished and the memorial can currently be viewed in the Victoria and Albert Museum. The textual component of this piece is located in its lower half, while above it two sculpted areas show one woman knelt within a circular frame and above this, a relief depicts two women embracing. One of these upper figures represents justice with a pair of scales and the other, as the text suggests, is Mercy, while the cross at Calgary rises up in the background. The epitaph reads:

> Erected by a Sister in Memory of her beloved ANNA CECILIA, Daughter of CHRISTOPHER RHODES Esq; of *Chatham* in the county of *Kent* . She departed this Life June 2: 1796, aged 32. Her Remains were deposited in the 42 Vault of this Chapel. Distinguished by a fine Understanding, and a most amiable Disposition of Heart. She was the Delight of her Parents, and the Admiration of all who knew her. At the Age of 17, the Smallpox stripped off all the Bloom of youthful Beauty, And being followed by a dreadful Nervous-disorder withered those fair Prospects of earthly Happiness Which were expected from her uncommon Affection, Sensibility and Tenderness. After enduring this afflictive Dispensation many Years, When it was difficult to say which exceeded, her Sufferings or her Submission; Her Friends Concern for her Sorrows, or their Admiration of her Patience; she was released by Death, and received into that World where there shall be no more Pain, But GOD himself shall wipe away Tears from every Eye.

> *Alas! how vain are feeble Words to tell*
> *What once she was, and why I lov'd so well:*
> *None else but he who form'd the Heart can know*
> *How great her Worth, or how extreme my Woe!*
> *Blest Calv'y, on my Crimson Top I see,*
> *Suff'rings and Death, with Life and Love agree;*
> *Justice severe and smiling Mercy join,*
> *And thro' the Gloom we see the Glory shine.* [italics and capitals are shown here as in the original].

The words read as a dedication to the departed Anna Rhodes from her surviving sister. Here is a narrative that condenses a life into its final stages, where the beauty of youth is eroded by sickness. The bodily decline of a woman is arrested in death as she is released into the spiritual world, and thus her life is couched within the Christian framework of physical suffering, death and rebirth – themes amplified in the figurative components of the ensemble. Through the memorial, a woman's life becomes the story of her death and of her sister's loss.

The text is reflective, composed in retrospect, as its narrative trajectory reaches into the past only to acknowledge its own inadequacy within the present: 'Alas! how vain are feeble Words to tell What once she was'. By its own admission and reference to 'feeble words', the memorial fails to represent a person as she had seemed in life – rather the memorial preserves a set of social bonds, an approximation of relationships primarily between family members (especially two sisters and their father who is named) but also extending out to friends and acquaintances. As Bindman (1999) notes in the case of eighteenth-century monuments, these were not dedicated exclusively to the preservation of a particular individual's memory; rather, in varying degrees, they have served to memorialise (or to inflate the status) of family groups, political figures and their agendas, as well as the artists who were commissioned to make them.

The memorial to Anna Rhodes, while executed in enduring marble, undermines its own weight by elevating the spiritual, immaterial world into which she has been released. In this respect the words inscribed to carry this message mark a distance or movement of the deceased away from the beholder. The words refer to a domain of shining glory beyond that of the immediate earthly material sphere so that the memorial and the temporal world in which it resides are made to appear as insubstantial traces left in 'gloom'. The memorial acts as a reminder that full recognition and knowledge of a life can only be realised to its fullest extent in the eyes of God. Of course during the 'life' of this particular memorial, it would have worked upon memories in different ways depending upon its positioning within the world view of those who gazed upon it, read it, gave it only a swift glance, registered only its physical or visual appearance. The multiple meanings of such materials across successive generations remains to be explored. We can note, however, that at its moment of production, this memorial deployed words in the service of a particular conception of memory and its relation to materiality: words, however heavily inscribed in marble, are described as 'feeble'. They, and by implication the memorial that holds them, cannot encompass a life, rather they can gesture to an immaterial world where that life will be fully known. Executed within a 'permanent' format this writing refers to transformation from material body to spiritual entity – it instantiates difference, separation and distance.

We can compare this eighteenth-century instance of materialized words apprehended as insubstantial traces, or shadows, with twentieth-century memorials that mobilize inscriptions as a form of embodiment, or a located physical presence. In the examples which follow, words associated with the dead are comprised of material and incorporated into mourning practices such that they are made to 'live'.

The Vietnam Veterans Memorial, unveiled in November 1982 in Washington, is comprised of the names of those lost at war between 1959 and 1975. Carved into two walls of polished black granite (which form a V shape), the 58, 132 names are arranged in chronological order of death. Harrison notes that the memorial 'is not a tombstone, which for better or worse can presume to contain "all that was mortal" of the dead whose names it registers' (1997: 190) as the bodies of the deceased remain dispersed across a landscape of war and in some cases were never found. So how have inscribed names been positioned and read in relation to the bodies, identities and memories of those lost? Sturken asserts that the power of the memorial emanates from the staggering multitude of names inscribed upon its length of 500 feet, and this textual weight is reinforced in the stated aims of Maya Lin (the monument's designer) that it should 'read "like an epic Greek poem" and "return the vets to the time frame of the war"' (1991: 126–7). To inscribe the names in chronological order according to the time of death produces a narrative of war charted through particular physical losses. This arrangement also resists narrative closure in that the last name on the memorial is situated so that it leads, at the central part of the V, to the first name (Sturken 1991). Names, as markers of identity for individuals, are thus the words through which the mass destruction of the war is brought to memory.

The focus here is upon the inscribed name as a primary marker of individual personhood (recall the importance of the signature on early modern wills). The minimalist, abstract design of the memorial has generated protest, yet Hawkins observes that visitors to it are moved by its presence and, in particular, tend to reach out to touch the names that they read (Hawkins 1993). The materialized name appears to be sufficient to provoke deeply felt sensations of intimacy, sentiment and personal devotion and these reactions are manifested in the gifts of flowers, letters, toys and photographs that have been arranged near to the inscriptions. Hawkins notes that 'mourners would try to give those names the keepsakes of identity, as if to restore to the dead the intimate worlds they had lost' (Hawkins 1993: 755). These individualized gifts, including written materials, are small and transient in comparison to the bulk and fixity of the memorial, yet they have developed their own conventions of preservation in that notes initially left on vulnerable paper are now protected with plastic and framed (see Hawkins

1993: 755). The individual items are collected daily by the National Park Service and, as they amass to over 25,000 in number, requests have been made for a permanent museum exhibition to be established (Hawkins 1993).

The evocative reach of the inscribed name as a means of recalling the dead is here consolidated through its linkage to personal possessions. Again the dead are approached as 'living', embodied, persons. As Sturken (1991: 132) points out, 'To dis-member [in war] is to fragment a body and its memory; to remember is to make a body complete'. While this completion is impossible (in that physical death is irreversible) gestures towards it take place through symbolic association: the presence of the inscribed name as the physicality of those lost is enhanced through the accumulation of material gifts belonging to the domain of intimacy and everyday life. In this way, the memorial has come to acquire shrine- like qualities in that it is a focus of devotion and physical contact between the living and the dead.

While we have focused here upon the uses of particular durable material used in writing dedicated to memory, we can note the a vast and expanding range of materialized words that have become significant as a means of relating to persons after death. For instance, the NAMES Project AIDS Quilt (organized in 1987) mobilizes thread and fabric to form written messages, sometimes using the clothing of the deceased, in memory and identity making (Hawkins 1993). Martha Cooper and Joseph Sciorra (1994) have documented the 'spraycan memorials' in New York where graffiti (comprised of words and images) is elaborated into vibrant dedications such that buildings, walls and streets are appropriated as sites of memory. Memorial plaques are fixed to benches and trees, inscribing places of contemplation and 'natural' forms with personalized messages (Figure 7.2). What characterizes this memorial writing is its hybridity of form that integrates a diversity of images, objects and written words to create identity markers for individuals whilst maximizing impact and expressing private sentiment in publicly recognizable symbols and materials. This fusion of word, image and material plays into the dynamics of physical loss and recovery that shapes the field of memory making in diverse responses to death.

Gestures Written in Grief

This chapter has focused upon textual forms of memory making as significant aspects of material cultures associated with the dying process

Figure 7.2 Memorial inscription on living forms. Tree and memory plaque, Hull University grounds. Photograph: Hull University.

and the continued social lives of the dead. Current experiences of grief, mourning and remembrance in England also involve forms of writing that deserve further attention. We can refer, for example, to the cards of sympathy and condolence sent to friends and relatives after a death, the messages on small cards attached to funerary wreaths (wreaths that are themselves sometimes presented in the shape of names written in flowers), obituaries and memorials printed in newspapers (see Bytheway and Johnson 1996). These are perhaps more ephemeral devices mobilized in the immediate aftermath of a death and integrated into the ritualized practices of burial. They are forms of death and memory writing that, in the case of cards and wreath inscriptions, precede the permanent writing on the gravestone. Written dedications and memorials, which regularly appear in local newspapers on the anniversary of deaths, mark the time after deaths whilst recalling past lives and relationships. Such inscriptions, preserved on paper, have their own traditions and iconographies where, for instance, personal handwritten words on mass-produced cards appear in relation to printed verses and images of flowers, crosses, prayer books, church windows, gateways and doves (Figure 7.3). They are also subject to a variety of conventions of private and public display, written and intended for readers within particular communities of memory.

We can add that these material messages are also retained and collected for future reference so that cards record shared moments of intense grieving. Alternatively cards and letters received by the bereaved may be stored and kept unopened, only to be read later when a death is less overwhelming. As with many highly personalized, 'ephemeral' instances of materialized memory, such writing has not yet received scholarly attention but we can identify these forms as instances of vernacular texts, comparable to the diaries, notes, letters and poems that Camitta (1993: 228) has examined as 'central to transacting social relationships' and making meaning in social life. Camitta defines vernacular texts as 'neither elite nor institutional' writing that is 'traditional and indigenous to the diverse cultural processes of communities as distinguished from the uniform, inflexible standards of institutions' (1993: 228–9). When applied to the materialized writing of grief, we can recognize these characteristics – the cards and printed memorials mobilize a shared informal discourse drawing upon, but not confined to, canons of literary production, traditions of religious imagery and institutionalized funerary ritual. These are forms of memory making that are woven into and occupy spaces between the formalized rituals that surround death.

Sensations of proximity to deceased relatives and friends are often achieved, in contemporary Western societies, through the written word. Take, for instance, Laurie Sieverts Snyder's photographs, which stand as powerful records of her grandmother's and mother's possessions gathered from her deceased parent's house and including letters; keys to cabinets, drawers and suitcases; eyeglasses; embroidered tablecloths; bandages; books; photographs, official documents. Snyder (1998: 82)

Figure 7.3 Wreath card with a written message left at the graveside after the funeral. Cemetery in Norwich, 1999. Photograph: Dr Nigel Norris.

stated that 'I feel compelled to store these relics of times past' and she has done so in her series of photographs entitled *Some of My Mother's Things* . She confesses that she does not speak or write the language in which her grandmother and mother wrote, yet her photographs are filled with the printed and handwritten words that they had saved on fragments, sheets and piles of papers – sometimes overlapping and obscured by other writings or photographs, others stacked so that their bulk is visible but their words illegible. These are photographs that communicate the materiality of writing and highlight the importance of writing as a means of memory making purely in terms of the physical traces (shapes and unintelligible marks) left by the hands of loved ones. These are the materials and forms of writing, invoking powerful memories of the dead, which are usually eclipsed by publicly sanctioned inscriptions displayed at the graveside.

This chapter has traced some of the ways in which words have been deployed in the service of memory. Central to our argument is the recognition of death-related writing as material and visual forms that supply or amplify the memory making potential of words. We have also emphasized the performative dimensions of writing and speaking in the context of will making and memorial inscription. That writing has been performed, in its execution and reception, tends to connect (or gestures towards the connection of) the bodies of the dying, the dead and the bereaved. Memory writing, in the contexts explored throughout this chapter, emerges as a hybrid form where surfaces of inscription are enmeshed in networks of material objects sustained through embodied practices (including speech). We also note the dynamic aspects of memorial inscriptions in that even when words are 'fixed' at officially sanctioned sites of remembrance, they can be supplemented and 'reinscribed' through further written gestures – as in the case of 'ephemeral' words, which are brought to graves and monuments in the form of cards and letters. Furthermore, material inscriptions are not always assumed to be permanent or even adequate as memory forms. They may be apprehended as insubstantial, as pale traces of persons deceased, as matter that will inevitably dissolve. To appreciate the fluctuating power of written words within memories associated with death we need to attend to their relation to the body, the materials in which they are fashioned, the wider field of material objects in which they are positioned over time and the ways in which they are reframed and drawn into subsequent acts of remembrance.

Notes

1. Canterbury Cathedral Archive and Library, DCb. PRC39/37, 220v. Testamentary, Knowler, 1626.

2. Canterbury Cathedral Archive and Library, DCb. X.11.2, 230v. Testamentary, Wills, 1590.

3. Canterbury Cathedral Archive and Library, DCb. PRC39/42, 72v. Testamentary, White, 1631.

4. Canterbury Cathedral Archive and Library, DCb PRC 39/25, fo.56, 56v. Testamentary, Hailes, 1602.

5. Canterbury Cathedral Archive and Library, DCb. X.11.10, fo.104, Testamentary Nutt, 1607.

eight

Ritualizing Death: Embodied Memories

This chapter explores the ritualized movement of objects and bodies in space, mediating the living and the dead and forming memory processes. Rituals associated with death involve embodied action and the manipulation of material forms and it is the dimensions of memory, embodied in ritualized practices, with which we are concerned. We begin by highlighting processes of ritualization that surround death and involve the orientations and actions of the body as well as material objects. Ritualization is not confined to clearly demarcated phases of ritual but can be seen as a feature of 'everyday' life, in which even the most mundane objects, such as clothing, can facilitate the work of memory. Anthropological studies have identified embodied practice and material culture as central features of memory in non-Western contexts. We discuss instances of these and then suggest ways in which we might view European memory processes, comparatively, in terms of their significant embodied and material dimensions.

Making sense of death-related objects, images and practices involves attending to the context within which they are located, a task often undertaken within ethnographic accounts (see, for example, Du Boulay 1982, Huntington and Metcalf 1979: 56–7, Levi-Strauss 1973: 298–320). However, social actions in the field of death and memory encompass more than just immediate spatially and temporally located acts such as a funeral or the unveiling of a memorial. Rather, memory acts reoccur and are dispersed over time. As we have argued throughout this study, memory making forms processes unfolding within interconnected and shifting social contexts, and these contexts are related via embodied practices and material forms. Anthropologists have attended to ritual events and examined the meanings ascribed to material objects in these settings, but processes of ritualization are not confined to rigidly demarcated ritual times and spaces.

179

Rosaldo (1989) and Parkin (1992) suggest that those funerals that, from anthropological perspectives, seem to reveal culturally specific systems of order might instead be considered as cases where a particular death has been less socially disruptive. Rosaldo, for example, argues that Douglas' *Death in Murelaga* 'captures only one extreme in the range of possible deaths. Putting the accent on the routine aspects of ritual conveniently conceals the agony of . . . unexpected early deaths . . . ' (1989: 13). In place of the self-contained cultural units or discrete phases of action represented in many ethnographic accounts of death ritual, Rosaldo proposes a view of culture which encompasses 'a more porous array of intersections where distinct processes criss-cross from within and beyond its border' (1989: 20). In a similar vein, Serematakis asks us to think in terms of the diffuse ritualization of death, rather than simply demarcated or bounded death rituals. The concept of 'ritualization' here refers to the ways in which death is represented across time in a multiplicity of sites and through a variety of practices. This approach shifts emphasis from the 'public rites' associated with death to those socially meaningful (death related) performances that are situated 'within the flux and contingency of everyday events' (Serematakis 1991: 47). The cultural forms that death assumes are therefore understood as aspects of social and ideological systems that are both pervasive and fluid, rather than confined to fixed, spatial and temporal loci. The ritualization of death as a process encompasses formalized public performances and aspects of 'mundane', everyday practices, mobilizing material objects usually associated with sacred space as well as those located within domestic arenas (Serematakis 1991: 47, Hallam 1996).

In Parkin's view, ritual primarily comprises physical movement and spatial orientation (1992). For instance, in funerary ritual the corpse is oriented and directed through a spatialized route which ends with the burial. Physical movement through material spaces also operates metaphorically within rites of passage to convey movement within social and cosmological space. Parkin's approach seeks to 'extend the spatial idea of ritual to the human body itself, which as well as sometimes physically being moved, can be regarded as subject to journeys and passages even when it remains in one position' (Parkin 1992: 22). Thus it is through spatial movement and orientation that the body is ritually transformed. Temporal transmission is also significant when Parkin argues that objects can embody personhood across time, acting as material markers of identity and memory (see Chapter 2). In situations where individuals are forced to flee their homes 'the body has become a lifeless object incorporating traumatised person-hood' (1999: 315). Here material objects, often hurriedly snatched prior to flight, form foci for the re-articulation or recreation of refugees' personhood undertaken in a new and safer time and place. Under extreme threat, the customary elision of personhood and the body is thus culturally realigned, body becoming object and object standing in for personhood. To grasp this process of memory making, therefore, we need to recognise the ritualized, embodied processes that establish connections across times and spaces. Even the most mundane object, salvaged in situations of danger, can become sacred to those attempting to rebuild future lives and past memories in unfamiliar places.

Our discussion of memory focuses here upon 'ritualization' as embodied acts that create links between different times and spaces. To examine memory from this perspective is to explore emergent social and cultural meanings within linked contexts of performance, which maintain complex relationships between the past and the present. In the formation of memories, then, it is not to 'discrete' material contexts that we should attend but, rather, to the complex interplay between them. Lambek and Antze argue that to remember is to perform an act – 'of commemoration, of testimony, of confession, of accusation' (1996: xxv) – and as practice or performance, such acts locate individuals both temporally and spatially in relation to that which is otherwise set apart from the immediacies of here and now. Memory practices forge connections and have significant social repercussions. Therein lies their power, one that can constitute both a resource and a threat. Memory can be integral to the perceived stability of personal identity across time, as Parkin argues in his account of the objects which displaced persons take with them when they are forced to move from their homes (1999). On the other hand, memory *loss* through Alzheimer's disease can bring about the social death of the individual whose identity is disintegrating. As Lambek and Antze point out: '[i]t is memory and its tokens that provide the substantive grounds for claims to corporateness and continuity' (1996: xxv).

Memory practices can be regarded as attempts to counter loss caused by death, making connections with absent individuals and bringing them into the present; but in so doing they simultaneously evoke the gaps they have left behind (Ash 1996). The construal of continuous kinship with the dead cannot be relegated to the margins of spheres occupied by 'real' social relationships in that the two splice into one another continually (Simpson 1998). Often, to foster connection is to simultaneously evoke absence. Attempting to repair the social and emotional rupture of loss via memory making is also to confirm that loss and to stimulate pain. This is evidenced in data from a study located in a city in the north of England which examined the lives of older people bereaved of their partners of the opposite sex (Hockey, Penhale and Sibley 1999).

Bill, a widower in his late sixties, had been bereaved of his wife, Edna, through cancer eighteen months before he was interviewed. He was continuing to remember her via a sequence of ritualized practices, some of his own choosing, some in deliberate fulfilment of the requests she had made for, faced with the prospect of dying, Edna had laid plans for her own memorialization. In the sitting room where he was interviewed Bill drew attention to the potted Devonshire violets which she had grown:

> She was very much into growing these violet pot plants . . . there's a lot through in kitchen there. I've still . . . had the last one she . . . rooted it just when she . . . while she was ill . . . and I've looked after . . . I don't want to lose 'em now, they're part of me, you see. But whether it's a wise thing to do or not, I don't know. When I was talking to my youngest son yesterday, he said, 'What you want is me mother back, in't it?' I said, 'Aye, but that'll never happen'.

Although the plants were a powerful living reminder of the vital physical presence Edna had in the home, in his narrative, Bill recognized sensations of pain arising out of his maintenance of her 'presence'. Placed on the windowsill in front of his customary armchair, the plants framed his view of the outside world. As he told the story of their relationship and her recent death, its details were fleshed out in relation to the chairs, tables, pictures and plants that provided the material setting of the interview.

Bill sustained memories of Edna as an outcome of his response to the requests she had made, all of which aimed to preserve memories of her after her death. For example, Bill and Edna had been judges in competitions between local gardening societies and she wanted a memorial trophy shield to be donated in her name: Bill said, 'That was requested, Edna's request . . . she wanted to do that . . . the thing that she talked about when she was dying, you know. Weeks before, she said she wanted us to do that, didn't want to be forgotten.' He went on to say, 'In her will she give me six [months] . . . she specified in her will I'd got to dispose of her clothing in six months'. Bill said that all of the clothes had gone – 'I think I've done pretty well, really' – although he had kept the T-shirts she had bought as souvenirs from their foreign holidays, another source of Bill's highly valued memories. Furthermore, he intended to give Edna's jewellery to a grand-daughter and with regard to Edna's watch he said: 'it still ticks, still the battery that's ticking away and nobody said "Could they have it?" so I thought, "Well I'll keep that . . .".'

In this case Edna had communicated three further specifications to her husband before she died which concerned her funeral and those she would leave behind. At the time of the interview Bill had fulfilled two out of the three, but it had been emotionally difficult for him. On this point he drew in supporting evidence from his elderly mother: 'me mother, she'll say sometimes . . . she says "You did everything which Edna asked you to do, didn't you" . . . and she said, "It couldn't have been easy".'

First Edna had told Bill that he would not be in a position to entertain people on the day of the funeral and so he was to organize a buffet for eighty people at the local pub. She said he would find the money to pay for it at the back of her purse – and sure enough Bill found the money there. Second Edna had told him that she wanted him to scatter her ashes on a promontory of the local coastline. He was not to spread them on the beach but to throw them into the wind. She told him, 'I want to be free, I want to be like a bird.' Afterwards Bill was to go to a pub on the coast and have the same meal which the two of them would always have after their New Year's Day walks by the sea. Third, he was to visit her brother in New Zealand who had been ill, and this request he had yet to carry out: 'But whether I shall get I don't know . . . it's a long way to fly when you . . . I've never done it non-stop . . . and I don't know if I could face a stopover on me own or not . . . it's still very early, you know.'

In fulfilling Edna's 'requests', Bill reconfigured the key social connections which once made up their shared married life. Through a process of embodied, spatialized movements Bill brought versions of the past into the present via a set of ritualized practices. Gatherings at the pub and visits to the coast had once been regular features of Bill and Edna's life together. In repeating these actions after her death their meaning was both transformed and intensified. The disrupted annual routine of the past – a walk by the sea followed by the 'same' meal at the 'same' pub – provided the vehicle through which the ritual disposal of Edna's ashes could be made memorable. For Bill to perform these actions was to enact the ritualized disposal his wife had mapped out during the period before her death.

In that Bill had willed himself to carry out all of her various instructions, Edna acquired considerable post-mortem agency. Temporally and spatially separated, the couple can be seen to have enacted a set of shared memory-making practices that took place in carefully targeted spaces: the local pub, a key coastal location that had been linked with a significant calendrical marker of time's passage, and the celebratory meal that the two of them would eat in a specific setting each year. That he had had difficulty in carrying out these requests and considered her third request to be particularly challenging gave them added import. That Edna had specifically laid down her instructions, and indeed paid for them to be carried out was, for Bill, not only testimony of her courage in facing death but also a challenge and a specific, previously anticipated connection with her.

This chapter highlights the uses of 'mundane' spaces and material forms within ritualized memory-making – or at least argues that investments in memories surrounding death work across and connect formalized ritual practices and 'sacred' spaces with those actions (and aspects of material environments) which are usually considered to be 'routine'. Following Serematakis (1991) this approach foregrounds the significance, in memories, of everyday social practices that are commonly assumed not to be death related. Recent ethnographic data, which reveal patterns of bereavement in northern England (Hockey, Penhale and Sibley, 1999), reinforce our discussion of Western contexts where an apparent profusion of spaces linked to the dead emerges, mapped out by people through highly personalized memory practices – these spaces may acquire sacred qualities alongside, or as counterbalances to, institutionalized or officially sanctioned spaces dedicated to the dead (see Chapter 4). While it might seem, in the late twentieth century, that death has been sequestrated to the cemetery, the mortuary and the funeral director's premises, memory investment in spaces, material objects and habitual actions that sustain connections with the deceased constitute a much broader field of ritualization.

Rosaldo has suggested that a death ritual can be understood as 'a single step in a lengthy series of ritual and everyday events' (1989: 17–18). It is this interconnected series that we wish to foreground in order to explore the ways in which embodied social practice can engender memories and foster remembering. We show how memory can be 'amassed' in the body through conventionalized gestures and performances, a 'mnemonics of the body' that enables the recollection and re-enactment of the past in the present (Connerton 1989: 74). Although rituals are subject to change, anthropological accounts often reveal their characteristic rules that demarcate spaces and guide embodied action (Parkin 1992). This perspective can be used to address a wide range of rituals, from public ritual and ceremonial, including funerals, pilgrimage and ritualised visits to sacred sites and memorials – to those associated with personal bereavement, for example, the changed use of domestic space, deathbed ritual and the re-enactment of a dead individual's habitual actions, such as cooking, gardening, or paperwork. Through historical and contemporary examples we discover the multi-dimensional nature of the material forms through which memory is evoked and come to understand, for example, the interplay of the treasured effects of the dead with times of calendrical or life cycle significance, as well as the collective processes through which the dead come to be commemorated. The following sections present and compare ethnographic examples of non-Western and Western death rituals, focusing upon bodily actions within their material environments. We then move on to examine processes of ritualization that indicate that the actions of the body in memory evocation are not confined to non-Western or pre-industrial societies, rather they come to form meaningful responses to death in contemporary European contexts.

Death Rituals: Cross-cultural Perspectives

Here we engage with debates about the nature and role of 'ritual' as a way of making connections, or of establishing orientations of the body in relation to the past and in anticipation of the future. In this section we refer to particular anthropological studies to consider the ways in which bodily and material dimensions of death and ritual have been addressed in non-Western settings. Our discussion is informed by Nora's proposition that embodied memories have been sustained mainly as part of 'environments' within oral or 'traditional cultures' (1989). Our references, in this section, to Western practices associated with death and memory prefigure later sections of this chapter which argue that the body, as a significant site of recall, has not been fully displaced by what Nora (1989) defines as modern forms of materialized memory sites (such as archives and monuments).

Bloch's ethnographically grounded account of memory and identity among the Sadah of the Yemen and the Bicolano of the Philippines, places analytic emphasis upon varying conceptions of memory (1996: 215–33). Bloch (1996: 218) reminds us that in Western societies, for example, we find two traditions: the Platonic notion of memory as the recall of 'original and unchanging truth' and the Aristotelian view of memory as built up over time in relation to an external world. The relationships between material forms and mental representations cannot therefore be taken as a given, but need to be teased out as an important aspect of the context of remembering. Bloch's non-Western data reveal the Sadah belief in innate, internal memory. They perceive themselves to be not only intimately linked with a particular lineage but also profoundly influenced by the attributes of forebears in terms of their own potential constitution (1996: 219–20). For them, memorizing Quranic texts (the fixed words of God) is a process that preserves connection with the divine. This text must be instilled, then, within the self, in ground already prepared for it through kinship connection. By contrast the impoverished Bicolano understand their connections with kin in terms of adaptation and openness to change. They *become* social individuals by responding to the vagaries of a more powerful external world – and their memories are mental inscriptions which overlay one another, each set of recollections potentially obscuring the previous one.

With reference to his fieldwork among the Merina of Malagasy, Bloch identifies combinations of these two conceptions of memory (1996: 226). His discussion is highly suggestive when it comes to wider questions of ritual and memory. The Merina, like the Bicolano, are open to change. Their responsiveness to the external world is a source of transformative power, and for them, as Bloch argues, 'kinship is created little by little throughout life and is only fixed after death in the final placing of the dead in the tomb' (1996: 225). Thus connectedness is *created* – ultimately, via the interment of the dried bones of their predecessors in megalithic tombs. While the living are open to transformation – for example, through adoption or the choice between connection with their father's or their mother's line – the dead fuse with the stone of the tomb, fixed absolutely in the space associated with a descent group's social identity. The soft, wet, mobile body is ritually separated at death from the boniness of the skeleton, its subsequent dryness then becoming one with the stone of the ancestral tomb which in its turn merges with localized Merina territory.

For the Merina, then, 'events flow round them' but they also retain a presence in the future, along with their forebears through their maintenance of the material structure of the tombs. While the dead are ritually opposed to the vital and responsive living Merina, they are not their polar opposites. Rather, this relationship is a gradual process of transformation which allows the memory of 'immobile ancestral traditions' (Bloch, 1996: 228) to become ineradicably sedimented into the bodies of the living. After their deaths they, like their ancestors, will become as one with the stone megaliths that house their bones. Bloch states that a Merina tomb is 'not a memorial of the dead, it is a memorial of the way the living have been abolished by transcendental stone' (1996: 228). Thus, for example, the receiving of blessing which takes place at the site of the tomb is a ritual practice involving contact between the soft flesh of the living and the dry stone which encompasses Merina forbears. This 'process of gradual invasion' is transformative. Over time it 'abolishes' the living Merina whose malleable identity, at death, becomes ultimately fixed and enduring through fusion with the materiality of the tomb and the land (1996: 227–8). In this account, the relationships between the living and the dead are formulated across the life course as they move gradually towards eventual fusion with one another. Crucial to this formulation of these relationships is the way in which memory and personhood are understood. As Bloch (1996: 229) notes, forms of memory which extend beyond the boundaries of an individual life are inextricably linked up with the way in which the nature of the self and its relationship with the wider social environment are understood.

Further anthropological studies have stressed the significance of bodily and material dimensions in non-Western death rituals. Turner's work, for instance, explored the bipolar nature of ritual symbols that combine the physiological/emotional and the abstract/conceptual domains in African contexts (1967: 19–17). Here, the potency of ritual symbols was evidenced in the effective fusion of the physiological and the conceptual that naturalized culturally specific sets of meanings. For example, in his account of the Ndembu women's fertility ritual *Isoma*, Turner described the specific symbolic resonances of each of its constituent elements for the Ndembu (1969). *Isoma*, performed as a cure for infertility mobilised symbolic forms known as blazes. These were perceived to have an embodied, material significance, and referred to the marks made by a hunter that allowed him to find his way between the unknown territory of the bush and the village. Blazes had further metaphoric resonance, connoting links between the immediate social world and the dangerous domain of the society's dead members. Given that the dead, as 'shades', could cause infertility if they were neglected by the living, the *Isoma* ritual was used to reconnect with and placate the dead. Women wishing to become pregnant would thus establish contact with their deceased kin. The desired changes in a woman's body were brought about through the blazes that linked her with the powerful domain of the shades. Turner views the restoration of fertility via re-connection with the dead as a means to manage broader social tensions between a woman's natal village and her husband's family.

In this case, the manipulation of ritual symbols re-established links between living bodies and the shades so that the Ndembu dead continued to exert influence upon fertility and reproduction. Rituals such as *Isoma*, then, integrated the dead into the present and anticipated the future as experienced by the living. If, as Turner argues, all rituals are rites of passage: whether they concern life course transitions, healing or seasonal change, in each case the past, the present and the future all come into play. Activating a symbolic yet materially grounded apparatus, rites of passage mark out transformations from a previous social status to a future one.

Parkin (1992) has more recently foregrounded the physicality of ritual and bodily movements that comprise particular ritual performances. Movements combined with their imaginative effects are key dimensions in rituals understood as 'the capacity to create and act through idioms of passage, movement, including exchange, journey, axis, concentricism, and up-and-down directions' (Parkin 1992: 18). Highlighting variation in ritual performances and the possibilities for spatial reshaping, Parkin indicates the scope for performers' agency, possibly in the formation of new ritual practices. In the example of the Giriama people who live along the coast of Kenya, burial ritual takes one of three different forms, depending upon which subgroup is performing the rite (Parkin 1992: 20). For example, among the group who live in the agricultural zone, converts to Christianity literally jostle for position in the procession of pallbearers so that they can say prayers before the body is speedily buried and the individual's transition to the world of ancestors accomplished. In addition, the varying spatial alignment of bodies reflects not only gender differences but also the local diversity of religious and cultural identities. Indeed members of the same family group may belong to different religions with the result that multiple death rituals can take place simultaneously, but in different homesteads.

The movement Parkin describes here is a bodily enactment; but he also highlights the centrality of metaphoric movement. Even when the body remains in a particular position, it can, via ritual engagement, move through 'journeys and passages' (1992: 22). The power of ritual therefore, in his view, operates through the body, not only in terms of the movement of individual participants in space but also in the 'ordering' of the body – for example, via bodily partition practices such as the dispersal and burial of human remains. An emphasis upon bodily movement and orientation can also be detected in contemporary Western practices where individuals appropriate traditional ritual acts when disposing of a relative's ashes, in ways which facilitate a realignment of their relationship with a deceased relative (see Chapter 4). Western technological changes in the manner of disposing of the dead via cremation have opened up opportunities for individuals to reinvent death rituals (Davies 1997: 28). In these instances, there may also be a negotiation of ritual 'ruling' (see Parkin 1992: 24) where spatially located practices of disposal are contested. We can see this in the unauthorized burying of ashes in institutionalized sites of memory and in privately organized scatterings in venues usually associated with leisure activities.

Roach (1996) also addresses embodied action in death rituals performed in circum-Atlantic settings. He examines the ways in which elements of ritual might create or recreate relationships between the living and the dead, and so repair the social gaps left behind after a death. Discussing public funeral processions and carnival, he uses the concept of substitution or surrogation to describe how the lost but remembered past is reinstated within the present via the actions of living bodies or through effigies of the dead. For example, in African-American jazz funerals in contemporary New Orleans the coffin bearing the corpse is surrounded by a brass band and mourners from the wider community, standing as an 'embodiment of loss' which is both material and symbolic (Roach 1996: 14). Once the body is 'cut loose', or allowed to proceed on its way with closer family members, there is a 'burst of joyous music, dance, and humour' that allows a renewal of cultural codes through the movement of the living bodies (Roach 1996: 61–2). And in this context festive celebration becomes a form of embodied countermemory that resists 'Eurocentric' forms of memorialization (Roach 1996: 61–2).

To read replication or repetition into these performances would, however, be to ignore the selectivity of memory, the prejudices, fears and aspirations which result in the privileging or recasting of certain recollections at the cost of others. As Roach argues, '[n]ew traditions may ... be invented and others overturned. The paradox of the restoration of behaviour resides in the phenomenon of repetition itself: no action or sequence of actions may be performed exactly the same way twice; they must be reinvented or recreated at each appearance' (1996: 29). Ritual therefore comprises creative forms of substitution that, for example, form genealogical links acting to mitigate the sense of cultural indeterminacy following a loss. Important in Roach's account of the ritualization of death and memory is the notion of performance that situates memories within the body's actions, yet acknowledges the 'invented' quality of embodied recollections. In this view, memories are discursively transmitted via embodied practices that serve both to incorporate and disseminate particular representations of whoever and whatever has been lost.

The anthropological studies examined here indicate the diverse ways in which bodily actions and aspects of material cultures are brought into play within rituals of death. Different anthropological approaches highlight the various materialized relations that have been sustained between the living and the dead in non-Western settings. Thus Bloch (1996: 227) explores bodily processes whereby, across the life course, 'the living become the dead and the dead become the living'. Turner's account of ritual processes reveals the interconnected domains of the living and the dead, which are symbolically reconfigured to sustain the bodily health and fertility of a social group. Again, in Parkin's work there is an emphasis on the actions, movement and spatial positioning of bodies as central to ritual. In Roach's analysis, the bodies of the living and the dead are performed in funerary ritual to both transmit and renew embodied memories.

From cross-cultural comparisons of death rituals we can gather that the body and its material surroundings become significant in the orientation of persons, both deceased and alive, in relation to their past, present and future. Here we can note Bloch's observations that 'there is no one way of relating to the past and the future and therefore of being in history. There is, therefore, no one way by which one wants to inscribe memory in the public world' (1996: 229). While the embodied, material dimensions of death rituals are examined within anthropological studies based in non-Western contexts, these dimensions are also deserving of attention in European settings. In the following section we provide an extended discussion of Seremetakis' anthropological study (1991) based in rural Greece, which focuses upon women's engagement with death and memory. Throughout this study she highlights the analytic importance of the concept of ritualization (rather than ritual) in understanding significant embodied practices in a twentieth-century context. We then consider the positioning of the body and material aspects of death within ritualized memory making in further Western settings shaped by women.

Processes of Ritualization: Women Making Memory

As already argued, static models of ritual as an event fixed in time and space have been criticized as limited accounts that fall a long way short of insiders' experiences and, in particular, side-step their emotional responses (Rosaldo 1989). Similarly, Seremetakis (1991: 48) has problematized the theorizing of death rituals as discrete units, arguing that the 'performative elaboration [of death] can haunt society and become an essential collective metaphor of social experience beyond the margins of ceremonial performance'. In her critique of anthropological accounts of death ritual in traditional societies, Seremetakis highlights the neglected issues of change and agency within processes of ritualization and points out the limitations of approaches that make spatially and temporally bounded rituals their sole focus. Therefore her account of mourning among the women of Inner Mani embraces a diverse range of interrelated practices such as: 'dreaming, lament improvisation, care and tending of olive trees, burying and unburying the dead, and the historical inscription of emotions and senses on a landscape of persons, things and places' (1991: 1). Significant within Seremetakis' account are the improvised laments of women at the time of death, yet these are woven into a rich field of social relations and cultural representations which extend well beyond phases of formalised ritual events.

Throughout her ethnographic fieldwork and over time Seremetakis recognized that her difficulty in identifying the 'beginning' of ritualization processes reflects their temporal and spatial complexity and lack of linearity. A system of 'warnings' indicates an impending death and initiate the process of ritualization. The sound of a bird call, for example, heard by a relative can act as an initial trigger for the ritualization of a subsequent death, although such signs are not detected by the dying person. After the death has occurred, funeral laments, the verses of which are the province of women, provide key cultural vehicles that allow emotional power and bodily symbolism to be combined. Through these, women are able to make truth claims, a form of resistance to long-term processes of colonization and a way of grounding their historical consciousness. Further, to 'cry one's fate' is not a solitary practice; rather, the expression of pain through sound and at the site of the body creates affective communities among women. It is the exchange of 'help' that binds such communities of pain, a principle that informs the practice of agricultural labour and is key to the tasks of disposal, from laying out the body through to exhuming it.

Lamenting, which produces 'proper pain', involves 'linguistic, acoustic and corporeal interaction' between a solo mourner and a chorus, all of whom are women, several of whom will step into the solo role in the course of the ritual (Seremetakis 1991: 100). Without a chorus it is felt that singing cannot express sufficient intensity of pain, the chorus and their responses serving to validate the pain expressed by the soloist. It is through a shared 'screaming the dead' that the 'good death' can be produced, an acoustic and bodily performance that both separates mourners from the rest of society and sacralizes the relationship between the living and the polluted dead in such a way that shared substance with the corpse is declared. This is affirmed repeatedly within the lament through the phrase 'come close', an invitation to establish contact with the dead and the affective space of the ritual. Those with few relatives to survive them are at risk of 'silent' death, a death ritual at which there is no lament, or a lament sung without the 'help' of a chorus. This is the bad death of those who will be forgotten as members of the community.

Ritualized disposal also involves exhumation, which allows for the possibility of post-mortem residues, traces of which are remembered or reconfigured, often at the site of the body and the grave. Referring to Hertz (1960 [1907]), Seremetakis (1991: 177) says: 'what appears as separation is in effect a series of gradual transformations that maintain the efficacy of the body as a social nexus, a signifying centre, while endowing it with a new value.' Thus the dead are remembered through the exhumation of their bones, a process that resituates them in time and space. Indeed the affective community of mourning women is intimately connected with a community of the dead who return, repeatedly, through the practice of exhumation at successive bereavements. Shared pain and desire provide the emotional substance of the relationship between the living and the dead. Each exhumation intensifies the memories of those who mourn and are mourned for, their identities encoded in the laments, some of which are perceived as part of a tradition reaching over the past 200 years.

Exhumation is, therefore, a practice through which memories of the dead are consolidated. Bones are brought up out of the damp and dark earth, carefully cleaned and made visible, memorable, in the bright light of the sun. Although this encounter with the corpse triggers intense grief, the dead are not seen as annihilated. Rather they are reconstituted, materially, the residue of the body evidencing the past moral status of the deceased; for example, black undissolved flesh is seen to indicate evil actions performed when alive. Once exhumed, the dead can become an important force within the everyday lives of survivors. In these contexts of embodied memory making, the active social presence of the dead is something that is welcomed by the living.

Seremetakis' analysis foregrounds the temporal dimension of death ritual. Initiated by the warning, something communicated by ambiguous signs to persons on the periphery of the death itself, temporal passage is alluded to in the funeral lament that also has the mnemonic capacity to create oral history. Seremetakis (1991: 105) notes how women repeat the last words of the verses she has taped and played back to them, 'taking it in their mouths as shared substance'. Words thus shift away from something inscribed to something incorporated through performance (see Connerton 1989). After burial and the 'last separation' of the deceased from the mourners, women wander through the graveyard 'reading' the dead, and their places in the memory of the living, from the signs upon the graves. In this way, they talk to the dead and introduce one another to those who have gone before.

Material objects, including aspects of the corpse itself, are made meaningful as part of memory processes that extend over time. These are also imbued with emotional resonance, a quality of memory objects which we see in further social contexts. Seremetakis (1991: 217), for example, refers to 'an archaeology of feeling' to encapsulate the process whereby Inner Mani women store memories of the dead in the 'ornaments', which everywhere betoken kinship and connection via the dressing or adornment of the living body, and other material forms such as olive trees and towers. To divest oneself of ornament – for example the red strip of cloth on the hem of a dark skirt, which signals a woman whose kin are all alive – is to reveal one's losses in death; and in death rituals, mourners are reinvested with 'emotions and artefacts of feeling such as language and narrative' (Seremetakis 1991: 215).

Seremetakis has, then, identified a diverse field of discursively related bodies, material objects, visual signs and words which comprise mourning and shape memories. She describes practices within this field as forms of cultural empowerment exercised by women and as articulations, from the 'margins', which develop in the context of modernisation. We move on now to discuss instances of ritualised memory-making which are not formalised as part of public death ritual but, nevertheless, come to assume the status of meaningful practices especially from women's perspectives.

Juliet Ash (1996) has provided a personal account of the way in that her dead partner's ties enfold both his presence and his absence, forming a materially grounded, sensual metaphor which encapsulates the embodied nature of remembering. Parkin (1999) has also described the way in which children's clothing, nappies, toys and favourite cushions were washed and packed by mothers at Auschwitz as they prepared to move with their children to a new camp. Charged with the tasks of social continuity, these mothers were in a sense conducting rites of anticipatory mourning in that a change of camp signalled a strong possibility of extermination. Past life and future life were thus condensed in what Parkin describes as 'tasks of tender enfolding' (1999: 314). These instances of memory making, which involve the body and its material environments in sensations of recall, seem intimately related to gendered domains of bodily care, clothing, domestic work and emotional expressivity. Memories of the deceased sustained by women through actions within inhabited domestic spaces and via habitually familiar objects would appear to be pronounced, yet marginalized in relation to more publicly visible ritualized practices.

As noted in Chapter 5, Carol Mara (1998) has described how parental bereavement can reconfigure the relationship between material spaces and times. Her narrative provides personal retrospective reflections on a series of memories experienced after the death of her son. Mara writes that, when she sees particular garments in the shops, she experiences a temporal relocation and responds to them as objects of desire for her thirteen-year-old son. And simultaneously she recalls his death and the three years that have since been added to the time of his 'life/ death' that might have led him to reject her choice of clothing. Enfolded in his remaining and his remembered clothing are the details of his death: some items returned to her after being analysed as 'forensic evidence', and some items returned but with the marks of the roadside accident that killed him (see Chapter 5).

Here Mara describes how, among her son's other clothes, there are some that she has lovingly washed, ironed and stored; some she has enclosed in plastic to preserve the smell of his body; some she has reanimated by handing them down to other family members. Through their proximity to her son's body in life and in death these material items sustain Mara's memories of her son despite the passage of time. Yet, as Mara concludes, '[g]radually, I know, I will divest the drawers of these clothes when they no longer hold the terrible potency that they assumed one Saturday in September. But not just yet' (1998: 60). The title of Mara's account, 'Divestments', captures an anticipated act of deliberate forgetting, as Mara lives with the hope that she will be able to finally remove the clothing from their chest of drawers.

This account is highly gendered and is indicative of processes of ritualization that draw the dead into memory in quite specific ways, and in contexts which unfold beyond public, institutionalized acts of memorialization. As materials from the everyday world are drawn into ritualized memory making, their resonance and emotional affectivity are intensified and inflected with personal meanings to form private sites of women's remembrance. As accounts such as Ash's (1996) and

Mara's (1998) indicate, fabrics, in their very materiality, are situated in relation to times and memories. Metonymically partaking of the body's substance, they remain as fragments that highlight the transience of human life. And yet, in their persistent presence, they stand for those who are 'gone' and thereby offer some resistance to the erasure of persons from memory over time. Thus, these materials, as mementoes of the dead, also retain a memento mori aspect, orienting survivors towards their own deaths, reminding them of the fate of their own possessions and raising questions about the meaning of the memento or the heirloom for those who survive. Even Mara, so intensely confronted by her son's recent death, refers to his remaining clothes as 'the pile of used fabric that in time they will become' (1998: 60). In this statement lies anticipatory anxiety provoked when the future anonymity of highly charged personal objects is imagined.

The materiality of the body and its linkages with other material objects is pivotal in these processes of Western ritualization. The ritualization of death in the sustenance of memory draws upon notions of bodily continuity with material surrounds (such as clothing and domestic spaces) to provide connections between the past and the present. This embodied, materialized linkage of bodies past and present is also a feature of memory-making in public spaces such as cemeteries (see Chapter 6). Thus, the various positionings of the body as a memory resource is evidenced, not only in anthropological accounts of non-Western death ritual but also, as the work of Serematakis, Ash and Mara suggests, in further social settings, where women's ritualised memory-making is significant.

Ritualization in Western Contexts: Messages from the 'Margins'

The centrality of the bodies of both the living and the dead in ritualized actions, which forge memory connections, is thus apparent in certain Western contexts. To further interpret these dimensions of contemporary death and memory, however, we need to place them in relation to what have been identified as predominant features of modern Western memory. Nora, for instance, argues that modern memory has been divested of bodily and collective dimensions to become 'indirect' and deeply reliant upon 'exterior' material sites of memory such as museums, archives, cemeteries, monuments (Nora 1989: 12) (see Chapter 5). Furthermore, the emergence of modern memory is seen to take place within the 'deritualization' of Western societies, so that these externalized sites of memory become 'devotional institutions', marking 'the rituals of a society without ritual' (Nora 1989: 12).

This analysis sets up stark contrasts between non-Western societies (where 'real memory' is embodied, 'social and unviolated') and Western societies (where traditional memory is lost) (Nora 1989: 8). If, in the modernized, rapidly changing societies of the West we no longer 'live within memory' through embodied gestures where '[m]emory installs remembrance within the sacred' (Nora 1989: 8–9), then Western forms of memory become radically different to those experienced in 'so-called primitive or archaic societies' (Nora 1989: 8–9). Hervieu-Léger elucidates this argument with regard to the implications of modernization for Western social memory:

> The differentiation of a specialized religious field, the gradual pluralization of institutions, communities and systems of religious thought historically – and exactly – correspond to the differentiation of total social memory into a plurality of specialized circles of memory. Industrialisation, urbanisation, the spread of trade and interchange mark the waning of the social influence of religion and the piecemeal destruction of communities, societies and even ideologies based on memory. (Hervieu-Léger 2000: 127)

If, in Western modernity, we have seen the breakdown of collective memory, this is linked to 'secularization' and 'rationalization'; and the consequences for new forms of memory are twofold. On one level, memory becomes subject to homogenizing processes. For instance, technologies of mass communication and media image production lead to a saturation, tending to 'obliterate meaningful continuity' (Hervieu-Léger 2000: 128). The immediacy of vast amounts of information and images is overwhelming and focuses attention on a perpetual present: ['t]he image enables any event or any catastrophe wherever it occurs to be instantly available to all and in the process immediately neutralizes whatever preceded it' (Hervieu-Léger 2000: 128). On another level, however, there is an increasing fragmentation of memory for individuals and different social groups that seek to construct and represent their pasts in a variety of ways and in the face of rapid social change. Recognizing these apparently contradictory tendencies, Hervieu-Léger goes further to propose that in contemporary societies there are socially significant attempts to re-constitute meaningful memory experiences:

forms of compensation . . . develop in reaction to the symbolic vacuum resulting from the loss in depth and in unity of collective memory in modern societies. And the reaction is the sharper because the gouging of memory, as experienced, is contradicted by the subjective sense of duration felt by individuals who are now in the main longer-lived. It is a contradiction that must be resolved by invoking substitute memories, multiple, fragmentary, diffuse and disassociated as they are, but which promise that something of collective identification, on which the production and reproduction of social bonds depends, can be saved.'
(Hervieu-Léger 2000: 141)

The impulse imaginatively to reconstruct means of connection with the past is then heightened when continuity of social identity is threatened by the speed of change. Finally, Hervieu-Léger asserts that while the 'imaginative search for partial continuity has escalated', new Western forms of memory making are *partial* because there is no way back to a 'total' or seemingly unified social memory. If the constitution of diverse means of memory making in Western contexts takes place in relation to sensations of loss and change as Hervieu-Léger indicates, then experiences of death would seem to further heighten the search for continuity.

We would argue that the imaginative constitution of and investment in personally meaningful memories occurs markedly in contemporary death-related practices. And in attending to the resources through which memory links with the dead are generated, we see that there is a proliferation of practices that engage bodies and their familiar material 'extensions' (for example, clothing). That, in the contemporary West, the body has become a major 'site of memory' is acknowledged (Lambek and Antze 1996: xiii) alongside the recognition that bodily inscriptions (such as tattoos) are now perceived, in a wildly fluctuating world, to be more enduring projections of self (Mellor and Shilling 1997). These are not the 'exterior' materialized sites of memory to which Nora refers. Rather, these are sites of subjective involvement that seek to provide means to 'live within memory' and also, when engaged in ritualized processes, they acquire something of the sacred – features of memory that Nora implies are confined to pre-modern or non-Western societies. The mobilization of bodies and their associated material possessions in memory linkages with the dead constitutes part of the imaginative searching for continuity that Hervieu-Léger sees as characteristic of contemporary memory. Embodied memory making might also register as attempts to 'reconsecrate the profane', a tendency that Mellor and

Shilling identify in 'advanced modern forms of sociality.' (1997: 26, 161)

We argue, then, that ritualized embodied acts of memory are significant in what have become a diverse range of Western cultural practices associated with death and the maintenance of social relationships with the dead. Our final example of memory making through the ritualized actions of clairvoyants in contemporary England reveals the ways in which the body and material objects figure prominently in the connections made between the deceased and their survivors.

The work of clairvoyants, as informal ritual specialists, can be described as the performance of spoken narratives through readings of the living body that activate memory processes and work to redefine or clarify their clients' personal and social relationships, including relationships with the departed (Hallam, Hockey and Howarth 1999; Hallam 2001). A study conducted by Hallam, which began in 1993, focused on the activities of clairvoyants and their clients in an East Midlands town in England, and revealed that clairvoyants are regularly consulted at times of life crisis: when relationships have broken down, during periods of sickness and after the deaths of relatives (see Hallam 2001). As in the context that Serematakis (1991) discusses, it is women who are predominantly involved in the ritualized processes of reading the past and the future at the site of the body during phases of personal tension, anxiety or change. However, in this case it is not the dead but the living body and its associated objects such as rings and watches that provide the material substance or grounding for the spoken narratives that connect women not only to the living but also the dead.

Clairvoyants perform their readings in their homes or in the houses of clients. The domestic settings of the kitchen or sitting room are temporarily transformed into ritual spaces in which the client's life is 'told' using a range of symbolic tools, from tarot cards to crystals. The palms of the hands, under the gaze of the clairvoyant become visible maps of the life the client has led and is about to face. Alternatively, or in addition, the clairvoyant will offer to read the client by holding and absorbing 'impressions' from a personal possession that has been in close bodily contact with the client. The clairvoyant's ability to see and sense events and relationships that are remote in time (which have either happened in the past or are about to unfold in the future) is crucial in her task: that is, to provide a reading which will be effective in helping a client to reorient herself in the present.

The names of deceased relatives and their messages to the client often enter the clairvoyant's reading. Clients are sometimes prompted with questions about relatives or friends who have 'passed away', so clients tell versions of their own memories, and these are further incorporated into the reading. Deceased persons associated with the client might be detected in tarot cards or traces of them seen in crystal balls by the clairvoyant. Overall, the effect of such ritualized readings is to provide clients with a life story to which a client will often respond by searching and reworking her memories in the context of the present. The reworking of the past through ritually reconstituted memories further serves to situate the client in relation to her projected or desired future.

Clairvoyants' practices and their participation in ritualized readings of the body, which shape memories of the dead, have a deeper history. Techniques used to contact the dead, and to nourish memories of them, extend back to the nineteenth century through the development of spiritualism. The materialization of spirits was sought by mediums in the 1870s at seances that would bring the departed powerfully back into view (Owen 1989). In this context, the perceived receptivity of the female body to the spirit world facilitated connections between the living and the dead. Fascination with the 'body' of the spirit and its visual or material traces was amplified in spirit photography (on the latter, cf. Roberts 1998), and the development of technologies, such as the telegraph, devoted to the transmission of auditory messages between the spatially separated living, ran parallel to the medium's reception of the temporally distant dead. Thus the system of sensation and perception that was expressed through spiritualism, together with technologies available for the linking of different spaces and times in the present, reinforced perceptions of the dead as accessible entities, available for recall in the eyes and bodily sensations of the living. The materiality of the devices used by mediums accentuated the tangible aspects of the departed. As Peters notes, '[m]ediums employed a diversity of media for spanning the chasm, including table turning, writing, speaking, drawing, singing, dancing, the displacement of animate and inanimate objects, and musical instruments' (Peters 1999: 97).

Winter identifies a growth in spiritualism in England during and immediately after the First World War, which, he argues, was a means for bereaved survivors to cope with extensive human losses (Winter 1998). Public interest in communication with the dead intensified and facing the trauma of war and mass death, women and men were 'prepared to go beyond conventional materialism and theology' to maintain communication with their lost relatives (1998: 54). The ability to contact or see material traces of the dead influenced certain forms of commemoration after the war and here Winter refers to spirit photographs taken in London in 1922. During the ritualized two-minute silence observed by the masses gathered at Whitehall on Remembrance Day, these photographs captured what were seen as spirits floating above the crowds. Such forms of memory making were registered through visually sustained contact with the departed and were underpinned, in Winter's view, by recourse, to 'the magical and the mythical realm' during a socially and emotionally difficult period of physical destruction and loss (Winter 1998: 76).

While not all contemporary clairvoyants are mediums, some do seek to develop their capacities as 'channels' for communication with the dead. Late twentieth-century spirituality and the persistence or reinvention of magical practices, such as clairvoyant readings, offer alternative means of sustaining memories of the dead. It is through ritualized practices involving the living body, as well as contact with material objects and media, that manifestations of the dead are rendered visible and therefore available as memory resources. Clairvoyants' practices involve a predominantly oral form of memory fashioning and transmission that is firmly rooted in the embodied experiences of their clients. But they are also crucially reliant upon a particular conception of the material object world in that objects of both a mundane and a magical nature are seen, within the clairvoyant's vision, as part of an interconnected network of relations which spans spaces and times. As Luhrmann has observed, with regard to twentieth-century Western magic:

> The magician's world view is an interdependent whole, a web of which no strand is autonomous. Mind and body, galaxy and atom, sensation and stimulus, are intimately bound . . . Individual objects are not fixed but fluctuating, constantly responding to their surroundings, bundles of relationships, rather than settled points. To treat objects as isolated and unique is a Western distortion in magicians' eyes. (1989: 118)

Within the ritual spaces marked out by clairvoyants for the purposes of reading or telling, bodies and their associated material objects are perceived to be enmeshed in past, present and future relationships and events. It is this conception of sustained and emotionally meaningful connection, registering through the material world, that establishes clairvoyants' readings as a potent means by which the dead are maintained in social lives and living memories. It is this framework of understanding that, however marginalized in relation to dominant discourses of science or rationality, might provide tangible access to the dead otherwise unavailable within sceptical, secularized societies. Furthermore, the ritualized readings that clairvoyants provide for their clients do not remain within a 'bounded' ritual space; rather the readings are remembered by the client and retold in further settings, often among female friends or members of their family. The transmission of the ritualized reading into further social settings where memories are discussed is facilitated when clairvoyants offer to tape-record the initial reading. Such tapes can then be played back, rewound, listened to, commented upon and interactively refashioned as time passes and events unfold.

This chapter began with the assertion that processes of memory making, in relation to death and the dead, are not confined to institutionalized, public rituals. The case of Bill and Edna (Hockey, Penhale and Sibley 2000) exemplified the point that personally meaningful actions, though usually associated with mundane aspects of social life, can be ritualized in creative attempts to maintain memories of persons deceased. Here we examined the significance of the body and 'everyday' material objects that become memory resources in patterns of ritualization. Our cross-cultural comparisons of death rituals in non-Western societies highlighted the diverse ways in which the bodies of the living and the dead have been aligned and related in the recall of the deceased. The work of anthropologists has been receptive to the various positionings of the body and its related materialities in non-Western death rituals, indicating their significance in the constitution of memories. Dimensions of embodiment, the material and sensual qualities of women's practices in the broader field of death and memory, have been explored within what Seremetakis defines as ritualized processes. The concept of ritualization, which embraces death-related actions unfolding beyond the 'confines' of formalized ritual, is useful in the interpretation of women's materialized memory-making practices in the contemporary West.

Studies of modern memory forms have emphasized the dissolution of collective memory and the emergence of diversified, fragmented attempts to connect past and present. We can see, through ethnographic studies of Western social practices surrounding death, that memory connections are being forged in diverse, and increasingly personalized ways. Here there are imaginative attempts to remember the deceased, to maintain their social presence and to reintegrate shifting memories of them into the flow of ongoing lives. The cultural resources that are drawn upon to sustain and regenerate memories of the deceased are notable in their materiality. As we have argued, the body and its material extensions can come to form the substance of memories, not just as an aspect of 'traditional', non-Western ways of living in memory, but also in the construction of continuities in the contemporary West. The Western examples through which we have highlighted the significance of materialized memories also reveal certain gendered dimensions. Ritualized memory making in these cases tends to take place at the site of the female body and in the social spaces within which women reside and work. Maintaining embodied memories of the dead might also become the concern of informal ritual specialists, such as clairvoyants whose (marginalized) magical world view activates a domain of 'sacred' material objects through which the dead are recalled and enlivened.

Memories and Endings

The ways in which dying, death and bereavement engage material-ized memories have been the central concern of this volume. Material cultures of death and their relation to memories are, however, complex and varied in their constitution, depending upon their social and cultural contexts. The materials of memory discussed throughout this book range from things perceived as beautiful to those considered 'vile' or disturbing in their broken condition. These aesthetic qualities of objects are, as we have suggested, culturally defined, yet we can refer back to one medieval conception of memory – that the things most readily remembered are those that are seen as extreme in their emotive capacities (see Chapter 3). As we have shown, material objects associated with dying, death and grief vary in mnemonic potency – from those that occasionally provide 'fleeting' sensations of proximity with the deceased, to those that are perceived as threatening or overwhelming in their association with life's ending. Death tends to throw into relief the values assigned to material possessions, belongings are unhinged and redistributed, death calls for the production and use of dedicated materials, it instigates strategies of salvage and forces questions about what can be kept in the face of loss. Identifying broad domains of death-related materials that work within and upon memories, we are con-fronted by objects of varying complexity – from the intricacies of hair jewellery to the simplicity of a single amber bead. Objects that are made to decay, such as coffins, are remembered alongside those materials appreciated for their visible qualities of endurance. Examining the symbolism and the effects of time, the marking of spaces and the spatial arrangement of memory materials, this study has explored aspects of the visual, textual and embodied processes of memory making. It is to the dynamics of preservation and decay, of fragmentation and framing, of inscription and erasure that we have attended in teasing out the extent to which memories are materialized.

This concluding chapter discusses significant themes within contemporary accounts of memory, memorial resources and the materials through which the dead are remembered. In Chapter 8 we noted the contention that in the later twentieth century mass media and the proliferation of transient images, through television and other technologies, have affected social memories, increasing fragmentation and reducing their depth (see Hervieu-Léger 2000). Here we reconsider aspects of media technologies with regard to their memory effects and then return, in particular, to twentieth-century responses to death within domains of material culture. The formation of sites of memory through increasingly eclectic and interconnected cultural displays can be viewed as deeply felt responses to the 'ephemeral' aspects of contemporary living. The latter section of this chapter then provides an overview of some of the main themes and arguments pursued throughout the volume.

Ephemerality, Mass Media and Contemporary Memento Mori

While it has been claimed that acts of forgetting stand as central issues in twentieth-century social and political relations (Forty 1999), developments in mass electronic media and commodity culture have been highlighted as major contributory factors in memory loss within Western societies (see Frow 1997). For example, Frow summarizes this problem with regard to television: '[n]ewsreel footage, the sound-bite, but also costume re-enactment and archive-based documentary all remove the past from its lived context to replay it within an electronic space of multiple possible worlds without ontological hierarchy or fixed relation' (1997: 219). The constructed nature of media images, then, is seen to continuously scramble and invent the past from the perspective of the present.

Yet, as Frow points out, mass media connects with and generates personal memories. Citing an instance in which family experiences were recalled after watching a television programme about the Second World War, Frow (1997) alludes to the private memory effects of mass media. The linkages made between the publicly broadcast funeral of Diana, Princess of Wales, as a media event in 1997, and the ritualized disposal of ashes as an act of personalized remembrance, were explored in Chapter 4 of this volume. This case points to the reception of mass media images as triggers for meaningful, localized memory-making. Similarly, Tacchi has explored experiences of radio in south-west

England, which becomes an aspect of the 'material culture of the home' and 'can act as a referencer of memories and feelings, of other places and other times' (1998: 26). The uses made of diverse media such as radio, television and video, in the environment of the home, and with regard to the formation of memories requires further ethnographic investigation. In contexts where access to a diverse range of techniques for personal record making is available, for example, photography, home film and video making, it is not the case that materially based memorializing has been displaced. As we have argued, constituting memories of the deceased in the later twentieth century often brings into play interrelated, hybrid forms (such as grave displays) and these can comprise material objects, writing and two-dimensional visual images (see Chapters 6 and 7).

The work of Huyssen (1995) provides relevant insights with regard to the impact of media technologies on memory as well as concurrent attitudes towards material culture in Western societies.

> At a time when the notion of memory has migrated to the realm of silicon chips, computers, and cyborg fictions, critics routinely deplore the entropy of historical memory defining amnesia as a dangerous cultural virus generated by the new media technologies. The more memory stored on the data banks and image tracks, the less of our culture's willingness and ability to engage in active remembrance, or so it seems. (Huyssen 1995: 249)

The representation of media technologies as debilitating and disabling in terms of active memory making, is challenged by Huyssen as he goes on to reveal not amnesia but a sustained fascination with memory and an 'obsession with the past' (1995: 253). Contemporary concerns with and heightened interest in memory are linked to 'accelerating technical processes' (Huyssen 1995: 7). Memory making, particularly via the sensory materials associated with memorialising, are part of efforts to slow the pace of material life and 'to recover a mode of contemplation outside the universe of simulation and fast speed information' (Huyssen 1995: 7). To provide a sense of temporal and spatial 'anchoring' in an increasingly mobile society, Huyssen argues that 'solid' or 'permanent matter' becomes an important focus for the articulation of memory (1995: 7, 255). The stone of monuments and the materiality of museum objects come to form significant alternatives to throw-away consumer culture and the immaterial, fleeting images circulated within mass communications.

Rather than moving into decline, later twentieth-century memorials and museums have undergone considerable transformation: during the 1980s 'ever more museums were planned and built as the practical corollary to the "end of everything" discourse' (Huyssen 1995: 14). In this context, the boundaries between museums, memorials and other sites and practices engaged in the display or consumption of the past are permeable, to the extent that Huyssen suggests 'a museal sensibility seems to be occupying ever larger chunks of everyday culture and experience' (Huyssen 1995: 14). This sensibility is evident in, for example, the restoration of buildings, the emergence of museum villages, the interest in antiques and second-hand trade and, at the personal level, the use of video recorders and diaries. The museum is now enmeshed in what Huyssen refers to a 'hybrid memorial-media culture' where diverse forms of cultural display and exhibition are consumed by a wide range of social groups fascinated by these spectacles (1995: 255). Important, here, is the stress upon the materiality of displayed objects (especially those that are aged) that possesses a 'register of reality' and a 'temporal aura' compared with the fleeting simulations of television or discarded consumer products. It is in the display and reception of material objects – practices that 'reenchant' objects and facilitate repeated and ritualised contemplation – that memories can be fuelled. And furthermore, it is 'this gaze at museal things also [that] resists the progressive dematerialization of the world which is driven by television and the virtual realities of computer networking'[1] (Huyssen, 1995: 33).

If the museum in its broader conception places emphasis on materiality and time depth, this orientation can be situated in contrast to modern consumption, which, as Appadurai has argued 'seeks to replace the aesthetics of duration with the aesthetics of ephemerality' (1996, 85). Fashion changes and the marketing of endless novelties stimulate desires for new commodities which are 'pristine' and 'unsullied by use' (Lupton 1998: 141). Yet once acquired, 'new' commodities might rapidly loose their appeal as further objects of desire are introduced. Huyssen (1995: 254) refers to this process as 'planned obsolescence' and its effect is to radically reduce the temporal reference or reach of material objects. In reaction to this, sites of cultural display and preservation become meaningful in attempts to articulate relationships with the past. And, whilst highlighting patterns of preservation, museums also reveal the transitory aspects of material life. It is in this sense that museums might operate as 'memento mori' and as such provide a 'ground for reflections on temporality and subjectivity, identity and alterity' (Huyssen 1995: 16).

Taking up the argument that contemporary cultural displays are not contained in bounded museums, but rather that they emerge in an interrelated field of materialized memory practices, the following section discusses aspects of those displays that are generated in relation to dying and death.

Death, Memory and Cultural Displays

As discussed in Chapter 8, while the pressures of modernization are seen to result in the loss of deeply rooted collective memory, this gives way to the specialized recreation of memories by interested social groups. Persons within different social groupings will creatively draw upon and deploy a range of cultural resources in attempts to fashion their distinctive identities and past affiliations. If, in the twentieth century, memory is 'composed of bits and pieces', in Hervieu-Léger's view, it is also a process of constant reinvention which is made more urgent in the face of accelerated social change (2000: 129):

> modernity's imaginative projection of continuity presents itself in an interlacing of shattered memories, memories that have also been worked upon and invented and constantly reshaped in response to the demands of the present which is increasingly subject to the pressures of change. (Hervieu-Léger 2000: 143)

Here, memory is presented as a process of continuous 'working', 'reshaping' and 'inventing', which takes place in relation to emergent factors in the present. Thus, it would seem, not only have materials of memory become increasingly broad but they are also subject to continuous manipulation in the fashioning of distinctive memory communities.

Attempts to create increasingly differentiated memorials that aptly capture or express aspects of individuals to whom they are dedicated are evident in cemeteries in contemporary England. For example, headstones in one Nottinghamshire cemetery are now engraved with messages and pictorial scenes or motifs that have been selected in order to create more distinctive memorial stones (see Chapter 6). Working within the constraints defined by local councils, local memorial masons and sculptors will advertise a range of services and memorial 'products' that cater to diverse tastes – from the highly 'traditional' to the innovative. Alluding to the use of traditional raw materials, such as granite, in combination with 'modern' machinery and techniques for engraving, memorial masons are keen to underline their provision of personalized, individual items – for example in the engraving and painting of flowers, religious figures, military motifs, illustrations of hobbies, landscape scenes or animals on headstones.

Styles of memorial display and the materials used in burial have also received public commentary in the form of exhibitions and media publicity. In March 2000 an exhibition in London, *Dead – An End to Conveyor Belt Funerals*, featured artists' work made to challenge what they see as the limitations imposed by the funerary business upon burial practices. Organised by artists /activists, in the group 'Welfare State International', their material compositions provided imaginative alternatives to the caskets and shrouds produced by the lucrative funeral industry. Not only represented as overly expensive, conventional 'grave goods' were also exposed as limited in their expressivity by artists who presented instead 'objects and ceremonies that were both celebratory and practical' (*Independent*, 2 March 2001). These included, for example, a funeral boat and a DIY coffin assembled from fruit boxes. In response to this exhibition, which aimed to display funerary objects that were not dominated by 'maudlin Victoriana', a leading director of an undertaker's firm was quoted: 'There is a new openness among our clients to having more personal rituals, like releasing doves at the grave, or balloons at children's funerals' (*Independent*, 2 March 2001).

Mass merchandising and consumerism may indeed impact upon material cultures of death as well as the materialized means through which memories are forged. The pace of material change and the fast turnover of disposable consumer goods have perceived effects upon preferred memorials. For instance, after the death of Diana, Princess of Wales, journalists speculated about appropriate 'new' memorial forms in comparison to gravestones and memorial plaques that had become 'curiously dated' (*Independent* magazine, 29 August 1998: 16). Given the 'rush to go on living', it was proposed that such 'dated' sites of memory are routinely overlooked and '[i]n such an instant and throw away culture, the flowers with which people chose to mourn the "Queen of Hearts" are an entirely instant and throw away memorial, brilliantly colourful one day, eclipsed and swept away the next' (*Independent* magazine, 29 August 1998). This commentary on flowers (that they have been used as brief expressions of grief which are little more than transient consumer items) then leads to suggestions that the time spent remembering the dead is drastically reduced in later twentieth-century consumer cultures.

Yet we have seen from contemporary perspectives on memory making in England that consumer goods are deployed as gestures of continuity and endurance. Dedicated displays of flowers and other mass-produced objects at graves (such as toys, household ornaments, plastic windmills, lanterns, glass angels, and Christmas decorations) are used to construct a sense of enduring personhood for deceased relatives and friends (see Chapter 6). In these instances, selected commodities are appropriated and incorporated within patterns of mourning, grief and remembrance. Grave displays combine objects that were already in the possession of the deceased before their death with new items that are purchased after their death to complement and elaborate existing ones. Bringing together disparate objects that are highly attuned to individuals' perceived biographies and social identities, grave displays sustain the social presence of the deceased. This is a manifestation of continuity registered through the changing arrangement and decoration of graves. Here the 'traditional' grave components, for example the inscribed headstone, are embellished with new gifts expressing desires to participate in a persistent shaping and personalizing of memorials. Configurations of materialized memories in this context tend to be 'open ended' rather than finalized and fixed, allowing for the shifting articulation of relationships between the living and the dead.

Highly eclectic and hybrid grave displays in America have recently been documented by photographer Martha Laugs (2000). Her published photographs reveal the clustering of household objects, such as crockery, ornamental ceramics and vases, alongside sculpted figures from Christian iconography, cans of Coca-Cola, flags, artificial and fresh flowers, placed on and around a varied range of headstones. The scenes and lettering engraved in stone and wood grave-markers reveal the diverse ways in which persons' memorials are linked, as deemed appropriate, with sport, the military, music and animals. At one grave a motorbike is set in concrete and at another, figures of Mickey Mouse are set on top of the headstone. Again, traditional religious motifs share the spaces of graves with mundane materials from the home, and as Kletke points out, with regard to the memory materials photographed by Laugs, 'the past and the present, the archaic and the futuristic stand side by side – and the ones who are gone are addressed as though they were still living' (2000: 7). Whilst such displays register highly personalized memory making by drawing upon and reinscribing material objects associated with the deceased, there is also an articulated awareness that the graves are visited and appreciated by those outside particular communities of mourners. One of the graves in Laugs' collection of photographs carries an inscription addressed to the wider public: 'Visitors Welcome. Photos Allow' [sic]. The distinctive headstone, fashioned in metal, is clearly dedicated to a child, yet the name of the man who made the memorial is also highly visible. In this case, innovations in memory making at the grave side express more than a set of personal connections between the deceased and their circle of relatives/friends – here the display openly addresses unknown visitors, anticipating wider interest and welcoming their attention. Contemporary artists may draw upon funerary artefacts in their exhibitions, but here the grave display is signalled as a place for visual contemplation that might exceed its memory functions: memorial displays begin to enter the territory of site-specific art.

Twentieth-century memorial displays, then, are characterised by processes of appropriation whereby an increasing range of materials are selected and re-positioned in gestures of connection with the deceased. New materials used to register the permanence of memories and the preservation of persons' social identities after death are incorporated into sites of memory. Freshly cut flowers are displayed at graves alongside those made of silk or plastic, as Kletke claims '[t]he latest aesthetic achievement for this particular kind of decoration are artificial "dew drops", made of silicone and able to withstand even the hottest midday sun' (2000: 4). Plastic and cellophane, used as a materials of memory, indicate the extensive reach of contemporary artefactual domains mobilized in response to death. Despite the association of plastic with modern mass-produced and often functional objects, this material has become part of the apparatus of personal memory making that gestures to both the past and the future. In some instances, as in the display of plastic toys at the grave, it is not necessarily the compositional material that matters; rather it is the shape and colour of the toy that is significant in its mnemonic capacity. However, the enduring qualities of plastic, its resistance to erosion is fully exploited as a means to convey the notion of 'the ever-lasting'. Flowers, cards, written messages and other objects are often covered in cellophane or placed in transparent plastic bags to protect them for as long as possible. Laidlaw (2000) has argued that cellophane has become a socially recognizable marker of the sacred or a means by which the special nature of grave flowers, or those placed at the sites of fatal accidents, is made immediately apparent. A further innovation has been to keep the wreath cards given with flowers at funerals in small cellophane wrappers and to attach, them with sticky tape, to the headstone. Here the messages written by mourners at the time of the burial are fused with the words inscribed in stone – modern materials used in this way facilitate the longer term display of written materials linked inextricably to the early, heavily ritualised, phases of grief (see Chapter 7).

As Huyssen (1995) argues, the later twentieth century has witnessed the development of a widespread 'museal sensibility' where, in diverse arenas and spaces, displays of material objects articulate relationships with the past. Increasingly eclectic graveside practices and artists' public engagement with the materials associated with death indicate the participation of different social groups in defining and transforming the ways in which memories are made. Artist's exhibitions of 'grave goods' may attempt a radical break with established styles and compositions, but the graveside displays discussed here tend to combine elements of the traditional and the new. While the latter might be drawn from a spectrum of 'ephemeral' consumer items, they are positioned at sites of burials as markers of endurance and connection with lives past. They also register a widespead search for materials that provide for the bereaved very real sensations of contact with the deceased.

Death, Memory and Material Culture

Miller has pointed to the importance of studies that examine the social and cultural contexts in which 'particular artefacts or artefactual domains' matter (1998: 10). With regard to materials that engage memory making and, in particular, relate to social experiences of dying and death, this study has highlighted a diverse and historically shifting field of material forms. In identifying domains of death-related material cultures, we have attended to the materials *deliberately* produced for the purposes of ritualized will making, bodily disposal, memorialization and mourning. We have also drawn attention to those material objects that *become* vehicles of memories by virtue of their entanglement or association with persons deceased – for instance, clothing and jewellery. Memory making in the anticipation and in the aftermath of deaths has taken shape via a wide range of materials that comprise written, visual and tactile dimensions.

Material cultures of death are increasingly difficult to delimit in that, as Nora has observed for the modern period, virtually any object can become a material of memory. Nora claims that '[t]he imperative of our epoch is ... to keep everything, to preserve every indicator of memory' (1989: 14). Lupton's (1998) study of emotional investment in everyday objects is also suggestive in this respect. Processes of interaction between persons and their material environments tend to imprint objects with traces such that almost any personal possession can carry memories. Yet, as Lupton points out, objects that acquire a heightened emotional charge or intimate association with individuals are those that are worn; those that 'enclose' the body, such as dwelling places; those with which persons interact on a daily basis, such as furniture; and those that express relations with others, for example postcards and handwritten letters (1998: 144). This provides an indication of the range of objects that might materialize memories after the death of the person with whom they had built up personal associations. The historical and ethnographic material discussed throughout this study indicates that those materials selected as potent in terms of their mnemonic capacities are those associated with the body – although this is by no means a straightforward assertion given the historically shifting perceptions of the body and its relation to material environments both in life and death.

Metaphors of memory, as discussed in Chapter 2, have shaped the ways in which remembering has been imagined and communicated in various historical contexts. Here we noted the metaphorical connections established between memory, material domains and the body as well as the persistence of visual and spatial dimensions in Western understandings of recall. The imagery of time and its passage has inflected the apprehension of remembering and the selection of materials which capture and convey memories in relation to death. The effects of time upon the body and, indeed, all material objects, together with the inevitability of death and decay were central concerns of early modern memento mori (see Chapter 3). While established within Christian beliefs, the imagery of the body returning to dust and linked to flowers and trees, the passage of time from night to day or through the seasons, and the relations between preservation and decay can still be discerned in materials of memory, despite processes of secularization. The appreciation of materials that remain at the end of a life to be taken up and held within memory has, however, been influenced by changing aesthetics, which tend to mask physical decomposition.

Materials of memory are possessed of complex temporal dimensions and, as explored in Chapter 4, spaces of memory are diverse: the spatial location of the dead, especially in terms of burial, shapes the topography of remembrance, and spaces associated with the dying process or the event of death are open to memorializing through ritualized practices. The location of material objects, associated with the dead, within public as well as domestic spaces concentrates memorializing within certain settings but these are seldom static. Rather, spaces of memory are dynamic in that their meanings can be reinscribed and contested. With the passage of time, public memorials might become 'invisible', while further memory practices, such as the scattering of ashes, establish links between personalized memories and selected locations. Throughout this study we have worked with a broad conception of material culture – one that encompasses visual images and written words as well as objects. Indeed, we have sought to explore the material dimensions of images and texts within different contexts of memory making. A diversity of visual and textual or inscribed memories was traced in Chapters 6 and 7, highlighting the relationships between these forms and the actions of living bodies as well as the cultural reworking of the dead body.

While materialized memories of the dead have been actively sought as means to sustain social and personal connections over time, we have seen that death-related objects are often difficult to manage. Memory-making in the fields that we have explored can become fraught with difficulty and unresolved anxiety. Once required as part of religious and moral instruction, the call to remember death and the proximity of objects that resonate with physical decay (see Chapter 3), can be perceived as threatening to modern sensibilities. Certain highly charged material forms, which might function to counteract the absence of a person, can simultaneously be felt as burdensome or disturbing in their powers of evocation. In Chapter 5 we explored the disturbing territories of objects, especially those associated with accidental or sudden deaths, that appear to possess agency in terms of their effects upon persons, actions and patterns of remembrance.

Drawing attention to the diversity of materials and material objects that have been made, reworked, assigned different meanings and associations in the forging of death-related memories also involves the identification of cultural patterns and transformations. We can argue, as does Sheringham, that '[t]o remember is to engage with what is already other' (1993: 313) in that the past belongs to what has gone and thus remains different in relation to the present. The transformative effects that deaths have upon lived material environments can also render the most familiar objects strange or disturbing by degrees. What was once a well-worn comfortable pair of shoes might become, after the death of their owner, the most powerful register of loss. Attempts to counteract sensations of loss, as we have seen, involve a range of cultural strategies – to sustain (partial) physical connection; to replicate and 'freeze' deceased persons; to mark disconnection and realize the differences that deaths make; to build a 'living' social presence for the deceased; to 'replace' or reconfigure previous damage. These strategies may coexist and overlap, they may be rejected, contested or embraced, depending upon the context in which they are enacted but they are all heavily dependent upon material forms.

Memory making through the production, manipulation and reorganization of material objects, as well as the embodied actions engaged in these processes, also involves further complexities which we have highlighted throughout this study. Relations of gender, social status and wealth are often marked and articulated through the materialization of memories. In the maintenance of memory spaces, the care of memory objects and in the ritualized making of memories at the site of the body (see Chapter 9), women's participation has often been significant. Yet in order to recover this significance, attention has to be paid to those spaces, materials and ritualized practices beyond those of the public and the institutionalized.

Throughout this book we have sought to explore relationships between death, memory and material culture, primarily in Western contexts. That memories are generated and experienced through material forms and as part of social and cultural processes is a central assertion of our study. Furthermore, we have seen that dying, death, disposal and mourning are experienced as tangible life crises that instigate or demand acts of memory making. However, memories, even in their materialized forms, are difficult to hold on to. As we have seen, in a variety of social settings, the materials of memory are complex, referring to the past, shaping the present and reaching into futures in various ways. The losses anticipated in the face of death and felt in its aftermath reverberate in the physical domains occupied by the body and its lived material environment. The intensity of death finds its inevitable expression at the level of the material where, at the very least, a person's physical being can be experienced as 'elsewhere' – their living, embodied personhood becomes a thing of the past. Yet, as we have argued, memory making as a response to death, ensures that persons are given a place within the present and to fashion memories in material forms constitutes gestures that grant the deceased a future often possessed of a powerful physicality.

Note

1. It is worth noting here that virtual memorials have been developed to provide memory resources available at Web sites. Here there are significant allusions or references to the concrete materials used in death-related memory making, for example, images of flowers, books and architectural memorials that users can select and customize as personalized markers of relative's deaths.

Bibliography

Alpers, S. (1989 [1983]) *The Art of Describing: Dutch art in the seventeenth century*, London: Penguin Books.

Appadurai, A. (1986) 'Introduction: commodities and the politics of value', in A. Appadurai (ed.) *The Social Life of Things: Commodities in cultural perspective*, Cambridge: Cambridge University Press.

Appadurai, A. (1996) *Modernity at Large: Cultural dimensions of globalization*. Minneapolis: University of Minnesota Press.

Ariès, P. (1983 [1977]) *The Hour of Our Death*, trans. H. Weaver, Harmondsworth: Peregrine Books.

Ariès, P. (1985) *Images of Man and Death*, trans. J. Lloyd, Cambridge MA: Harvard University Press.

Ash, J. (1996) 'Memory and Objects' in P. Kirkham (ed.) *The Gendered Object*, Manchester: Manchester University Press.

Aston, M. (1988) *England's Iconoclasts. Volume 1. Laws Against Images*, Oxford: Clarendon Press.

Bachelard, G. (1994 [1958]) *The Poetics of Space: The classic look at how we experience intimate spaces*, Boston: Beacon Press.

Bakhtin, M. (1984 [trans. 1965]) *Rabelais and his World*, trans. H. Iswolski, Bloomington: Indiana University Press.

Ball, M. (1976) *Death*, London: Oxford University Press.

Battersby, C. (1993) 'Her Body/Her Boundaries: Gender and the metaphysics of containment', *Journal of Philosophy and the Visual Arts*, 31–9.

Belk, R. W. (1994) 'Collectors and collecting', in S. M. Pearce (ed.), *Interpreting Objects and Collections*, London: Routledge.

Bindman, D. (1999) 'Bribing the Vote of Fame: Eighteenth century monuments and the futility of commemoration' in A. Forty and S. Küchler (eds), *The Art of Forgetting*, Oxford: Berg.

Binski, P. (1996) *Medieval Death: Ritual and representation*, London: British Museum Press.

217

Bloch, M. (1996) 'Internal and External Memory', in P. Antze and M. Lambek (eds), *Tense Past: Cultural essays in trauma and memory*, London: Routledge.

Botting, F. (1996) *Gothic*, London: Routledge.

Bourdieu, P. (1977) *Outline of a Theory of Practice*, Cambridge: Cambridge University Press.

Bourke, J. (1996) *Dismembering the Male: Men's bodies, Britain and the Great War*, London: Reaktion Books.

Bradbury, M. (1993) 'Contemporary representations of "good" and "bad" death', in D. Dickenson and M. Johnson (eds), *Death, Dying and Bereavement*, London: Sage.

Bradbury, M. (1996) 'Representations of "good" and "bad" death among deathworkers and the bereaved', in G. Howarth and P. Jupp (eds), *Contemporary Issues in the Sociology of Death, Dying and Disposal*, London: Macmillan.

Braunstein, P. (1988) 'Toward Intimacy: The fourteenth and fifteenth centuries', in G. Duby, *A History of Private Life. II. Revelations of the Medieval World*, Cambridge Massachusetts: The Belknap Press of Harvard University.

Bronfen, E. (1992) *Over Her Dead Body: Death, femininity and the aesthetic*, Manchester: Manchester University Press.

Brown, B. (1998) 'How to Do Things with Things (A Toy Story)', *Critical Inquiry*, 24 (Summer), 935–64.

Burns, S. B. (1990) *Sleeping Beauty: Memorial photography in America*, Altadena: Twelvetrees Press.

Bytheway, B. and Johson, J. (1996) 'Valuing Lives? Obituaries and the life course', *Mortality* 1(2), 219–234.

Camitta, M. (1993) 'Vernacular Writing: Varieties of literacy among Philadelphia high school students', in B. Street (ed.), *Cross-cultural Approaches to Literacy*, Cambridge: Cambridge University Press.

Camporeisi, P. (1994) *The Anatomy of the Senses: Material symbols in medieval and early modern Italy*, Cambridge: Polity Press.

Cannadine, D. (1981) 'War and Death, Grief and Mourning in Modern Britain', in J. Whaley (ed.), *Mirrors of Mortality*, London: Europa Publications.

Cardinal, R. (1994) 'Collecting and Collage-Making: The case of Kurt Schwitters', in J. Elsner and R. Cardinal (eds), *The Cultures of Collecting*, London: Reaktion Press.

Cardinal, R. (1995) 'Thinking Through Things: The presence of objects in the early films of Jan Švankmejr', in P. Hames (ed.), *Dark Alchemy. The films of Jan Švankmajer*, Trowbridge: Flicks Books.

Carruthers, M. J. (1990) *The Book of Memory: A study in memory in medieval culture*, Cambridge: Cambridge University Press.

Clark, T. (2000) 'Deconstruction and Technology', in N. Royle (ed.), *Deconstructions: A users guide*, Basingstoke: Palgrave.

Cohen, K. (1973) *Metamorphosis of a Symbol: The transi tomb in the late middle ages and the Renaissance*, Berkeley: University of California Press.

Comaroff, J. (1994) 'Aristotle Re-membered', in J. Chandler, A. I. Davidson and H. Harootunian (eds), *Questions of Evidence: Proof, practice, and persuasion across the disciplines*, Chicago: University of Chicago Press.

Connerton, P. (1989) *How Societies Remember*, Cambridge: Cambridge University Press.

Cooper, M. and Sciorra, J. (1994) *R. I. P. New York Spraycan Memorials*, London: Thames & Hudson.

Cressy, D. (1997) *Birth, Marriage and Death: Ritual, religion and the life-cycle in tudor and stuart England*, Oxford: Oxford University Press.

Cullen, C. (1996) 'Counter intuitive interpretations of memory', *Symposium on Recovered Memories*, British Psychological Society Annual Conference, Leicester: The British Psychological Society.

Damasio, A. R. (1994) *Descartes' Error: Emotion, reason and the human brain*, London: Papermac.

Davie, G. and Martin, D. (1999) 'Liturgy and music', in T. Walter (ed.), *The Mourning for Diana*, Oxford: Berg.

Davies, D. (1997) *Death, Ritual and Belief*, London: Cassell.

Davies, J. (1993) 'War Memorials' in D. Clark (ed.), *The Sociology of Death*, Oxford: Blackwell Publishers/The Sociological Review.

Davis N. Z. and Starn, R. (1989) 'Introduction', *Representations. Special Issue: Memory and counter-memory*, 26, 1–6.

Du Boulay, J. (1982) 'The Greek Vampire: A study of cyclic symbolism in marriage and death', *Man* , XVII, 219–38.

Edwards, E. (1999) 'Photographs as Objects of Memory', in M. Kwint, C. Breward and J. Aynsley (eds), *Material Memories: Design and evocation,* Oxford: Berg.

Fabian, J. (1983) *Time and the Other: How anthropology makes its object*, New York: Columbia University Press.

Fabian, J. (1991) *Time and the Work of Anthropology: Critical essays 1971–1991*, Chur, Switzerland: Harwood Academic Publishers.

Fentress, J. and Wickham, C. (1992) *Social Memory*, Oxford: Blackwell.

Finucane, R. C. (1996) *Ghosts: Appearances of the dead and cultural transformation*, New York, Prometheus Books.

Forty, A. (1999) 'Introduction' in A. Forty and S. Küchler (eds), *The Art of Forgetting*, Oxford: Berg.

Foucault, M. (1986) 'Of Other Spaces', *Diacritics*, Spring, 22–7.

Francis, D., Kellaher, L. and Neophytou, G. (2000) 'Sustaining Cemeteries: The user perspective', *Mortality*, 5(1), 34–52.

Frow, J. (1997) *Time and Commodity Culture: Essays in cultural theory and postmodernity*, Oxford: Clarendon Press.

Geary, P. (1986) 'Sacred Commodities: The circulation of medieval relics', in A. Appadurai (ed.), *The Social Life of Things: Commodities in cultural perspective*, Cambridge: Cambridge University Press.

Geertz, C. (1968) 'Religion as a cultural system', in M. Banton (ed), *Anthropological Approaches to the Study of Religion*, ASA Monographs 3, London: Social Science Paperback.

Gell, A. (1998) *Art and Agency: An anthropological theory*, Oxford: Clarendon Press.

Gillis, J. (1993) (ed.) *Commemoration: The politics of national identity*, Princeton: Princeton University Press.

Gold, A. G. and Gujar, B. R. (1997) 'Wild Pigs and Kings: Remembered landscapes in Rajastan', *American Anthropologist,* 99 (1), 70–84.

Goody, J. (1986) *The Logic of Writing and the Organization of Society*, Cambridge: Cambridge University Press.

Goody, J. (1987) *The Interface Between the Written and the Oral*, Cambridge, Cambridge University Press.

Guthke, K. S. (1999) *The Gender of Death: A cultural history in art and literature*, Cambridge: Cambridge University Press.

Hacking, I. (1994) 'Two Souls in One Body', in J. Chandler, A. I. Davidson and H. Harootunian (eds), *Questions of Evidence: Proof, practice, and persuasion across the disciplines*, Chicago: University of Chicago Press.

Hallam, E. (1994) *Crisis and Representation: Gender and social relations in Canterbury and its region, 1580–1640*. PhD thesis, University of Kent at Canterbury.

Hallam, E. (1996) 'Turning the Hourglass: Gender relations at the deathbed in early modern Canterbury, *Mortality*, 1(1), 61–82.

Hallam, E., Hockey, J., Howarth, G. (1999) *Beyond the Body: Death and social identity*, London: Routledge.

Hallam, E. (2001, forthcoming) 'The Eye and the Hand: Memory, identity and clairvoyants' narratives in England', in J. Harbord and J. Campbell (eds), *Temporalities: Autobiography in a postmodern age*, Manchester: Manchester University Press.

Hansen, J. and Porter, S. (1999) *The Physician's Art: Representations of art and medicine*, Durham: Duke University Medical Center Library and Duke University Museum of Art.

Harris, C. (1987) 'The Individual and Society: A processual approach', in A. Bryman, B. Bytheway, P. Allatt and T. Keil (eds), *Rethinking the Life Cycle*, London: Macmillan.

Harrison, R. P. (1997) 'The Names of the Dead', *Critical Inquiry*, Autumn, 176–90.

Hawkins, P. S. (1993) 'Naming Names: The art of memory and the NAMES Project AIDS Quilt', *Critical Inquiry*, Summer, 752–79.

Hertz, R. ([1907]1960) *Death and the Right Hand,* New York: Free Press.

Hervieu-Léger, D. (2000) *Religion as a Chain of Memory*, Cambridge: Polity Press.

Hirsch, M. (1997) *Family Frames: Photography, narrative and postmemory*, Cambridge Massachusettes: Harvard University Press.

Hockey, J. (1990) *Experiences of Death: An anthropological account*, Edinburgh: Edinburgh University Press.

Hockey, J. (1992) *Making the Most of a Funeral,* London: Cruse: Bereavement Care.

Hockey, J. (1996) 'Encountering the "Reality of Death" Through Professional Discourses: The matter of materiality', *Mortality*, 1(1), 45–60.

Hockey, J. and James, A. (1993) *Growing Up and Growing Old: Ageing and dependency across the lifecourse*, London: Sage.

Hockey, J., Penhale, B. and Sibley, D. (1999) 'Home, Space and Memory: A study of the changed experience of space among older adults bereaved of an opposite sex partner', Paper given at the British Gerontological Society Conference, 'Traditions and Transitions', Bournemouth.

Houlbrooke, R. (1998) *Death, Religion and the Family in England, 1480–1750*, Oxford: Clarendon Press.

Howarth, G. (1996) *Last Rites: The work of the modern funeral director,* New York: Baywood Publishing Company.

Humm, M. (1987) 'Autobiography and Bellpins', in V. Griffiths, M. Humm, R. O'Rourke and J. Batsleer, F. Poland, and S. Wise (eds), *Feminist Biography 2: Using life histories,* Manchester: Studies in Sexual Politics, University of Manchester.

Huntington, R. and Metcalf, P. (1979) *Celebrations of Death: The anthropology of mortuary ritual*, Cambridge: Cambridge University Press.

Hutton, P. H. (1987) 'The Art of Memory Reconceived: From rhetoric to psychoanalysis', *Journal of the History of Ideas*, 371–92.

Huyssen, A. (1995) *Twilight Memories: Marking time in a culture of amnesia*, London: Routledge.

Illich, I. (1975) *Medical Nemesis: The expropriation of health*, London: Caldar & Boyars Ltd.

Jamison, K. R. (2000) *Night Falls Fast: Understanding suicide*, London: Picador.

Jennings, E. (1967) *Collected Poems*, London: Macmillan.

Jones, B. (1999) 'Books of Condolence', in T. Walter (ed.), *The Mourning for Diana*, Oxford: Berg.

Jordanova, L. (1997) 'Happy Marriages and Dangerous Liaisons: Artists and anatomy, in D. Petherbridge and L. Jordanova (eds), *The Quick and the Dead: Artists and anatomy*, London: South Bank Centre, National Touring Exhibitions.

Kellehear, A. (1990) *Dying of Cancer*, Chur: Harwood Academic Publishers.

Kemp, M. (1995) '"Wrought by No Artist's Hand": The natural, the artificial, the exotic, and the scientific in some artefacts from the Renaissance', in C. Farago (ed.), *Reframing the Renaissance: Visual culture in Europe and Latin America 1450–1650*, New Haven: Yale University Press.

King, A. (1998) *Memorials of the Great War*, Oxford: Berg.

King, A. (1999) 'Remembering and Forgetting in the Public Memorials of the Great War', in A. Forty and S. Küchler (eds), *The Art of Forgetting*, Oxford: Berg.

King, C. (1997) 'The Death of a King: Elvis Presley (1935–1977)', in P. C. Jupp and G. Howarth (eds), *The Changing Face of Death*, Basingstoke: Macmillan.

Klass, D. (1996) 'Grief in an Eastern Culture: Japanese ancestor worship', in D. Klass, P. R. Silverman, S. L. Nickman (eds), *Continuing Bonds: New understandings of grief*, Washington: Taylor & Francis.

Kletke, D. (2000) 'Life After Death', text in M. Laugs, *America After Life*, Munich: Kehayoff.

Kristeva, J. (1982) *Powers of Horror: An essay on abjection*, New York: Columbia University Press.

Kwint, M. (1999) 'Introduction: The physical past', in M. Kwint, C. Breward and J. Aynsley (eds), *Material Memories: Design and evocation*, Oxford: Berg.

Laidlaw, P. (2000) 'Catch your Death', *Ibca Journal*, Winter, 4–8.

Lakoff, G. and Johnson, M. (1980) *Metaphors We Live By*, Chicago: University of Chicago Press.

Lambek, M. and Antze, P. (1996) 'Introduction: Forecasting memory', in P. Antze and M. Lambek (eds), *Tense Past: Cultural essays in trauma and memory*, London: Routledge.

Latour, B. (1993) *We have never been modern*, New York: Harvester Wheatsheaf.

Laugs, M. (2000) *America After Life*, Munich: Kehayoff.

Lawton, J. (1998) 'Contemporary Hospice Care: The sequestration of the unbounded body and "dirty dying"', *Sociology of Health and Illness*, 20(2), 121–43.

Lawton, J. (2000) *The Dying Process: Patients' experiences of palliative care*, London: Routledge.

Legg, C. (1998) *Psychology and the Reflective Counsellor*, Leicester: BPS Books.

Le Goff, J. (1992) *History and Memory*, New York: Columbia University Press.

Levi-Strauss, C. (1973) *Tristes Tropiques*, London: Jonathan Cape.

Lewis, C. S. (1961) *A Grief Observed*, London: Faber & Faber.

Leys, R. (1994) 'Traumatic Cures: Shell shock, Janet, and the question of memory', *Critical Inquiry*, 20 (Summer), 623–62.

Littlewood, J. (2000) 'Just and old-fashioned love song or a "harlequin romance"? Some experiences of widowhood', in J. Hockey, J. Katz and N. Small (eds), *Grief, Mourning and Death Ritual*, Buckingham: Open University Press.

Llewellyn, N. (1991) *The Art of Death: Visual culture in the English death ritual c.1500 - c.1800,* London: Reaktion Books.

Lupton, D. (1998) *The Emotional Self*, London: Sage

Luhrmann, T. M. (1989): *Persuasions of the Witch's Craft: Ritual magic in contemporary England*, Cambridge MA: Harvard University Press.

Luthi A. L. (1998) *Sentimental Jewellery: Antique jewels of love and sorrow*, Princes Risborough: Shire Publications.

MacGregor, A. (1985) 'The Cabinet of Curiosities in Seventeenth-Century Britain', in O. Impey and A. MacGregor (eds), *The Origins of Museums: The cabinet of curiosities in sixteenth and seventeenth-century Europe*, Oxford: Clarendon Press.

McCormack, C. (1985) 'Dying as Transformation to Ancestorhood: The Sherbro Coast of Sierra Leone', *Curare*, Sonderband 4:117–26.

Mara, C. (1998) 'Divestments', in K. Dunseath (ed.), *A Second Skin: Women write about clothes*, London: The Women's Press.

Melion, W. and Küchler, S. (1991) 'Introduction: Memory, cognition, and image production', in Küchler S. and Melion, W. (eds), *Images of Memory: On remembering and representation*, Washington: Smithsonian Institution Press.

Mellor, P. (1993) 'Death in High Modernity: The contemporary presence and absence of death', in D. Clark (ed.), *The Sociology of Death*, Oxford: Blackwell/Sociological Review.

Mellor, P. and Shilling, C. (1997) *Reforming the Body: Religion, community and modernity*, London: Sage.

Merrin, W. (1999) 'Crash, bang, wallop! What a picture! The death of Diana and the media, *Mortality*, 4(1), 41–62.

Miller, D. (1998) 'Why some things matter', in D. Miller (ed.), *Material Cultures: Why some things matter*, London: UCL Press.

Miller, W. (1998) 'Fixin' to die', plenary paper given at the 4th International *Death, Dying and Disposal Conference*, Glasgow Caledonian University.

Mollon, P. (1996) 'Clinical complexities in the memory debate', *Symposium on Recovered Memories*, British Psychological Society Annual Conference, Leicester: The British Psychological Society.

Moore, H. (1996) *Space, Text and Gender: An anthropological study of the Marakwet of Kenya*, New York: The Guilford Press.

Morley, J. (1971) *Death, Heaven and the Victorians*, London: Studio Vista.

Mulkay, M. (1993) 'Social death in Britain', in D. Clark (ed), *The Sociology of Death*, Oxford: Blackwell/Sociological Review.

Morrison, B. (1993) *When Did You Last See Your Father?* London: Granta Books.

Muxel, A. (1996) *Individu et Memoire Familiale*, Paris: Nathan.

Nettleton, S. (1998) *The Body in Everyday Life,* London: Routledge.

Nora, P. (1989) 'Between Memory and History: Les lieux de memoire', *Representations*, 26, (Spring), 7–25.

O'Hara, D. (1992) 'The Language of Tokens and the Making of Marriage', *Rural History*, 3(1), 1–40.

Okely, J. (1983) *The Traveller-Gypsies*, Cambridge: Cambridge University Press.

Olalquiaga, C. (1999) *The Artificial Kingdom: A treasury of the kitsch experience*, London: Bloomsbury Publishing.

Ong, W. (1982) *Orality and Literacy: The technologizing of the word.* London: Methuen.

Owen, A. (1989) *The Darkened Room: Women, power and spiritualism in late nineteenth century England*, London: Virago.

Parkes, C. M. (1972) *Bereavement: Studies of grief in adult life,* Harmondsworth: Penguin.

Parkin, D. (1992) 'Ritual as spatial direction and bodily division', in D. de Coppet (ed), *Understanding Rituals*, London: Routledge.

Parkin, D. (1999) 'Mementoes as Transitional Objects', *The Journal of Material Culture*, 4(3), 303–20.

Pels, P. (1998) 'The Spirit of Matter: On fetish, rarity, fact, and fancy', in P. Spyer (ed.), *Border Fetishisms: Material objects in unstable spaces*, London: Routledge.

Peters, J. D. (1999) *Speaking into the Air: A history of the idea of communication*, Chicago: University of Chicago Press.

Pointon, M. (1999) 'Materializing Mourning: Hair, jewellery and the body', in M. Kwint, C. Breward and J. Aynsley (eds), *Material Memories: Design and evocation*, Oxford: Berg.

Ranum, O. (1989) 'The Refuges of Intimacy', in R. Chartier (ed.), *A History of Private Life, III. Passions of the Renaissance*, Cambridge MA: The Belknap Press of Harvard University.

Reichardt, R. (1998) 'Light Against Darkness: The visual representations of a central Enlightenment concept', *Representations*, Winter, 61, 95–148.

Riches, G. and Dawson, P. (1996) 'Communities of Feeling: The culture of bereaved parents', *Mortality*, 1(2), 143–61.

Riches, G. and Dawson, P. (2000) *An Intimate Loneliness: Supporting bereaved parents and siblings*, Open University Press: Buckingham.

Ricoeur, P. (1981) *Hermeneutics and the Human Sciences*, Cambridge: Cambridge University Press.

Roach, J. (1996) *Cities of the Dead*, New York: Columbia University Press.

Roberts, J. (1998) 'Remain in Light', *Frieze*, 40, 56–61, London: Durian Publications Ltd.

Robinson, D. (1995) *Saving Graces*, New York: W. W. Norton & Co.

Rosaldo, R. (1989) *Culture and Truth: The remaking of social analysis*, Boston: Beacon Press.

Rosenzweig, M. R., Leiman, A. and Breedlove, S. (1999) *Biological Psychology: An introduction to behavioural, cognitive and clinical neuroscience*, Sunderland, Mass: Sinauer Associates, Inc.

Rowlands, M. (1999) 'Remembering to Forget: Sublimation as sacrifice in war memorials', in A. Forty and S. Küchler (eds), *The Art of Forgetting*, Oxford:Berg.

Roy, A. (1997) *The God of Small Things*, London: Flamingo.

Ruby, J. (1995) *Secure the Shadow: Death and photography in America*, Cambridge MA: MIT Press.

Salvo, D. (1997) *Home Altars of Mexico*, London: Thames & Hudson.

Sarbin, T. R. (1986) 'Emotion and Act: Roles and rhetoric', in R. Harré (ed.), *The Social Construction of Emotions*, Oxford: Basil Blackwell.

Sawday, J. (1995) *The Body Emblazoned: Dissection and the human body in Renaissance culture*, London: Routledge.

Seale, C. (1995) 'Heroic Death', *Sociology*, 29(4), 597–613.

Seremetakis, C. N. (1991) *The Last Word: Women, death and divination in inner Mani*, Chicago: University of Chicago Press.

Seremetakis, C. N. (1994) (ed.) *The Senses Still: Perception and memory as material culture in modernity*, Chicago: The University of Chicago Press.

Shelton, A. (1995) (ed.) *Fetishism: Visualising power and desire*, London: Lund Humphries Publishers.

Sheringham, M. (1993) *French Autobiography: Devices and desires*, New York: Oxford University Press.

Simpson, B. (1998) *Changing Families*, Oxford: Berg.

Skultans, V. (1998) *The Testimony of Lives: Narrative and memory in post-Soviet Latvia*, London: Routledge.

Snyder, L. S. (1998) 'Some of My Mother's Things', *Diacritics*, 28(4), Winter, 82–9.

Sontag, S. (1979) *On Photography*, Harmondsworth: Penguin.

Sontag, S. (1978) 'The double standard of ageing', in V. Carver and P. Liddiard (eds), *An Ageing Population*, Milton Keynes: Open University Press.

Spyer, P. (1998) 'Introduction', in P. Spyer (ed.), *Border Fetishisms: Material objects in unstable spaces*, London: Routledge.

Stafford, M. (1994) *Artful Science: Enlightenment entertainment and the eclipse of visual education*, Cambridge MA: MIT Press.

Stallybrass, P. and White, A. (1986) *The Politics and Poetics of Transgression*, London: Methuen.

Stewart, S. (1994) 'Death and Life, in that Order, in the Works of Charles Willson Peale', in J. Elsner and R. Cardinal (eds), *The Cultures of Collecting*, London Reaktion Books.

Stewart, S. (1998 [1993]) *On Longing: Narratives of the miniature, the gigantic, the souvenir, the collection*, Durham: Duke University Press.

Stewart, S. (1999) 'Prologue: From the museum of touch', in M. Kwint, C. Breward and J. Aynsley (eds), *Material Memories: Design and evocation*, Oxford: Berg.

Stimming M. and Stimming, M. (1999) (eds) *Before their Time: Adult children's experiences of parental suicide*, Philadelphia: Temple University Press.

Street, B. (1993) (ed.) *Cross-cultural Approaches to Literacy*, Cambridge: Cambridge University Press.

Stroebe, M. and Schut, H. (1995) 'The Dual Process Model of Coping with Loss.' Paper presented at the International Workgroup on Death, Dying and Bereavement, Oxford, UK.

Sturken, M. (1991) 'The Wall, the Screen, and the Image: The Vietnam veterans memorial' *Representations*, Summer, 35, 118–142.

Tacchi, J. (1998) 'Radio Texture: Between self and others', in D. Miller (ed.), *Material Cultures: Why some things matter*, London: UCL Press.

Tambiah, S. J. (1981) *A Performative Approach to Ritual*, London: Oxford University Press.

Taylor, L. (1983) *Mourning Dress: A costume and social history*, London: George Allen and Unwin.

Thomas, K. (1985 [1971]) *Religion and the Decline of Magic: Studies in popular beliefs in sixteenth and seventeenth-century England*, Harmondsworth: Penguin Books.

Tonkin, E. (1995 [1992]) *Narrating our pasts: The social construction of oral history*, Cambridge: Cambridge University Press.

Turner, B. (1998) Plenary paper given at the *After the Body Conference*, University of Manchester.

Turner, V. (1967) *The Forest of Symbols*, New York: Cornell University Press.

Turner, V. (1969) *The Ritual Process*, Harmondsworth: Penguin.

Turner, V. (1974) *Dramas, Fields and Metaphors: Symbolic action in human society*, Ithaca: Cornell University Press.

Vincent, G. 1991: 'A History of Secrets?' in A. Prost and G. Vincent (eds), *A History of Private Life. V. Riddles of Identity in Modern Times*, Cambridge, Massachusetts: The Belknap Press of Harvard University Press.

Walter, T. (1990) *Funerals and How to Improve Them*, London: Hodder & Stoughton.

Walter, T. (1991) 'Modern Death: Taboo or not Taboo?', *Sociology*, 25(2), 293–310.

Walter, T. (1994) *The Revival of Death*, London: Routledge.

Walter, T. (1996) 'A New Model of Grief: Bereavement and biography', *Mortality*, 1(1), 2–26.

Walter, T. (1997) 'Emotional Reserve and the British Way of Death', in K. Charmaz, G. Howarth and A. Kellehear (eds), *The Unknown Country: Death in Australia, Britain and the USA*, Basingstoke: Macmillan.

Warner, M. (1995) 'The unbearable likeness of Being', *Tate: The art magazine*, Issue 6, Summer, 40–47.

Warner, M. (1996) *The Inner Eye: Art beyond the visible*, National Touring Exhibitions, South Bank Centre.

Watt, T. (1994 [1991]) *Cheap Print and Popular Piety, 1550–1640*, Cambridge: Cambridge University Press.

Whitaker, A. (1984) *All in the End is Harvest: An anthology for those who grieve*, Darton, Longman and Todd/Cruse: London.

Wikan, U. (1988) 'Bereavement and Loss in Two Muslim Communities: Egypt and Bali compared', *Social Science and Medicine*, 27(5), 451–60.

Wilkinson, J. D. and Campbell, E. A. (1997) *Psychology in Counselling and Therapeutic Practice*, Chichester: John Wiley & Sons.

Winter, J. (1998 [1995]) *Sites of Memory, Sites of Mourning: The Great War in European cultural history*, Cambridge: Cambridge University Press.

Worden, J. W. (1991) *Grief Counselling and Grief Therapy*, London: Routledge.

Wouters, C. (1992) 'On Status Competition and Emotion Management: The study of emotions as a new field', *Theory, Culture and Society*, 9, 229–52.

Young, J. E. (1989) 'The Biography of a Memorial Icon: Nathan Rapoport's Warsaw Ghetto monument', *Representations*, 26 (Spring), 69–106.

Wertheimer, A. (1991) *A Special Scar: The experiences of people bereaved by suicide*, London: Routledge.

Yates, F. (1992 [1966]) *The Art of Memory*, London: Pimlico.

Zelizer, B. (1998): *Remembering to Forget: Holocaust memory through the camera's eye*, Chicago: Chicago University Press.

Index